Object-Oriented
Programming
in Oberon-2

Hanspeter Mössenböck

Object-Oriented Programming

in Oberon-2

Foreword by
Niklaus Wirth

Translation by
Robert Bach

Springer-Verlag
Berlin Heidelberg New York
London Paris Tokyo
Hong Kong Barcelona
Budapest

Prof. Dr. Hanspeter Mössenböck
Institut für Computersysteme
ETH-Zentrum, CH-8092 Zürich

With 104 Figures

Title of the Original German Edition:
Objektorientierte Programmierung in Oberon-2
© Springer-Verlag Berlin Heidelberg 1993

ISBN 3-540-56411-X Springer-Verlag Berlin Heidelberg New York
ISBN 0-387-56411-X Springer-Verlag New York Berlin Heidelberg

Library of Congress Cataloging-in-Publication Data

Mössenböck, Hanspeter, 1959–
(Objektorientierte Programmierung in Oberon-2. English) Object-oriented programming in Oberon-2 / Hanspeter Mössenböck; foreword by Niklaus Wirth; translation by Robert Bach. p. cm.
Translation of: Objektorientierte Programmierung in Oberon-2.
Includes bibliographical references and index.
ISBN 0-387-56411-X
1. Object-oriented programming. 2. Operating systems (Computers) 3. Oberon. I. Title.
QA76.64.M67 1993 005.13' 3-dc20-93-10033 CIP

© Springer-Verlag Berlin Heidelberg 1993
Printed in Germany

Cover Design: Konzept & Design, Ilvesheim
Typesetting: Camera-ready by author/translator
Exposed by Text & Grafik B.E.S., Heidelberg
33/ 5 4 3 2 1 0 - Printed on acid-free paper

Foreword

Without a doubt the idea of object-oriented programming has brought some motion into the field of programming methodology and enlarged the set of programming languages. Object-oriented programming is nothing new—it first arose in the sixties. The motivation came from the simulation of discrete event systems. The concept first manifested itself in the language Simula 67. It took nearly two decades for the method to gain impetus, and today object-oriented programming is an important concept and a powerful technique. Meanwhile, we can even speak of an over-reaction, for the concept has become a buzzword. But buzzwords always appear where there is the hope of exploiting ill-informed clients because they see the new approach as the solution to all their problems. Thus object-oriented programming is often hailed as a panacea. And so the question is justified: What is really behind it?

To let the cat out of the bag: There is more to object-oriented programming than merely putting data as objects in the fore-ground, instead of algorithms to which the data are subject. It is more than purely an alternative view of programmed systems. To identify the essence of object-oriented programming, is the subject of this book. This is a textbook that shows in a didactically skillful way which concepts and constructs are new, where they can be employed reasonably, and what advantages they offer. For, not all programs are automatically improved by merely recasting them in an object-oriented style. On the contrary, the new method can only be applied sensibly where complex data structures are present. It would be unwise to prematurely discard the conventional view.

It is to the author's credit that he introduces the concepts of object-oriented programming in a constructive way, demonstrates them in an evolutionary manner, and uses suitable examples to show how these concepts can be employed judiciously. The programming language Oberon-2 provides an excellent foundation because it adds only the few typically object-oriented concepts to those of conventional procedural programming but no more. The reader should always be aware that not the language but the methodology and discipline constitute the essential concern of the book. The language only serves the purpose of formulation in a clear and concise manner. We speak of a language supporting a method; Oberon-2 supports object-oriented programming.

The object-oriented paradigm holds so much promise especially for complex systems, because the technique of object-oriented programming makes it possible to create modular systems that are truly extensible. By extensible we mean that not only new operations can be added that build on old ones, but that the same is true for data types and their instances. These comments indicate that object orientation comes to full fruition only when combined with modularity and strict typing of data.

This book is a well-organized introduction to this new field. It is obvious that the author draws on a wealth of experience gained in years of intensive work in the area and in successful teaching. The book is an enrichment for anyone interested in modern programming techniques.

Niklaus Wirth, Zurich, 1993

Preface

Object-oriented programming (OOP) has become a buzzword that is prominently displayed in numerous journals and advertisements. What is OOP all about? Is it merely a marketing fad, or does it really denote something new and useful, perhaps even a new panacea?

To be short, OOP is no panacea. Contrary to the claims made by some vendors, it does not make programming a trivial task. OOP requires a sizable portion of ability and experience—perhaps even more than traditional programming techniques do. However, OOP definitely has its strengths: it often permits more elegant solutions than are possible with conventional techniques; it promotes modularity and thus readability and maintainability of programs; and it contributes to the extensibility and reusability of software.

This book is aimed at students of computer science as well as at practitioners who want to gain a perspective on new software development methods. Since more and more languages are being extended to include object-oriented features, this book also addresses programmers who want to make better use of these new features.

The goal of this book is to convey the fundamentals of OOP, namely classes, inheritance and dynamic binding. The emphasis is on the concepts rather than on the specifics of a particular programming language. In addition, readers should learn to determine for which problems OOP is most suitable, and which problems would be better solved with conventional means.

Object-oriented programming is programming in the large. Although its principles can be explained on the basis of small examples, wider reaching examples are necessary in order to convey the power and elegance of this technique. This is precisely what is missing in most books on the subject. Chapter 11 thus presents the design and implementation of an adequately large system, including source code, in order to drive home the ideas behind object-oriented programming.

The examples in this book are not coded in any of the widespread languages such as Smalltalk or C++. Instead, *Oberon-2*, a language in the tradition of Pascal and Modula-2, was selected: The reason for this choice is that Oberon-2 is more compact than most of the other object-oriented languages; in fact, it is even smaller than Pascal, which makes it possible to master the language quickly. Object-oriented elements are smoothly integrated into the language without displacing proven constructs such as records, arrays and procedures. Once the reader has understood the concepts presented in this book, it should be easy to transfer them to any other language.

However, if the reader takes a liking to Oberon-2, the Oberon System, complete with compiler, editor and several other tools, can be obtained at no charge. Implementations are available for several platforms (see Appendix D). The case study printed in Chapter 11 is also available as source code.

The Oberon System was developed by Professors *Niklaus Wirth* and *Jürg Gutknecht* 1985-1987 at ETH Zürich [WiG92]. It consists not only of the Oberon language, but also of an operating system with the same name. The design of Oberon reflects the experience of the man who developed Algol W, Pascal and Modula-2. In Oberon-2, the author of this book added several extensions to the Oberon language that make it more suitable for object-oriented programming.

This book is neither a general introduction to programming nor a handbook for Oberon-2; these tasks are covered by other texts [ReW92, Rei91]. The reader is assumed to be familiar with an imperative language such as Pascal or Modula-2. Chapter 2 explains Oberon-2 only enough to enable comprehension of the examples in this book. Appendix A contains the complete language definition.

I want to express both gratitude and admiration for the two designers of Oberon for their elegant design of the operating system and the language, as well as for the ergonomic and efficient implementation that makes working with Oberon a pleasure.

I owe many of the examples to my assistants, *Robert Griesemer, Clemens Szyperski* and *Josef Templ*. Josef Templ also contributed valuable ideas for Oberon-2.

Last but not least, I want to thank Prof. *Peter Rechenberg*, Prof. *Jörg R. Mühlbacher*, Dr. *Martin Reiser*, Dr. *Günther Blaschek*, and Dr. *Erich Gamma* for their careful reading of the manuscript and for their numerous suggested improvements.

Zürich, 1993   Hanspeter Mössenböck

Contents

1 Overview

What is the essence of object-oriented programming? What are its typical applications, and what benefits can we expect from it? How does object-oriented thinking differ from traditional, procedure-oriented thinking? These are the questions that will be explored in this chapter.

1.1 Procedure-Oriented Thinking

Since the beginnings of programming we have been used to thinking in a procedure-oriented way. We decompose programs into procedures that transform input data into output data (Fig. 1.1). *Decomposing programs into procedures*

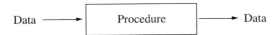

Fig. 1.1 Procedure-oriented thinking

In order to compute the area of a figure f, we write

    a := Area(f)

The procedure *Area* is the focus of attention, while the data a and f tend to be relegated to the background.

This approach is quite practical and usually leads to good programs. However, problems arise when a program has to deal with *several* kinds of figures (e.g., rectangles, triangles, circles, etc.). In conventional languages, it is not possible to use the same procedure for different figure types; instead, a separate procedure is required for each kind of figure (e.g., *RectangleArea*, *TriangleArea*, *CircleArea*, etc.). *Problems*

Furthermore, wherever a surface area is to be computed, the various kinds of figures must be differentiated and the respective procedure must be invoked. We have to write something like

```
IF f is rectangle THEN a := RectangleArea(f)
ELSIF f is triangle THEN a := TriangleArea(f)
ELSIF f is circle THEN a := CircleArea(f)
END
```

This means that we have to perform an extensive case analysis, which not only inflates the code but also causes the types of figures to be statically bound to the program. If later on ellipses are to be handled due to changed requirements, a new case will have to be inserted *at every location* where the computation of an area occurs:

```
...
ELSIF f is ellipse THEN a := EllipseArea(f)
...
```

Modifications of this nature are troublesome and easy to overlook.

Finally, the data type for figures would also need to be changed in order to accommodate ellipses. This could mean that all programs that use figures would have to be adapted to the new type or at least to be recompiled.

1.2   Object-Oriented Thinking

Decomposition into objects that fulfill contracts

The object-oriented way of thinking focuses on the data rather than on the procedures. The data and the operations applicable to them constitute *objects* that can be asked to handle certain requests and to return data as their result (Fig. 1.2).

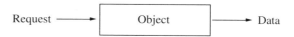

Fig. 1.2 Object-oriented thinking

The point here is that one does not have to bother about the type of the object to which a request is sent. Every type of object handles the request in its own way and carries out the correct operation: rectangles handle *Area* by computing the area of a rectangle, circles by computing the area of a circle, etc. Special notation is used to express this view. The statement

```
a := f.Area()
```

means that figure f is asked to handle an *Area* request. We also say that we send f the message *Area*. It does not matter whether f is a rectangle, a triangle, or a circle. Even if we later add ellipses as an additional type of object and then assume that f is an ellipse, the statement $a := f.Area()$ remains unchanged. The statement is properly executed as long as ellipses understand the message *Area*. This means that the introduction of ellipses *does not affect existing code*.

Our small example already suggests some of the advantages of object-oriented programming: Object-oriented programs have to contend less with case analysis and are more extensible than procedure-oriented programs.

1.3 Object-Oriented Languages

Our next question is: What is an object-oriented programming language? This is not as easy to answer as it seems. Common OOP languages differ in many details that are not by any means all necessary for object-oriented programming. Which minimum set of features must a language provide in order to qualify as object-oriented? The most significant features are information hiding, data abstraction, inheritance, and dynamic binding.

Information hiding means that the implementation of complex data is encapsulated in objects and that clients have access only to an abstract view of it (Fig. 1.3). Clients cannot directly access the encapsulated data, but must use procedures that are part of the respective object. Thus clients are not troubled with implementation details and are not affected by later changes in the implementation of the object.

Information hiding

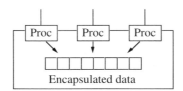

Fig. 1.3 An object with encapsulated data and a procedural interface

Information hiding was propagated by David Parnas [Par72]. It is not restricted to object-oriented languages but also supported by numerous other modular languages such as Modula-2 with its *modules* and Ada with its *packages*.

Data abstraction

Data abstraction is the next step after information hiding. The objects described above exist only once, yet sometimes multiple copies of them are needed (Fig. 1.4).

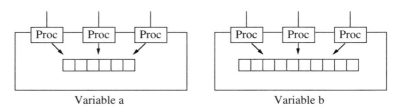

Variable a   Variable b

Fig. 1.4 Two variables *a* and *b* of an abstract data type

Just as we can declare any number of variables of a specific data type Integer, we want to be able to declare multiple variables of an abstract data type *Binary Tree*. As the operations +, -, * and DIV belong to *Integer*, a *Binary Tree* should provide operations such as insertion, deletion and searching for elements.

Integer   +, -, *, DIV, MOD, =, #, <, <=, >, >=
Binary tree   Insert, Delete, Search, Traverse, ...

An abstract data type is thus a unit consisting of data and the operations applicable to them. Multiple variables of such a type can be declared. Abstract data types are likewise not an invention of the object-oriented camp; they also can be realized in Modula-2 and Ada.

Inheritance

Inheritance is a concept not found in any conventional programming language. It means that an existing abstract data type can be extended to a new one that inherits all the data and operations of the existing type. The new type can include additional data and operations and can even modify inherited operations. This makes it possible to design a type as a semi-finished product, store it in a library, and later extend it to produce various final products (Fig. 1.5).

An important consequence of inheritance is that the extended type is compatible with the original one. All algorithms that work with objects of the original type can also work with objects of the new type. This greatly promotes the reusability of existing algorithms.

The fourth characteristic of object-oriented programming languages is *dynamic binding* of messages (requests) to procedures. When the message *Area* is sent to an object, the decision regarding which procedure is to carry out the request is made at run time, i.e., dynamically.

Dynamic binding

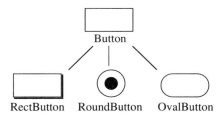

Fig. 1.5 A base type *Button* and various extensions

The compatibility between a type and its extensions makes it possible to store in a variable of type T not only objects of type T, but also objects of any extension of T. Thus a variable can be *polymorphic* (i.e., containing objects of multiple types). Depending on the type of the object stored in a variable at run time, messages are carried out differently. If variable f contains a *Rectangle* object, $f.Area$ invokes the *Area* procedure for rectangles (Fig. 1.6 a); if f contains a *Circle* object, $f.Area$ invokes the *Area* procedure for circles (Fig. 1.6 b).

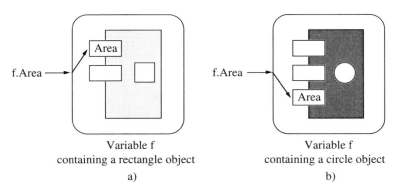

Fig. 1.6 Dynamic binding: the message *f.Area* is carried out by the *Area* procedure of the object that is stored in the variable *f* at run time

Dynamic binding has also been known for a long time in the form of procedure variables. The activation of a procedure variable causes the invocation of the procedure contained in it at run time. Working with procedure variables, however, is troublesome and error-prone, while dynamic binding in object-oriented languages represents an elegant and reliable solution.

Extensible abstract data types with dynamically bound messages are called *classes*. Classes are the basic building blocks of object-oriented programming. They will be treated in detail beginning in Chapter 4. In summary we can say:

Object-oriented programming means programming with abstract data types (classes) using inheritance and dynamic binding.

1.4   How OOP Differs from Conventional Programming

Object-oriented terminology

Upon first contact with OOP, one immediately notices its unaccustomed terminology. We work with *classes* instead of data types, and we send *messages* instead of calling procedures. These terms were introduced in Smalltalk [GoR83], one of the first object-oriented languages, and have gained widespread acceptance despite the fact that (apart from subtle differences) conventional terminology would have sufficed.

Table 1.7 translates the most important terms of object-oriented languages into conventional terminology. The object-oriented terms are usually more concise and handier than their conventional counterparts. Therefore we will use them throughout this book. The reader should be aware, however, that these terms do not represent radically new concepts, but have their corresponding terms in conventional programming.

Object-oriented term	Conventional term
Class	Extensible abstract data type
Object	Instance of a class
Message	Procedure call (dynamically bound)
Method	Procedure of a class

Table 1.7 Object-oriented terminology

Another difference is the unaccustomed syntax of procedure calls in object-oriented languages. In order to invoke a procedure that draws a circle with a given *color* , we write:

```
circle.Draw(color)
```

We say that we send the message *Draw* to the object stored in *circle* (or simply to the object *circle*). The message merely represents a request rather than a procedure. It is the object that determines which procedure is to carry out the request. Because the object is the focus of attention, *circle* is written in front of the message name.

These differences, however, are of minor importance. Instead, the following properties are more essential:

- concentration on the data
- emphasis on reusability
- programming by extension
- distributed state and distributed responsibilities

Object-oriented programming focuses on the *objects* rather than on the procedures. In fact, there are programmers who insist that no procedure should exist that is not associated with some object. This goes too far, for there are certainly situations in which the algorithm bears more weight than the data. Nevertheless, data are usually the central points of object-oriented design around which the procedures crystallize.

Concentration on the data

Object-oriented design strives harder to achieve reusability than conventional design does. The goal of most conventional design methods, such as stepwise refinement [Wir71], is to find a customized solution to a specific problem. This results in tailored programs that are usually correct and efficient but very sensitive to changes in the requirements. Even a small change in the specifications could scrap the entire design.

Emphasis on reusability

In object-oriented design, the goal is not to tailor the classes to the clients, but rather to design the classes independently of their context and adapt the clients to the classes. One strives to make the classes more general than would be necessary for a specific application. This requires additional time during development, but pays off long term: the classes can be reused in other programs for which they were not originally designed.

Object-oriented software is seldom written from scratch. OOP typically means extending existing software. Components such as windows, menus and switches are usually available as semifinished products in a library; they can be extended to meet specific requirements. Whole frameworks of classes can be taken from such libraries and extended to a complete program.

Programming by extension

Distributed state
and distributed
responsibilities

In conventional programs the program state is stored in the global variables of the main program. Although the main program invokes procedures, the procedures usually do not have a state of their own, but either transform input data into output data, or work on global data (Fig. 1.8).

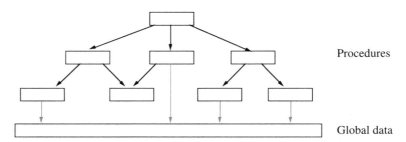

Procedures

Global data

Fig. 1.8 Calling graph of procedures working on a set of global data

In object-oriented programs the state is distributed among multiple objects. Each object has its own state (its own data) and a set of procedures working on that state. The object is responsible not only for a single computation, but for a whole set of services.

Both state and responsibilities are more distributed in object-oriented programs. The main program and its global data are less important and often do not even exist. Objects communicate with one another in order to perform a specific task (Fig. 1.9). An object knows *what* other objects are responsible for, but does not know *how* they fulfill these responsibilities.

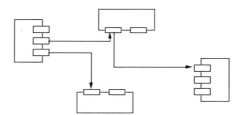

Fig. 1.9 Objects communicate by means of messages. Each object is responsible for a set of services that it provides to other objects.

Let us examine the example of a window system that, among other things, processes mouse clicks. An object-oriented window system registers such clicks, but it does not process them itself. It is not aware of the specific window types and hence does not know how they would react to mouse clicks (perhaps by positioning an insertion point, by marking selected text, by drawing a figure, etc.).

Thus it passes the click on to the respective window object and leaves further processing to that window. Processing mouse clicks is not the responsibility of the window system, but of the window in which the mouse key was pressed.

1.5 Classes as Abstraction Mechanisms

Classes allow the modeling of real world entities. It is interesting to look at their history in programming languages. The driving force behind the introduction of classes was the striving for abstraction and the desire to bridge the *semantic gap* between problem-oriented specifications and machine-oriented programs.

Semantic gap

Initially, abstractions for data and for operations were developed independently, but for some years there has been the tendency to combine them. Object-oriented programming is a consequence of this trend (Fig. 1.10).

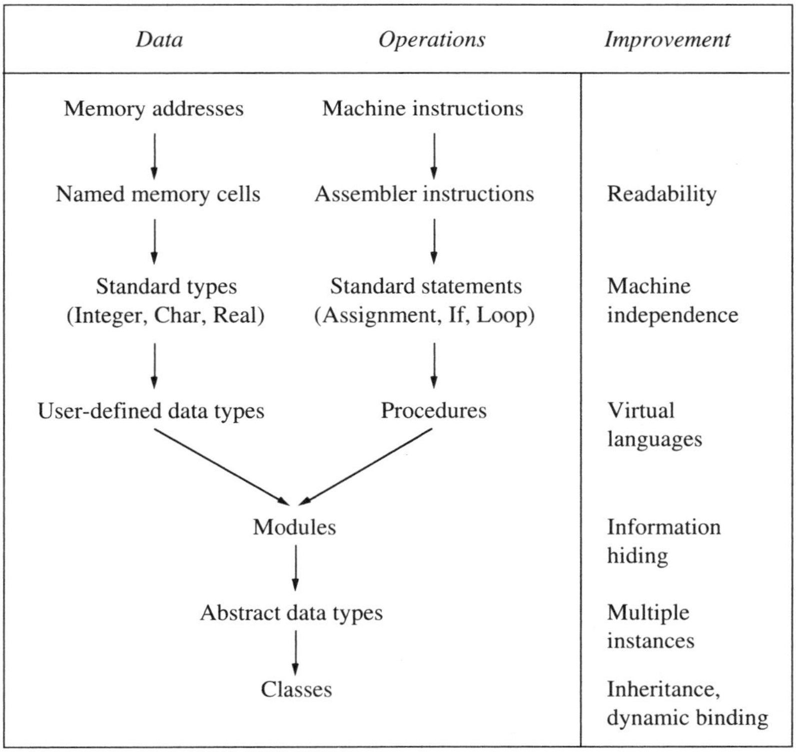

Data	*Operations*	*Improvement*
Memory addresses ↓	Machine instructions ↓	
Named memory cells ↓	Assembler instructions ↓	Readability
Standard types (Integer, Char, Real) ↓	Standard statements (Assignment, If, Loop) ↓	Machine independence
User-defined data types ↘	Procedures ↙	Virtual languages
	Modules ↓	Information hiding
	Abstract data types ↓	Multiple instances
	Classes	Inheritance, dynamic binding

Fig. 1.10 The development of abstractions in programming languages

The earliest programs used memory cells as data and machine instructions as operations. The greatest problem in programming was to map real-world entities such as a customer or an account onto the machine level. There was a broad gap between the problem domain and the program.

Variable names and mnemonic operation names

The first improvement came with assemblers, which made it possible to give memory cells a name and a primitive structure, and replaced binary instruction codes with mnemonic instruction names. This improved the readability of programs, but contributed little to reducing the semantic gap.

Standard types and standard operations

Only with the advent of higher programming languages such as Fortran could the semantic gap be reduced. Now arithmetic expressions could be written in common mathematical notation rather than needing to be reduced to a sequence of machine instructions. The first simple data types such as Integer and Real were introduced along with a set of operations that could be applied to them. Although the data types and operations were determined by the programming language, the machine independence that was achieved represented immense progress in the level of abstraction.

Note that Integer has almost all the properties of an abstract data type. Users of Integer variables do not need to know whether the most significant bit is left or right, or which machine instructions are used to realize the + operation. The only difference with regard to abstract data types is that Integer is built into the programming language, while abstract data types are defined by the programmer.

User-defined data types and procedures

In the 1960s languages like Pascal were developed that allowed the programmer to create a virtual language. One no longer had to restrict oneself to the data types and operations of a particular language; instead, the programmer could define custom data types and custom operations in the form of procedures. The resulting virtual language was tailored to a specific problem domain and thus more problem-oriented than a concrete language.

Modules

So far, data and operations had developed separately, although it is interesting to note that similar developments took place almost simultaneously in the two branches. First they achieved better readability, then machine independence, and finally more problem orientation. At the end of the 1970s it was recognized that data and their associated operations should be combined into modules. This brought more order into programs. Being collections of data and operations, modules are better suited to modeling real-world entities than procedures are. Modules are taken for granted in most modern programming languages; without them the development of large program systems would be much more complicated and error-prone.

The problem with modules is that there is only one instance of them. If multiple copies are needed, one has to use abstract data types which, like modules, consist of data and operations, but can be used to declare several variables of this type. Abstract data types already existed in languages such as Modula-2 and Ada.

Abstract data types

Object-oriented languages introduced the concept of classes. Classes are abstract data types supporting inheritance and dynamic binding. They are perfectly suitable to modeling real-world entities such as sensors, switches, or displays in software. The semantic gap between the problem domain and the program nearly disappears.

Classes

1.6 History of Object-Oriented Languages

Object-oriented programming is by no means new. The term was coined in the early 1970s in connection with Smalltalk [GoR83], a programming language developed by a research group at Xerox PARC. The roots of OOP, however, go back even farther to the language Simula [BDMN79], which was developed at the University of Oslo in 1967. Simula already had, in essence, all the properties of today's object-oriented languages. Thus OOP was around already a quarter of a century ago, which makes it even more surprising that the approach only recently began to gain widespread acceptance. This probably stems from the fact that Simula and Smalltalk were considered specialized languages: Simula was designed as a simulation language, and Smalltalk was viewed as a toy by many computer scientists. The value of classes for general programming was recognized only later.

Smalltalk became the prototype of object-oriented languages. It still is one of the most consistent OOP languages, for all its data types are classes and all its operations are messages. Smalltalk is usually interpreted, making its execution slow. Although newer Smalltalk systems do generate machine code, message dispatching is still interpretative. Furthermore, Smalltalk does not allow static type checking. This limits its suitability for larger software systems.

Smalltalk

Hybrid languages	In the mid-1980s many new object-oriented languages emerged; most of them were *hybrid* in nature and were extensions of existing languages such as Pascal and C. Hybrid languages include conventional data types (such as Integer and arrays) in addition to classes, and procedures in addition to messages. These languages permit type checking at compile time. Programs are translated into machine code, improving their efficiency over interpreted systems. The ease of switching from a familiar language like Pascal to a dialect like Object-Pascal [Sch86] contributed to the acceptance of such extensions and thus of object-oriented programming in general. Object-oriented dialects are now available for a wide range of languages.

Oberon-2	Oberon-2, the language used in this book, is also a hybrid. In fact, Oberon-2 is even closer to conventional languages because it does not have a special class construct: Classes are simply records that contain procedures in addition to data.

1.7   Summary

The most significant properties of OOP are the following:

(1) Data and operations are combined into classes that serve as types for objects.

(2) Classes can be extended to create new classes containing additional data and operations. Objects of an extended class can be used wherever objects of their base class are permitted.

(3) Operations on objects are usually not performed by procedure calls; instead, objects are sent messages. A message is a request, and it is up to the receiving object to determine which procedure is to handle the request. Objects communicating via messages are more loosely coupled than software components statically connected via procedure calls.

2 Oberon-2

Throughout this book we will use the programming language Oberon-2, an object-oriented language in the tradition of Pascal and Modula-2

This chapter introduces the reader to Oberon-2. We do not provide an introduction to programming, but assume that the reader is already able to read and write programs. Anyone who understands Pascal or, better yet, Modula-2 can read Oberon-2 programs without difficulty. Thus Oberon-2 is only described informally on the basis of several examples. Answers to more detailed questions can be found in the language definition in Appendix A.

Oberon-2 evolved from Oberon, which, like its predecessors Pascal and Modula-2, was developed by *Niklaus Wirth* [ReW92]. Several features of Modula-2 such as variant records, enumeration types and subrange types were omitted in Oberon. The language concentrates on the essentials and is thus well suited for both education and practice. New features in Oberon include the concept of type extension (inheritance); Oberon-2 finally adds type-bound procedures (methods).

Oberon is not only a programming language, but also an operating system that provides a run-time environment with command activation, garbage collection, dynamic loading of modules, and certain run-time data structures [Rei91, WiG92; see also Appendix A.12.4]. In Oberon the language is interwoven with the operating system. For the user to fully enjoy the power of Oberon, the language needs to be combined with the Oberon System, under which both Oberon and Oberon-2 programs run.

2.1 Features of Oberon-2

Oberon-2's most important features are block structure, modularity, separate compilation, strong type checking at compile time, type extension, and type-bound procedures.

Block structure allows nested procedures with separate scopes for identifiers. *Modules* permit the decomposition of large programs into smaller, comprehensible parts that can be compiled separately. The compiler ensures that their interfaces match. This is called *separate* compilation to distinguish it from *independent* compilation, in which no interface checking takes place (such as in Fortran or C).

Strong type checking means that the compiler checks at every operation (assignment, arithmetic, relational, etc.) whether variables are used according to their declaration and hence according to the intentions of the programmer. In this way many errors can already be detected at compile time, which drastically reduces the cost of corrections.

The object-oriented features of Oberon-2 are not yet treated in this chapter. They are described in Chapters 4 to 6 and then used extensively throughout the rest of this book.

2.2 Declarations

Data types

All identifiers appearing in a program (i.e., all names of constants, types, variables, and procedures) must be declared before they are used. In their declaration they are assigned a data type. Oberon-2 has basic types and composite types. The basic types are listed in Table 2.1.

	Type name	Typical range
Integer numbers	SHORTINT	-128..127
	INTEGER	-32768..32767
	LONGINT	-2147483648..2147483647
Real numbers	REAL	$\pm 3.40282E38$ (4 bytes)
	LONGREAL	$\pm 1.79769D308$ (8 bytes)
ASCII characters	CHAR	0X..0FFX (0..255 hexadecimal)
Boolean values	BOOLEAN	TRUE, FALSE
Sets	SET	Sets of numbers in the range 0..31

Table 2.1 Basic types in Oberon-2

The ranges of the basic types are not defined by the language. On most machines, however, the values given in the right column of Fig. 2.1 apply. Composite data types are *arrays, records, pointers* and *procedure types*.

An *array* is a collection of elements all of the same type (the element type). The elements do not have individual names, but are selected via an index. Examples of array variables are:

Arrays

```
VAR
    a: ARRAY 10 OF CHAR;  (* a has 10 elements: a[0], ..., a[9] *)
    b: ARRAY 100, 100 OF INTEGER;
```

Arrays are indexed with integers, the first element having the index 0. The elements are referenced as $a[i]$ and $b[i, j]$, whereby the index values are checked to assure that they are within the declared range.

A *record* is a collection of named *fields* of arbitrary type, for example:

Records

```
TYPE
    Person = RECORD
        name: ARRAY 32 OF CHAR;
        idNumber: INTEGER;
        salary: REAL
    END;
```

IF r is a variable of type *Person*, its fields can be referenced as *r.name, r.idNumber* and *r.salary*. Records can be extended to create new types (see Chapter 5).

A *pointer variable* contains the address of a record or an array, or it has the value NIL, which means that it does not point to any record or array. Examples of pointer types are:

Pointers

```
TYPE
    PersonPtr = POINTER TO Person;
    Box = POINTER TO RECORD x, y, width, height: INTEGER END;
    Vector = POINTER TO ARRAY 100 OF INTEGER;
    String = POINTER TO ARRAY OF CHAR;
```

If p is a variable of type *PersonPtr*, then $p^\wedge$ is the (nameless) record of type *Person* (the pointer base type) to which p points. The field *name* is referenced with $p^\wedge.name$. For the sake of simplicity the symbol $\wedge$ can be omitted, leaving *p.name*. This is an abstraction from the fact that p is only a pointer to a record and not the record itself. However, one must be aware that in the assignment $q:=p$ only the pointer p is assigned and not the record $p^\wedge$. The invocation of the predeclared procedure NEW(p) allocates memory for $p\wedge$.

If s is a variable of type *String*, then $s\wedge$ is the array to which s points. The array has been declared without length and is thus called an *open array*. Its length is specified at run time. $s\wedge[i]$ denotes the element with index i. Here, too, the symbol $\wedge$ can be omitted, leaving $s[i]$. NEW(s, n) allocates memory for the array $s\wedge$ with n elements.

In Oberon, dynamically allocated memory is never explicitly deallocated. Instead, the Oberon System features a *garbage collector* that collects and recycles regions of memory that are no longer referenced by a pointer. This resolves a frequent source of errors: The programmer could deallocate memory to which some pointer still refers. Dereferencing via such a dangling pointer would lead to an error.

Procedure types   Variables of type procedure (*procedure variables*) contain as their value either a procedure or NIL (no procedure). When a procedure variable is invoked, the procedure currently stored in it is activated. In the following example the procedure *WriteTerminal* is assigned to the procedure variable *write*:

```
VAR write: PROCEDURE (ch: CHAR);

PROCEDURE WriteTerminal (ch: CHAR);
BEGIN ...
END WriteTerminal;

write := WriteTerminal;
write(ch);   (*activates WriteTerminal*)
```

2.3 Expressions

Expressions describe the computation of values and consist of operators and operands. There are four kinds of expressions, which are shown in Table 2.2.

	Operators	Result type
Arithmetic expressions	+, -, *, /, DIV, MOD	Numeric
Boolean expressions	&, OR, ~	BOOLEAN
Relational expressions	=, #, <, <=, >, >=, IN	BOOLEAN
Set expressions	+, -, *, /	SET

Table 2.2 Kinds of expressions in Oberon-2

The meaning of the arithmetic and relational operators is obvious. It should be noted, however, that the compatibility rules in Oberon-2 are less restrictive than in Pascal or Modula-2. In particular, numeric types (INTEGER, REAL, etc.) can be mixed in arithmetic expressions, and character arrays can be compared. The following examples will answer most questions. The detailed compatibility rules can be found in the language definition in Appendix A.

Arithmetic expressions and relational expressions

```
VAR
    i: INTEGER; j: LONGINT; r: REAL;
    set: SET;
    s: ARRAY 32 OF CHAR;
    sp: POINTER TO ARRAY OF CHAR;
    p, p1: PersonPtr;  (*see declaration in previous section*)
    proc: PROCEDURE (x: INTEGER);
```

Expression	Result type
3	SHORTINT
300	INTEGER
100000	LONGINT
0X	CHAR
i + j	LONGINT
i + 3*(r-j)	REAL
i DIV j	LONGINT
i / j	REAL
(s > "John") OR (s = sp^)	BOOLEAN
s = "a"	BOOLEAN
p # p1	BOOLEAN
proc = NIL	BOOLEAN
~ (i IN set)	BOOLEAN

The expression $\sim x$ means the negation of x. The operators & and OR are not commutative and are evaluated as follows:

Boolean expressions

```
a & b        if a then b else false end
a OR b       if a then true else b end
```

This is called *short circuit evaluation* because the evaluation of the expression stops as soon as its value is known; this proves especially useful for expressions like the following:

```
IF (p # NIL) & (p.name = "John") THEN ... END
```

If p = NIL, the second part of the expression is not evaluated; thus improper dereferencing of p is avoided.

Set expressions The set operators have the following meanings:

+	Union	$\{0..7\} + \{5..9\} = \{0..9\}$
-	Difference $(x-y = x*(-y))$	$\{0..7\} - \{5..9\} = \{0..4\}$
*	Intersection	$\{0..7\} * \{5..9\} = \{5..7\}$
/	Symmetric difference	$\{0..7\} / \{5..9\} = \{0..4, 8..9\}$
	$(x/y = (x-y)+(y-x))$	

The expression *i IN s* tests whether the number *i* is contained in the set *s*.

2.4   Statements

Oberon-2 provides elementary statements (assignment, procedure call, return, exit), as well as structured statements for selection (if, case) and iteration (while, repeat, for, loop). The meanings of these statements are so common that the following examples should suffice. The reader can find details as well as the meanings of the predeclared procedures (ORD, CHR, etc.) in the language definition (Appendix A).

```
p.name := "John"                               (*assignment*)
i := 10*i + ORD(ch)-ORD("0")

WriteInt(i, 10)                                (*procedure call*)
i := Length(text)

r := p MOD q;                                  (*while*)
WHILE r # 0 DO
    p := q; q := r; r := p MOD q
END

i := 0;                                        (*repeat*)
REPEAT
    s[i] := CHR(ORD("0") + n MOD 10);
    n := n DIV 10;
    INC(i)
UNTIL n = 0

FOR i := 0 TO LEN(s)-1 DO s[i] := 0X END        (*for*)

i := 0;                                        (*loop, exit, if, return*)
LOOP
    ReadChar(ch);
    IF i = LEN(s) THEN Error; RETURN
    ELSIF ch = 0X THEN EXIT
    END;
    s[i] := ch; INC(i)
END
```

```
CASE ch OF                                  (*case*)
   "a".."z", "A".."Z": ReadIdentifier
|  "0".."9": ReadNumber
|  " ' ", ' " ': ReadString
ELSE ReadSpecial
END
```

Note that string constants can be assigned to a character array of fixed length as long as the array is sufficiently long to hold the string and the terminal character 0X that is automatically inserted during the assignment.

Also note that every structured statement ends with a keyword (usually END) and may contain a whole sequence of statements. Contrary to Pascal, the statement sequence need not be bracketed in BEGIN ... END.

2.5 Procedures

For procedures, an example will also suffice. The procedure below converts a number n to a character array hex that represents the hexadecimal representation of the number.

```
PROCEDURE IntToHex (n: LONGINT; VAR hex: ARRAY OF CHAR);
   VAR i, k: INTEGER; s: ARRAY 8 OF CHAR;

   PROCEDURE Hex (i: LONGINT): CHAR;
   BEGIN (*0 <= i <= 15*)
      IF i < 10 THEN RETURN CHR(i + ORD("0"))
      ELSE RETURN CHR(i-10 + ORD("A"))
      END
   END Hex;

BEGIN (*IntToHex: assumes n >= 0*)
   i := 0;
   REPEAT s[i] := Hex(n MOD 16); INC(i); n := n DIV 16 UNTIL n = 0;
   k := 0;
   REPEAT DEC(i); hex[k] := s[i]; INC(k) UNTIL i = 0;
   hex[k] := 0X
END IntToHex;
```

Procedures consist of a declaration part, in which constants, types, variables and further procedures can be declared locally, and a statement part (the body), which is executed when the procedure is invoked. The parameters declared in the procedure heading (n and hex) are called *formal* parameters. They are considered local to the procedure. The parameters specified at the procedure call are termed *actual* parameters.

Scope

The *scope* of an identifier, i.e., the range in which the identifier can be used, extends textually from its declaration to the end of the block (procedure or module) in which it is declared. It overrides the scope of any identically named identifier declared in an outer block. The scope of the parameter *i* in *Hex* overrides the scope of the variable *i* in *IntToHex*. Nested scopes allow the declaration of arbitrary identifiers in every procedure without having to bother about whether an identifier was already declared outside the procedure. Good programming style suggests that a procedure work only with its own local variables (including its parameters) and that it not use global variables or—even worse—local variables of an enclosing procedure.

Parameters

In the procedure *IntToHex*, *hex* is called a *variable parameter* because it is declared with the symbol VAR. A variable parameter has the same address as its corresponding actual parameter, which must be a variable. Thus if *hex* is modified in the procedure, the actual parameter is modified, too. Variable parameters are used as output parameters.

n is a *value parameter* because during the procedure invocation the value of the actual parameter is assigned to *n*. Thus *n* contains a local copy of the actual parameter. Changing the value of *n* does not affect the value of the actual parameter. Value parameters are used as input parameters.

hex is an *open array* parameter. Its length is determined at run time and is equal to the length of the actual parameter, which must likewise be an array.

Function procedures

IntToHex is a procedure that is invoked as a statement. *Hex*, on the other hand, is a function procedure that is invoked as part of an expression. It returns a value that is used in the evaluation of the expression. The value that a function procedure is to return must be specified in a return statement. A function procedure is characterized by the declaration of a result type following its formal parameter list.

Recursion

Procedures can invoke themselves recursively. With each invocation, a new set of local variables is allocated, so that every invocation of the procedure works with its own local variables.

Standard procedures

A number of standard procedures such as ORD, CHR, LEN and COPY are predeclared. Their descriptions are given in Appendix A.10.3.

2.6 Modules

Large programs are normally decomposed into smaller units, called modules. A compiler, for example, consists of a scanner, a parser, a code generator, and a table handler (Fig. 2.3). Each of these modules works on a well-defined subdomain of the problem and is easier to understand than the compiler as a whole.

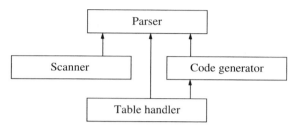

Fig. 2.3 Modules of a compilers: Arrows indicate the "is used by" relationship

A module is a unit with a clearly defined *interface*; it can be used without knowledge of how it is implemented, and it can be implemented without knowledge of the context in which it might later be used.

The module interface

In line with this definition, a module in Oberon-2 is a collection of constants, types, variables, and procedures that form a logical and syntactical entity. Its interface consists of the declarations of the identifiers that can be used by other modules. The module is said to *export* these identifiers.

Let us take the example of a module that represents the implementation of a dictionary in which word pairs can be entered and looked up. The first word serves as the key and the second as the value.

When designing a module like this, we first define its interface by writing a skeletal module consisting only of the declarations of the exported identifiers. For the dictionary this could be:

```
MODULE Dictionary;
    TYPE String* = ARRAY 32 OF CHAR;
    PROCEDURE Clear*; END Clear;
    PROCEDURE Enter* (key, value: String); END Enter;
    PROCEDURE Lookup* (key: String; VAR value: String); END Lookup;
    PROCEDURE Print*; END Print;
END Dictionary.
```

An identifier is marked as exported by adding an asterisk (*) after its name in its declarations. Thus the module exports the type *String*, as well as the procedures *Clear* for erasing the dictionary, *Enter* for entering a new word pair, *Lookup* to search for a word pair with a given key, and *Print* to output the dictionary on the terminal.

Implementation　　This skeleton is later complemented by further declarations and statements until the implementation is complete. Now let us tackle the full implementation of module *Dictionary*. For the sake of simplicity, it is implemented using an unsorted linked list.

```
MODULE Dictionary;
IMPORT IO;

TYPE
    String* = ARRAY 32 OF CHAR;
    Node = POINTER TO NodeDesc;
    NodeDesc = RECORD
        key, value: String;
        next: Node
    END;

VAR root: Node;

PROCEDURE Clear*;
BEGIN root := NIL
END Clear;

PROCEDURE Enter* (key, value: String);
    VAR p: Node;
BEGIN
    NEW(p); p.next := root; root := p; p.key := key; p.value := value
END Enter;

PROCEDURE Lookup* (key: String; VAR value: String);
    VAR p: Node;
BEGIN p := root;
    WHILE (p # NIL) & (p.key # key) DO p := p.next END;
    IF p # NIL THEN value := p.value ELSE value := "" END
END Lookup;

PROCEDURE Print*;
    VAR p: Node;
BEGIN p := root;
    WHILE p # NIL DO
        IO.Str(p.key); IO.Str("  "); IO.Str(p.value); IO.NL;
        p := p.next
    END
END Print;

BEGIN Clear
END Dictionary.
```

Note that the types *Node* and *NodeDesc* as well as the variable *root* are declared without an export mark and are therefore not visible outside *Dictionary*.

The interface of the module can be extracted from the implementation at any time using a *browser* (see Section 2.6). The browser simply collects the declarations of all exported identifiers and shows them in the following form:

```
DEFINITION Dictionary;
    TYPE String = ARRAY 32 OF CHAR;
    PROCEDURE Clear;
    PROCEDURE Enter (key, value: String);
    PROCEDURE Lookup (key: String; VAR value: String);
    PROCEDURE Print;
END Dictionary.
```

Note that this is not an Oberon-2 module, but only a special view of it, namely its interface. In languages like Modula-2 the programmer has to write the interface description (the definition module) manually and separately from the implementation of the module. Consistency between the two documents must be maintained manually. In Oberon-2 there is only one document per module: the implementation. The interface is only a special view on it; it is extracted automatically and therefore always consistent with the implementation. This is significant progress over the Modula-2 approach.

For the output of words, *Dictionary* uses the module *IO*, which is *imported* at the beginning of *Dictionary*. *IO*'s interface looks like this: *Import*

```
DEFINITION IO;
    PROCEDURE Str (s: ARRAY OF CHAR);
    PROCEDURE Int (i: LONGINT; w: INTEGER);
    PROCEDURE NL;  (*skip to next line*)
    ...
END IO.
```

All identifiers exported by *IO* can be used in *Dictionary* or any other module that imports *IO*. They only need to be *qualified* with the name of the exporting module. The procedure *Dictionary.Print* contains invocations of *IO.Str* and *IO.NL*, for example.

An important feature of Oberon-2 is that the compiler checks the correct use of interfaces. When a module is compiled, a description of its interface is written to a *symbol file* in machine-readable form. During the compilation of a client module, the compiler obtains the symbol files of the imported modules and   *Separate compilation with interface checking* thus knows the identifiers exported by those modules as well as their types. This permits type checking as if the exported identifiers had been declared in the importing module itself.

This is called *separate compilation*, in contrast to *independent compilation*, in which modules can be individually compiled, but the compiler does not check the interfaces.

During the compilation of *Dictionary* the compiler checks whether *IO* is used in accordance with its interface. If this interface happens to be modified later, then the previous check is no longer valid, and *Dictionary* has to be recompiled to recheck the correct use of *IO*. Meanwhile the operating system makes sure that *Dictionary* cannot be executed until it has been recompiled. Thus any modification in the interface of a module M would also require the recompilation of all its *clients* (all modules that import M).

Module body

In addition to its procedures a module can also contain its own code. This code is called the *module body* (the statement sequence at the end of *Dictionary*). The module body primarily serves to initialize the global data of the module. It is executed as soon as the module is loaded. Prior to that, however, the bodies of all imported modules are executed. (The imported modules need to be initialized before the importing module, or they could not be used in the body of the importing module.) This means that Oberon-2 does not permit cyclic import relationships among modules. The initialization sequence would otherwise be undefined.

Read-only export

A variable or a record field can be exported as read-only so that clients can read its data, but they cannot make modifications. This increases the reliability of the system, because the exporting module can be sure that clients will not destroy its data. Read-only variables and fields are marked with a minus sign (-) instead of an asterisk (*) in their declaration. A file system, for example, could write-protect its data as follows:

```
MODULE FileSystem;
TYPE
    File* = POINTER TO FileDesc;
    FileDesc* = RECORD
        name-: ARRAY 32 OF CHAR;
        length-: LONGINT;
        ...
    END;

VAR resultCode-: INTEGER;
...
END FileSystem.
```

The fields *name* and *length* as well as the variable *resultCode* can be read but not modified by clients. Only the exporting module *FileSystem* can modify them, because they are declared in that module. If a structured variable is read-only, this also applies to its components. Not only *file.name* but also *file.name[i]* is read-only.

In languages such as Modula-2, data that are not to be modified must be made available via access procedures. Read-only export is a more efficient solution.

What are modules for? First of all, they are a *structuring medium*. They group data and their associated operations together and help to create order in a program.

The purpose of modules

Modules are also an *abstraction medium*. They hide implementation details from other modules and provide their services via a simple interface. A module forms a wall. Identifiers declared within a module are visible outside only if they are exported. Identifiers exported by a module A are visible within a module B only if A is imported by B. Import and export make the coupling between modules visible.

Finally, a module is a *compilation unit*. Its source code is stored in a file and the resulting object code is written to another file. Thus modules are the smallest interchangeable components in a system. The code generator in Fig. 2.3 can be replaced with another one without recompilation, but not an individual procedure of the code generator.

2.7 Commands

The explanations thus far referred to the *language* Oberon-2; this section treats features of the Oberon *operating system*.

In most operating systems the smallest units that can be invoked in dialog with the computer are programs. In the Oberon System these units are *commands*. A command is any parameterless procedure P that is exported by a module M. In a typical Oberon environment a command is activated by typing its name ($M.P$) in a window and clicking it with the middle mouse button. Usually the name of the command is already displayed in some window and only needs to be clicked.

When the command $M.P$ is activated, the module M and all modules imported by M are loaded (if they are not already in memory) and the procedure P is executed. After P terminates, M remains loaded with all its global data and their values. If $M.P$ (or another command from M) is invoked again, M is not loaded anew. P finds the values of the global data just as they were left after P's last invocation.

Commands can thus communicate with one another via data structures in main memory rather than via files. This is simpler and more efficient and makes it possible to hide the data structure within the module to which the commands belong.

Let us now rewrite the *Dictionary* example of Section 2.6 so that *Clear*, *Enter*, *Lookup* and *Print* can be invoked as commands by the user. The interface of *Dictionary* would look like this:

```
DEFINITION Dictionary;
    PROCEDURE Clear;
    PROCEDURE Enter;
    PROCEDURE Lookup;
    PROCEDURE Print;
END Dictionary.
```

All four procedures are now commands and can be invoked like programs. But how do they obtain their arguments?

Command arguments

Each command can decide itself what kind of data it accepts as arguments: the text following the command name, the text in the current selection, the text at the insertion point, or some other marked object on the screen. The Oberon System provides appropriate procedures to read such arguments.

In our example, we obtain the arguments from the text following the command. The user activates the commands as follows:

```
Dictionary.Enter     book Buch
Dictionary.Lookup    book
```

Enter takes the word pair "book Buch" as its parameter and enters it in the dictionary. *Lookup* takes the word "book", searches for it in the dictionary, and returns the word "Buch". The command *Enter* is implemented as follows:

```
PROCEDURE Enter*;  (*read two words following the command text*)
    VAR s: IO.Scanner; p: Node;
BEGIN NEW(p);
    s.SetToParameters; s.Read; (*read first word*)
    IF s.class = IO.name THEN
        COPY(s.str, p.key ); s.Read; (*read second word*)
        IF s.class = IO.name THEN
            COPY(s.str, p.value);
            p.next := root; root := p  (*link p to the dictionary*)
        END
    END
END Enter;
```

IO.Scanner is a data type that allows convenient reading of names, numbers, characters, and strings (see Appendix C). The Scanner variable s is set to the text immediately following the command name by *s.SetToParameters*. *s.Read* reads the next symbol. Thus the command obtains its arguments and can proceed as in Section 2.6.

Note that *Dictionary* remains loaded after *Enter* terminates and the data of the dictionary thus retain their values. Succeeding invocations of *Enter* permit additional words to be entered, and with *Lookup* words can be searched for.

When is *Dictionary* removed from memory? Oberon's solution is that modules must be explicitly unloaded on user demand. The Oberon System provides a command for that purpose. After *Dictionary* is unloaded, a new version of it can be loaded.

Unloading modules

It should be noted that Oberon has a *linking loader* that links object modules with other modules only upon loading. There are no prelinked object files; rather, each object module is its own file.

Linking loader

The loader also makes sure that each module is in memory *only once*. If module A is loaded that imports an already loaded module B, then A is linked to the loaded B and B is not loaded anew. Since modules remain in memory after being loaded the first time, modules seldom have to be afterloaded. This reduces loading time and memory requirements for Oberon programs.

Commands are a useful language construct. They permit the creation of programs with multiple entry points. Commands can be invoked interactively without needing a main program. They prove especially practical in the creation of large systems consisting of several equally important services, such as an electronic mail system with services such as sending mail, reading mail, deleting mail, etc. Which of these services should become the main program and which should be subordinate? Commands allow offering all these services on the same level without the need to create an artificial superordinate main program.

Purpose of commands

3 Data Abstraction

Abstraction is the most effective weapon against complexity. It means concentrating on the essentials and ignoring the details. Large systems can only be made comprehensible by decomposing them into modules that are simple from the outside and hide all complexity within.

The principle of abstraction has been successfully applied to many technical things; e.g., anybody can operate a television set without understanding the circuitry within the device. The same should also apply to software. We strive for modules with simple interfaces that can be used without knowing their implementation. In other words, we want to abstract from *concrete* data structures and attain *abstract* data structures, or, even better, abstract data types or classes.

3.1 Concrete Data Structures

In older programming languages like Pascal, all data structures are visible. A programmer can define custom data types, yet their structure is known to other parts of the program; indeed, the structure must be known in order for the programmer to work with these data. We call these *concrete data structures*.

Let us consider an example of a nontrivial data structure, a *priority queue*, to which elements can be added in any order and then retrieved in the order of their priority. For the sake of simplicity, we assume that the elements are numbers that simultaneously express their priority (smaller numbers representing higher priority). One efficient data structure for the implementation of priority queues is the *heap* [Sed88]. A heap is a binary tree with n elements that are arranged in the tree such that the value of the parent is always less than or equal to the value of its two

Concrete data structure for a priority queue

children. The tree is almost balanced: there exists a number h such that all nodes have height h or $h-1$ (Fig. 3.1).

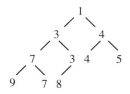

Fig. 3.1 Heap with 10 elements

Contrary to binary trees, there is no ordering between the two children of a node. The value of the left child could be smaller than, equal to, or greater than the value of the right child. However, the value of the parent is always less than or equal to the value of the children, which means that the root has the smallest value of the entire structure.

Fig. 3.1 shows that all levels of the tree except the last one are completely filled. The first level contains the element 1; the second level the elements 3 and 4; the third level 7, 3, 4 and 5; and so on. If the elements are stored in this sequence, an array can be used as concrete data structure, as shown in Fig. 3.2.

$$1\ \ 2\ \ 3\ \ 4\ \ 5\ \ 6\ \ 7\ \ 8\ \ 9\ \ 10$$

a | 1 | 3 | 4 | 7 | 3 | 4 | 5 | 9 | 7 | 8 |

Fig. 3.2 Array representation of the heap in Fig. 3.1

The advantage of this implementation is that pointers do not need to be stored; the children of elements $a[i]$ (if they exist) are located at $a[2*i]$ and $a[2*i+1]$. For a given element $a[i]$, the parent (if it exists) is located at $a[i\ DIV\ 2]$. The concrete data structure of a heap that can hold up to 127 numbers takes the following form:

```
VAR
    a: ARRAY 128 OF INTEGER;
    n: INTEGER; (*number of elements in the heap*)
```

A new element is inserted by storing it at the end of the heap (in $a[n+1]$) and then swapping places with its parent (propagating it upward) as long as the value of the new element is less than the value of its parent. As Fig. 3.3 shows, the number of swaps is of order $O(\log n)$.

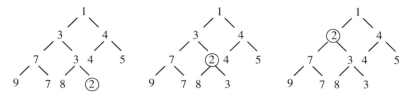

Fig. 3.3 Element 2 is appended to the end of the heap and then moved upwards until its parent element is of lesser or equal value

The following statements insert element x in heap a (we assume that the value MIN(INTEGER) is stored in $a[0]$ as a sentinel):

```
(*virtually insert x at a[n]*)
n := n + 1;
(*propagate x from a[n] upwards*)
i := n;
WHILE x < a[i DIV 2] DO
    a[i] := a[i DIV 2]; i := i DIV 2
END;
a[i] := x
```

A heap is used in situations that require elements to be removed from a set in ascending order of value beginning with the smallest. A typical example is a set of processes that are to be ordered according to time or priority.

The smallest element is always located at $a[1]$. When it is removed, the heap must be adjusted. This is done by moving the last element $a[n]$ to $a[1]$ and then swapping places with the smaller of its children (propagating it downward) as long as it is larger than (both) its child(ren) (Fig. 3.4).

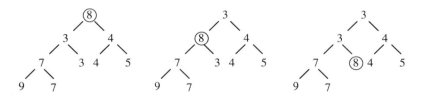

Fig. 3.4 Element $a[1]$ was removed. Element $a[n] = 8$ was moved to $a[1]$ and is now propagated downward in the tree

The following code segment removes the smallest element x from heap a:

```
x := a[1];
(*propagate a[n] from a[1] downwards*)
y := a[n]; n := n - 1; i := 1; ready := FALSE;
WHILE (i <= n DIV 2) & ~ ready DO
    j := i + i;
    IF (j < n) & (a[j] > a[j+1]) THEN j := j + 1 END;  (*select smaller child*)
    IF y > a[j] THEN a[i] := a[j]; i := j ELSE ready := TRUE END
END;
a[i] := y
```

Heap a and its number of elements n make up the concrete data structure for the priority queue. Clients can access the concrete data structure directly, but this is not recommended because of the following problems:

Clients are bothered with details

Clients must be familiar with both the declaration of the data structure and the algorithms for inserting and removing elements. This complicates working with the data and bothers clients with unnecessary details. The same code for accessing the data is often present in every module that uses the data, thus leading to duplication of code. Finally, clients may inadvertently destroy the consistency of the data (the heap order).

Modifications in the data affect the clients

Working with concrete data structures further has the disadvantage that modifications in the data affect the clients. If the implementation of the heap is changed from a fixed-length array to a tree in order to allow an arbitrary number of elements to be stored in it, then the access algorithms also change and all clients must be adapted. This is unpleasant because it requires knowing all locations where the data structure is used. It is easy to miss one.

The clients actually do not care how the priority queue is implemented. They simply want to use it as a black box. More important, they do not want to be affected by changes in its implementation. The concrete data structure thus needs to be hidden.

3.2   Abstract Data Structures

An abstract data structure is a unit consisting of data and procedures. The data are hidden within the unit and can only be accessed by means of dedicated procedures (Fig. 3.5). The data structure is termed abstract because only its name and its interface, but not its implementation, are known.

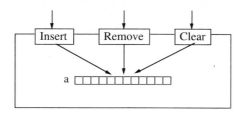

Fig. 3.5 Abstract data structure:
Heap *a* is accessible only via dedicated procedures

Abstract data structures support information hiding [Par72]. Their implementation is hidden behind an interface that remains unchanged, even if the implementation changes.

Information hiding

Abstract data structures have a *state* that can be modified by means of access procedures. The state is expressed in the values of the data structure and serves to store values between successive procedure invocations.

State

In Oberon-2, abstract data structures are implemented as *modules* that hide the data from clients by not exporting them. The priority queue thus becomes the module *PriorityQueue* with the following interface:

```
DEFINITION PriorityQueue;
    VAR n-: INTEGER;  (*number of elements*)
    PROCEDURE Insert (x: INTEGER);
    PROCEDURE Remove (VAR x: INTEGER);
    PROCEDURE Clear;
END PriorityQueue.
```

The module's three procedures *Insert* an element, *Remove* the smallest element, and *Clear* the queue, respectively. The number of elements is not provided by an access procedure, but directly as variable *n*. It is unlikely that its implementation will change, thus its type need not be hidden behind an access procedure. The variable is exported read-only, however, because clients could otherwise destroy the correctness of the module. The implementation of *PriorityQueue* takes the following form:

```
MODULE PriorityQueue;
CONST length = 128;
VAR
    n-: LONGINT; (*number of elements*)
    a: ARRAY length OF INTEGER;

PROCEDURE Clear*;
BEGIN n := 0, a[0] := MIN(INTEGER)
END Clear;
```

Priority queue as an abstract data structure

```
PROCEDURE Insert* (x: INTEGER);
   VAR i: INTEGER;
BEGIN
   IF n < length - 1 THEN
      n := n + 1; i := n;
      WHILE x < a[i DIV 2] DO
         a[i] := a[i DIV 2]; i := i DIV 2
      END;
      a[i] := x
   END
END Insert;

PROCEDURE Remove* (VAR x: INTEGER);
   VAR y, i, j: INTEGER; ready: BOOLEAN;
BEGIN
   IF n > 0 THEN
      x := a[1]; y := a[n];
      n := n - 1; i := 1; ready := FALSE;
      WHILE (i <= n DIV 2) & ~ ready DO
         j := i + i;
         IF (j < n) & (a[j] > a[j+1]) THEN j := j + 1 END;
         IF y > a[j] THEN a[i] := a[j]; i := j ELSE ready := TRUE END
      END;
      a[i] := y
   END
END Remove;

BEGIN Clear
END PriorityQueue.
```

The implementation of the data and the access algorithms is now hidden. Clients see *PriorityQueue* as a black box that is easy to use via its procedures *Clear*, *Insert* and *Remove*.

Advantages   This solution has several advantages:

(1) Clients do not need to be familiar with the implementation of *PriorityQueue*, which makes it easier for them to use the data structure.

(2) The implementation can be changed later without needing to adapt the clients. If *a* is implemented as a tree rather than as an array (Fig. 3.6), the clients do not notice anything as long as the interface of *PriorityQueue* remains unchanged.

(3) The data are encapsulated in the module *PriorityQueue* and protected there against inadvertent destruction.

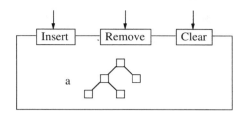

Fig. 3.6 Priority queue with modified implementation
but unchanged interface

Data abstraction also has some disadvantages: *Drawbacks*

(1) Using *PriorityQueue* is less efficient than using a concrete data structure because access to the data is now channelled through procedures. However, the cost of a procedure invocation is usually low in relation to the cost of the access algorithm.
(2) The data can only be accessed by the operations specified in the interface. If we later need to search for a particular element in the priority queue, say, this would be impossible because the module lacks an appropriate access procedure.

Information hiding should always be used with care and never for *Information hiding* its own sake. If all data are hidden as a matter of principle, the simplicity, the flexibility and the extensibility of a module may suffer. One should always be aware of the actual goal: to make the use of a module as easy as possible and to hide changes in its implementation from clients. The module *PriorityQueue* would not have been simplified if n had been exported as an access procedure rather than as a variable. The point is not that clients *must not* access private data, but that they *need not* do so in order to use the module.

3.3   Abstract Data Types

Of an abstract data structure there is only one instance. If we need multiple instances, we must use abstract data *types*. An abstract data type is likewise a unit consisting of data and procedures, but contrary to an abstract data structure, it can be used as a type; i.e., multiple variables of this type can be declared.

In Oberon-2 an abstract data type is implemented as a record whose fields can individually be hidden by not exporting them. The priority queue in our example can be implemented as an abstract data type as follows:

```
DEFINITION PriorityQueues;
   TYPE
      Queue = RECORD
         n-: INTEGER  (*number of elements*)
      END;
      PROCEDURE Insert (VAR q: Queue; x: INTEGER);
      PROCEDURE Remove (VAR q: Queue; VAR x: INTEGER);
      PROCEDURE Clear (VAR q: Queue);
   END PriorityQueues.
```

Queue is a record whose fields represent the data of the priority queue. Among these fields, n is exported read-only, while other fields are hidden (not exported). Note that each variable of type *Queue* has its own set of data.

The access procedures have an additional parameter q of type *Queue* designating the record to which the procedures refer. Because the data of the priority queue are changed by the procedures, q must be a variable parameter. The implementation of *PriorityQueues* looks like this:

Priority queue as an abstract data type

```
MODULE PriorityQueues;
CONST length = 128;
TYPE
   Queue* = RECORD
      n-: LONGINT; (*number of elements*)
      a: ARRAY length OF INTEGER
   END;

PROCEDURE Clear* (VAR q: Queue);
BEGIN q.n := 0, q.a[0] := MIN(INTEGER)
END Clear;

PROCEDURE Insert* (VAR q: Queue; x: INTEGER);
   VAR i: INTEGER;
BEGIN
   IF q.n < length - 1 THEN
      q.n := q.n + 1; i := q.n;
      WHILE x < q.a[i DIV 2] DO q.a[i] := q.a[i DIV 2]; i := i DIV 2 END;
      q.a[i] := x
   END
END Insert;
```

```
PROCEDURE Remove* (VAR q: Queue; VAR x: INTEGER);
    VAR y, i, j: INTEGER; ready: BOOLEAN;
BEGIN
    IF q.n > 0 THEN
        x := q.a[1]; y := q.a[n]; q.n := q.n - 1; i := 1; ready := FALSE;
        WHILE (i <= q.n DIV 2) & ~ ready DO
            j := i + i;
            IF (j < q.n) & (q.a[j] > q.a[j+1] THEN j := j + 1 END;
            IF y > q.a[j] THEN q.a[i] := q.a[j]; i := j ELSE ready := TRUE END
        END;
        q.a[i] := y
    END
END Remove;

END PriorityQueues.
```

Clients can now create multiple *Queue* variables, e.g.:

```
VAR negNumbers, posNumbers: PriorityQueues.Queue;
```

and use them separately:

```
PriorityQueues.Clear(negNumbers); PriorityQueues.Clear(posNumbers);
...
IF x < 0 THEN PriorityQueues.Insert(negNumbers, x)
ELSE PriorityQueues.Insert(posNumbers, x)
END
```

The abstract data type *Queue* can be used like any concrete data type (e.g., INTEGER). The language has been extended by a new data type and thus made better suited to solving a particular problem.

Extending the language by a new data type

However, abstract data types are again slightly less efficient than abstract data structures, because for each operation the object to which the operation refers has to be passed as a parameter. One should thus give consideration to when an abstract data *type* (i.e., multiple variables of this type) is needed and when an abstract data *structure* suffices. Examples of abstract data types include *Stack, Queue, Set, File, Window* and *Text*. On the other hand, for *Mouse* and *Terminal*, abstract data structures suffice because there is normally only one instance of them.

Abstract data types are often implemented not as records, but as pointers to records. Here, too, individual fields of a record can be hidden. The interface of the priority queue then takes the following form:

Abstract data types are often pointers

```
DEFINITION PriorityQueues1;
    TYPE
        Queue = POINTER TO QueueDesc;
        QueueDesc = RECORD
            n-: INTEGER;  (*number of elements*)
        END;
    PROCEDURE Insert (q: Queue; x: INTEGER);
    PROCEDURE Remove (q: Queue; VAR x: INTEGER);
    PROCEDURE Clear (q: Queue);
END PriorityQueues1.
```

The parameter q can be a value parameter here because it is not the pointer that is modified by the procedures, but only the fields of the record referenced by the pointer.

4 Classes

A problem with the notation for abstract data types is that data and procedures do not form a syntactic entity. Procedures are declared outside the record and without visible connection to it. Thus it is not immediately clear which procedures belong to a data type.

Therefore, Oberon-2 permits the declaration of special procedures (*methods*) that are syntactically connected to a record. Records that contain methods in addition to data fields are called *classes*. Values whose type is a class are termed *objects*.

Classes differ from abstract data types in that they are extensible and support the dynamic binding of messages to methods. We postpone the discussion of extensibility and dynamic binding to Chapters 5 and 6, respectively.

4.1 Methods

The procedures associated with a class are termed *methods* or *type-bound procedures* in order to distinguish them from ordinary procedures.

Methods

The type *Queue* in Section 3.3, for example, could be implemented as a class with the following interface:

```
DEFINITION PriorityQueues;
TYPE
    Queue = RECORD
        n-: LONGINT;
        PROCEDURE (VAR q: Queue) Insert (x: INTEGER);
        PROCEDURE (VAR q: Queue) Remove (VAR x: INTEGER);
        PROCEDURE (VAR q: Queue) Clear;
    END;
END PriorityQueues.
```

Methods are considered (constant) record fields whose type is a procedure type. At invocation they are accessed like record fields, e.g.:

    q.Insert(x)

Messages

We say that we send the message *Insert* to the object designated by q. The terminology should make clear that this is not a procedure call, but a request to an object. Only at run time will it be decided which method is to handle the request.

Receiver

The object to which a message is sent is called the *receiver*. Thus the object designated by q is the receiver of the message *Insert*. It reacts by invoking the *Insert* method of its class. Since the variable q can contain objects of various classes (see Chapter 5) the *Insert* message can lead to the invocation of different methods.

The receiver is a parameter of every method. In order to distinguish it from other parameters, it is declared in front of the method name:

    PROCEDURE (VAR q: Queue) Insert (x: INTEGER);

Separating the receiver from the other formal parameter seems justified since the corresponding actual receiver parameter is also written in front of the message name when the message is sent:

    q.Insert(x)

Note that the receiver plays a double role: Firstly, it is passed as a parameter to the method, and secondly, the object stored in it determines which method is invoked at run time (see Chapter 6).

Implementation of methods

Let us now look at the implementation of methods. Although they belong to records, it would be unwise to implement them directly in the record declaration. Statements would be in the midst of declarations. Thus in Oberon-2 methods are implemented outside records, but in the same module. Nevertheless, they are considered local to their record. To which record a method belongs can be seen from the type of its formal receiver parameter.

Oberon-2 goes even further and omits the procedure headings in the record declaration. The class interface at the beginning of this section is not an Oberon-2 program, but a piece of documentation created by the browser (see Section 2.6). The actual implementation of *PriorityQueues* takes the following form:

    MODULE PriorityQueues;
    CONST length = 128;

```
TYPE
    Queue* = RECORD
        n-: LONGINT; (*number of elements*)
        a: ARRAY length OF INTEGER
    END;

PROCEDURE (VAR q: Queue) Clear*;
BEGIN q.n := 0, q.a[0] := MIN(INTEGER)
END Clear;

PROCEDURE (VAR q: Queue) Insert* (x: INTEGER);
    VAR i: INTEGER;
BEGIN
    IF q.n < length - 1 THEN
        q.n := q.n + 1; i := q.n;
        WHILE x < q.a[i DIV 2] DO q.a[i] := q.a[i DIV 2]; i := i DIV 2 END;
        q.a[i] := x
    END
END Insert;

PROCEDURE (VAR q: Queue) Remove* (VAR x: INTEGER);
    VAR y, i, j: INTEGER; ready: BOOLEAN;
BEGIN
    IF q.n > 0 THEN
        x := q.a[1]; y := q.a[n];
        q.n := q.n - 1; i := 1; ready := FALSE;
        WHILE (i <= q.n DIV 2) & ~ ready DO
            j := i + i;
            IF (j < q.n) & (q.a[j] > q.a[j+1]) THEN j := j + 1 END;
            IF y > q.a[j] THEN q.a[i] := q.a[j]; i := j ELSE ready := TRUE END
        END;
        q.a[i] := y
    END
END Remove;

END PriorityQueues.
```

The receiver parameters in the procedure headings of *Clear*, *Insert* and *Remove* indicate that these are not ordinary procedures, but methods of the class *Queue*.

Why do we actually need a special method notation, since the operations of a class could also be implemented as procedure variables? For example:

Methods and procedure variables

```
TYPE
    Queue = RECORD
        n-: INTEGER;
        a: ARRAY length OF INTEGER;
        Insert: PROCEDURE (VAR q: Queue; x: INTEGER);
        Remove: PROCEDURE (VAR q: Queue; VAR x: INTEGER);
        Clear: PROCEDURE (VAR q: Queue);
    END;
```

This is a possible solution, but it has the following drawbacks:

(1) Procedure variables occupy storage in every object, although their values are the same for all objects of a class. Methods, on the other hand, belong to the *class* and are not stored in objects.

(2) Procedure variables must be initialized in each object; this means that they must be assigned procedures whenever an object is created. This is easy to forget. Methods need not be initialized.

(3) The operations of a class should be procedure *constants* rather than procedure *variables*. It should not be possible to exchange them at run time. Methods are constants while procedure variables are not.

Pointer types

Many object-oriented programs do not work with records, but with pointers to records. These are actually pointer-to-class types. For the sake of simplicity, we also refer to these pointer types as classes as long as this does not lead to confusion. Variables of these types point to objects. In the following example *Queue1* is declared as a pointer type:

```
DEFINITION PriorityQueues1;
TYPE
   Queue1 = POINTER TO QueueDesc;
   Queue1Desc = RECORD
     n-: LONGINT;
     PROCEDURE (q: Queue1) Insert (x: INTEGER);
     PROCEDURE (q: Queue1) Remove (VAR x: INTEGER);
     PROCEDURE (q: Queue1) Clear;
   END;
END PriorityQueues1.
```

If the type of the formal receiver parameter is a pointer type, the receiver must be a value parameter, whereas in the case of records it must be a variable parameter. The use of *Queue1* is analogous to *Queue*:

```
VAR q: Queue1;
...
NEW(q); ... q.Insert(x); ...
```

Comments on the notation for methods

Oberon-2 differs from most object-oriented languages in its notation for methods. Other languages pass the receiver as a hidden parameter with the predefined names *self* or *this*. Oberon-2 avoids hidden mechanisms and requires that the receiver be explicitly declared as a parameter. The declaration of the receiver also has the advantage that it can be given an expressive name. A name like q or *queue* provides better readability than *self*.

When the fields and methods of a receiver are referenced in Oberon-2, they must be qualified with the name of the receiver (e.g., $q.a$). Most object-oriented languages allow the programmer the option of referencing a field as *self.a* or only as *a*. This may be confusing since *a* could be a local or global variable as well.

Omitting the method headings in the record declaration avoids redundancy. The type declaration is kept short. Modifications cannot lead to inconsistent method headings. The browser permits viewing the class with all its methods by extracting this information from the program. This proves faster than flipping through pages of source code.

The fact that the class and module interfaces are not manually written by the programmer, but extracted from the source code, requires some readjustment, especially on the part of Modula-2 programmers. After getting used to the idea, however, anything else seems inconvenient. Programs increasingly tend to be read and written directly on the screen, which makes it practical to enjoy the screen's advantages over paper. Of course, the extracted information can also be printed to hardcopy.

4.2 Classes and Modules

Classes and modules bear certain similarities: they encapsulate data and make them available via access procedures. Are both constructs necessary, or could we scrap modules and employ classes as compilation units?

The question is justified, and some languages, such as Smalltalk, actually use only classes and not modules. Closer examination, however, reveals that using both constructs does make sense. They are complementary.

Classes are expected to support information hiding. In Oberon-2, however, classes are records; access to their fields is unrestricted. How does this agree?

Information hiding

In Oberon-2, not a class but the module in which the class is implemented is responsible for information hiding. Within a module all fields of private classes are visible, but other modules see only the exported fields. Within *PriorityQueues*, field *a* of class *Queue* is visible, but it is not visible for client modules. This makes sense because a module should only contain related data and procedures anyway. Why should we want to hide information among them?

For reasons of efficiency, it is sometimes necessary for a procedure to have *direct* access to the data of *two or more* classes. If the data were not visible outside the classes, an ordinary procedure could not access them. It would not help to make the procedure a method of one class, for then it still would not have access to the data of the other class. In Oberon-2 the procedure along with the classes to which it must have efficient access can be wrapped in one module. This allows the procedure to access the data of both classes while still keeping the data hidden from other modules. Thus modules permit the grouping of several classes and procedures to a subsystem.

Modules as collections of functions

Not all programs can be forced into the scheme of classes and methods. There are procedures (e.g., numeric functions) that are neither dependent on any state nor modify a state and thus cannot be naturally associated with any class. Modules make it possible to group such functions together, without having to resort to classes which would be an artificial imposition.

Global variables and procedures

Modules allow the use of global variables and procedures in connection with classes. Values that must be accessible for all objects of a class can be stored in global variables of a module without requiring storage in each object. Global procedures permit the execution of operations on a *class*; for example, a procedure could be used to create a new object of a class. Such operations cannot be implemented as methods because an object cannot be sent a message before it is created.

4.3   Examples

The following examples are intended to give the reader a better feel for working with classes.

The class Set

The standard type SET provides sets of integers between 0 and MAX(SET). If sets of arbitrary integers are needed, a class *Set* can be defined:

```
DEFINITION Sets;
TYPE
   Set = RECORD
      PROCEDURE (VAR s: Set) Init (max: INTEGER);
      PROCEDURE (VAR s: Set) CopyTo (VAR s1: Set);
      PROCEDURE (VAR s: Set) Clear;
```

```
        PROCEDURE (VAR s: Set) Incl (x: INTEGER);
        PROCEDURE (VAR s: Set) Excl (x: INTEGER);
        PROCEDURE (VAR s: Set) Contains (x: INTEGER): BOOLEAN;
        PROCEDURE (VAR s: Set) Add (s1: Set);
        PROCEDURE (VAR s: Set) Subtract (s1: Set);
        PROCEDURE (VAR s: Set) Intersect (s1: Set);
    END;
END Sets.
```

Note that *Set* is a record type, and thus the receiver parameter of the methods must be a variable parameter. The meaning of the operations is obvious, so that we can immediately go on to their implementation.

```
MODULE Sets;
CONST setSize = 32;  (*size of type SET*)
TYPE
    Set* = RECORD
        max-: INTEGER;  (*largest element allowed*)
        val: POINTER TO ARRAY OF SET
    END;

PROCEDURE (VAR s: Set) Init* (max: INTEGER);
BEGIN
    s.max := max;
    NEW(s.val, (max + setSize) DIV setSize)
END Init;

PROCEDURE (VAR s: Set) CopyTo* (VAR s1: Set);
    VAR i: INTEGER;
BEGIN
    s1.Init(s.max);
    FOR i := 0 TO s.max DIV setSize DO s1.val[i] := s.val[i] END
END CopyTo;

PROCEDURE (VAR s: Set) Clear*;
    VAR i: INTEGER;
BEGIN
    FOR i := 0 TO s.max DIV setSize DO s.val[i] := {} END
END Clear;

PROCEDURE (VAR s: Set) Incl* (x: INTEGER);
BEGIN
    IF (x > 0) & (x <= s.max) THEN
        INCL(s.val[x DIV setSize], x MOD setSize)
    END
END Incl;

PROCEDURE (VAR s: Set) Excl* (x: INTEGER);
BEGIN
    IF (x > 0) & (x <= s.max) THEN
        EXCL(s.val[x DIV setSize], x MOD setSize)
    END
END Excl;
```

```
PROCEDURE (VAR s: Set) Contains* (x: INTEGER): BOOLEAN;
BEGIN
    RETURN (x > 0) & (x <= s.max)
    & (x MOD setSize IN s.val[x DIV setSize])
END Contains;

PROCEDURE (VAR s: Set) Add* (s1: Set);
    VAR i, max: INTEGER;
BEGIN
    max := s.max; IF s1.max < max THEN max := s1.max END;
    FOR i := 0 TO max DIV setSize DO
        s.val[i] := s.val[i] + s1.val[i] END
END Add;

PROCEDURE (VAR s: Set) Subtract* (s1: Set);
    VAR i, max: INTEGER;
BEGIN
    max := s.max; IF s1.max < max THEN max := s1.max END;
    FOR i := 0 TO max DIV setSize DO
        s.val[i] := s.val[i] - s1.val[i] END
END Subtract;

PROCEDURE (VAR s: Set) Intersect* (s1: Set);
    VAR i, max: INTEGER;
BEGIN
    max := s.max; IF s1.max < max THEN max := s1.max END;
    FOR i := 0 TO max DIV setSize DO
        s.val[i] := s.val[i] * s1.val[i] END
END Intersect;

END Sets.
```

The field *val* of the class *Set* is not exported. Clients can modify it only by means of methods. *val* contains the actual sets of numbers; it is implemented as a dynamic array of sets that is allocated the necessary storage at run time. *max* is the largest element that can be stored in a *Set* object.

Class Figure   As a second example, let us consider a class for figures in a graphics editor. Here we only describe the interface (the module *OS*, which is used in the interface, is described in Appendix B):

```
TYPE
    Figure = POINTER TO FigureDesc;
    FigureDesc = RECORD
        selected: BOOLEAN;
        next: Figure;
        PROCEDURE (Q: Figure) Draw;
        PROCEDURE (Q: Figure) Move (dx, dy: INTEGER);
        PROCEDURE (Q: Figure) Select (x, y, w, h: INTEGER);
        PROCEDURE (Q: Figure) Deselect;
        PROCEDURE (Q: Figure) Load (VAR r: OS.Rider);
        PROCEDURE (Q: Figure) Store (VAR r: OS.Rider);
    END;
```

The class *Figure* is implemented as a pointer to a record. Thus the formal receiver parameters of the methods must be value parameters.

4.4 Common Questions

This section answers some questions that might have arisen in reading Chapter 4.

Q: Can a method and a procedure declared in the same module share the same name?

A: Yes. A method is local to the class to which it belongs. There is no name conflict with globally declared names or with names in other classes.

Q: Can a method be bound to a class that is declared in another module?

A: No. The locality of code and data is an important principle that makes maintenance of software easier. If the methods of a class were distributed among various modules, this would violate the principle of locality.

Q: Can a message be sent to a pointer object if the formal receiver parameter of the method is a record? I.e.:

```
TYPE
    Ptr = POINTER TO Rec;
    Rec = RECORD ... END;
VAR
    p: Ptr;

PROCEDURE (VAR r: Rec) M; ... END M;

    ... p.M ...  (*is this message legal?*)
```

A: Yes. The record referenced by p is passed as a variable parameter to M. On the other hand, a message must not be sent to a record object if the formal receiver parameter is a pointer. This means that the following situation is forbidden:

```
VAR r: Rec;

PROCEDURE (p: Ptr) M1; ... END M1;

    ... r.M1 ...  (*this is illegal*)
```

A record cannot be passed to a pointer. When both variables of type *Ptr* and variables of type *Rec* are used and messages are to be sent to both, the formal receiver parameter of the methods must be declared as a record.

5 Inheritance

So far we have used classes only as abstract data types. The remarkable feature of classes, however, is that they can be extended. The extensibility of classes is the new aspect of object-oriented programming and the reason that OOP proves superior to conventional programming in many situations.

5.1 Type Extension

In Oberon-2 a record type can be extended to a new type that contains new fields and methods, yet maintains its compatibility with the original type. In the declarations

Base type and extended type

```
TYPE
    T0 = RECORD ... END
    T1 = RECORD (T0) ... END
```

T1 is a (direct) *extension* of *T0*, and *T0* is the (direct) *base type* of *T1*. In the case of classes, the base type is also called *base class* or *superclass*, while the extension is called *subclass*.

Specifying the name of the base type in parentheses after the symbol RECORD means that the new type is an extension of the base type and thus contains, in addition to its own fields and methods, all fields and methods of the base type, as though they had been explicitly declared here. We say that the extended type *inherits* the fields and methods of the base type and thus also refer to type extension as *inheritance*. Type extension also works for pointer types. If we have

```
TYPE
    P0 = POINTER TO T0;
    P1 = POINTER TO T1;
```

and if $T1$ is an extension of $T0$, then $P1$ is also an extension of $P0$ and $P0$ is the base type of $P1$.

In the following example *RectangleDesc* is an extension of *FigureDesc* and *Rectangle* is thus an extension of *Figure*.

```
TYPE
    Figure = POINTER TO FigureDesc;
    FigureDesc = RECORD
        selected: BOOLEAN;
        PROCEDURE (f: Figure) Draw;
        PROCEDURE (f: Figure) Move (dx, dy: INTEGER);
        PROCEDURE (f: Figure) Store (VAR rider: OS.Rider);
    END;

    Rectangle = POINTER TO RectangleDesc;
    RectangleDesc = RECORD (FigureDesc)
        x, y, w, h: INTEGER;
        PROCEDURE (r: Rectangle) Fill (pat: Pattern)
    END;
```

Figure 5.1 shows that *RectangleDesc* contains all the fields and methods of its base type *FigureDesc* in addition to those declared directly in *RectangleDesc*.

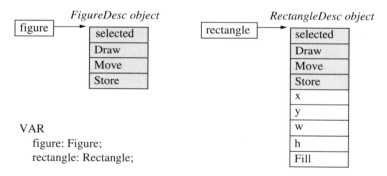

VAR
    figure: Figure;
    rectangle: Rectangle;

Fig. 5.1 Variables of types *Figure* and *Rectangle*

The fields and methods of the variable *rectangle* can be referenced as *rectangle.selected*, *rectangle.Draw*, *rectangle.x* or *rectangle.Fill*, for example.

In Fig. 5.1 the methods are represented as record fields in order to indicate that the first part of a *RectangleDesc* object is identical with a *FigureDesc* object. However, methods are actually not stored in each object, but only once per class (see Appendix A.12.4).

For the sake of simplicity, we subsequently also refer to the values of pointer variables as objects. When we speak of objects of class *Figure* or *Rectangle*, we actually mean objects of class *FigureDesc* or *RectangleDesc*.

Extensibility is transitive, so the type *TextBox* below is an extension of *Rectangle* and thus indirectly also of *Figure*.

Transitivity

```
TYPE
    TextBox = POINTER TO TextBoxDesc;
    TextBoxDesc = RECORD (RectangleDesc)
        text: ARRAY 32 OF CHAR
    END;
```

In addition to *Rectangle* any number of other types can be derived from *Figure*, e.g.:

```
TYPE
    Circle = POINTER TO CircleDesc;
    CircleDesc = RECORD (FigureDesc)
        x, y, radius: INTEGER
    END;
```

The inheritance relationship can be depicted graphically as follows (Fig. 5.2):

Graphical representation of a type hierarchy

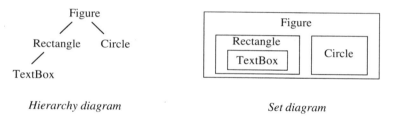

Hierarchy diagram   *Set diagram*

Fig. 5.2 Graphical representation of a type hierarchy

The set diagram in Fig. 5.2 shows clearly that every *TextBox* is also a *Rectangle* and every *Rectangle* is also a *Figure*. Inversely, however, not every *Figure* is a *Rectangle* for it could also be a *Circle*.

Is-a relationship

An extended type is a *specialization* of the base type: rectangles are specialized figures. We call this an *Is-a relationship*.

Subclasses allow not only the addition of new methods but also the redefinition of inherited methods. An inherited method can be redefined (*overridden*) by redeclaring it with the same name and with an identical parameter list in the subclass. Note that only methods, not data fields, can be overridden.

Overriding

The class *Figure*, for example, contains the method *Store*, which writes the fields of a figure to a file. When this method is inherited in *Rectangle*, it should also write the *Rectangle* fields x, y,

w and h to the file. Thus *Store* must be overridden in *Rectangle* as follows:

```
PROCEDURE (r: Rectangle) Store (VAR rider: OS.Rider);
BEGIN
    r.Store^ (rider);
    ... write r.x, r.y, r.w, r.h to rider ...
END Store;
```

Of course we do not want to rewrite *Store* from scratch; instead, we would like to reuse the inherited (and overridden) *Store*. However, this method can no longer be referenced as *r.Store*, for *r.Store* now designates the new *Store* of *Rectangle*. Therefore, it is referenced as

```
r.Store^ (rider)
```

The symbol $\wedge$ after the method name indicates that the *Store* method of the immediate superclass of *Rectangle* (the type of r) is to be invoked. Note that the meaning of $\wedge$ after a method name is different from its meaning after a pointer variable p, where $p^\wedge$ designates the variable to which p points.

5.2   Compatibility of a Base Type and Its Extension

The reader might wonder whether type extension is only a way to reduce the writing effort. Is there a difference between *Rectangle* and the following type *NewRectangle*, in which the fields and methods are explicitly redeclared instead of being inherited from *Figure*?

```
TYPE
    NewRectangle = POINTER TO NewRectangleDesc;
    NewRectangleDesc = RECORD
        selected: BOOLEAN;
        x, y, w, h: INTEGER;
        PROCEDURE (r: NewRectangle) Draw;
        PROCEDURE (r: NewRectangle) Move (dx, dy: INTEGER);
        PROCEDURE (r: NewRectangle) Store (VAR rider: OS.Rider);
        PROCEDURE (r: NewRectangle) Fill (pat: Pattern)
    END
```

There is a very important difference: *Rectangle* is compatible with *Figure* because it is an extension of *Figure*, while *NewRectangle* is not compatible with *Figure* although it contains the same fields and methods as *Rectangle*. *NewRectangle* is a completely different type.

Every Rectangle object is also a Figure object! This is the revolutionary aspect of object-oriented programming. It means that all algorithms that work with *Figure* objects can also work with *Rectangle* objects.

The compatibility between a base type and its extensions is particularly used in assignments. If *figureDesc* is a variable of type *FigureDesc* and *rectangleDesc* is a variable of type *RectangleDesc*, then the assignment

Record assignment

```
figureDesc := rectangleDesc
```

is permitted because *RectangleDesc* objects are (extended) *FigureDesc* objects and thus can be assigned to *FigureDesc* variables. The assignment works like a *projection*. That is, only those fields of *RectangleDesc* are assigned that also exist in *FigureDesc*.

The inverse assignment *rectangleDesc := figureDesc* is not permitted because a *FigureDesc* object is not a *RectangleDesc* object. (*rectangleDesc* contains more fields than *figureDesc*; the assignment would leave these fields undefined.) This error would be detected at compile time.

Passing an object as a value parameter is also an assignment. A procedures with a formal parameter of type *FigureDesc* can be invoked with a *RectangleDesc* object as its actual parameter.

The assignment compatibility between records is hardly ever used. Who wants to lose data in an assignment? Pointers, however, are another matter. If *figure* is of type *Figure* and *rectangle* of type *Rectangle*, then the assignment

Pointer assignments

```
figure := rectangle
```

is permitted because a *Rectangle* is an extended *Figure*. Here no data of the object *rectangle*^ are lost; instead, after the assignment *figure* simply points to *rectangle*^, whose first part is interpreted as an object of type *FigureDesc* (Fig. 5.3).

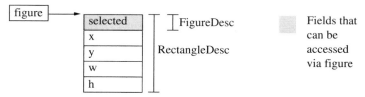

Fig. 5.3 Result of the assignment *figure := rectangle*

The fields x, y, w and h are still there in the object to which *figure* points after the assignment, but they cannot be referenced via *figure* because *figure* was declared as a variable of type POINTER TO *FigureDesc*, and *FigureDesc* contains no such fields.

The inverse assignment *rectangle := figure* is not permitted. *rectangle* would point to a *FigureDesc* object, and the fields x, y, w, and h would be undefined (Fig. 5.4). This kind of error is again detected by the compiler.

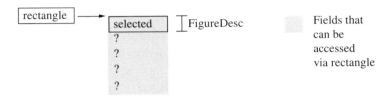

Fig. 5.4 Hypothetical effect of the assignment *rectangle := figure*

Records as variable parameters

There is another situation in which a base type and its extension are compatible: when a record is passed as a variable parameter. Let P be a procedure with the following interface:

PROCEDURE P (VAR figureDesc: FigureDesc);

This procedure can be invoked with a parameter of type *RectangleDesc*:

P(rectangleDesc)

With variable parameters no assignment takes place; instead the formal parameter *figureDesc* simply has the same address as the actual parameter *rectangle*Desc. No fields of *rectangleDesc* are truncated. As in a pointer assignment, the fields of the extension (e.g., *rectangleDesc.x*) are still there when P is executed, but they cannot be accessed via *figureDesc*. Passing records as variable parameters is used in Section 6.3 for message records.

Other examples of assignment compatibility

To discuss some more examples, let us return to the type hierarchy diagram of Fig. 5.2.

```
       Figure                    VAR
      /     \                        figure: Figure;
 Rectangle  Circle                   rectangle: Rectangle;
    /                                circle: Circle;
 TextBox                             textBox: TextBox;
```

Which of the following assignments is legal?

a) figure := rectangle   e) rectangle := circle
b) rectangle := figure   f) circle := rectangle
c) figure := circle   g) rectangle := textBox
d) figure := textBox   h) circle := textBox

Only assignments a), c), d) and g) are correct. Variables of an extended type can be assigned to variables of its base type, but not the other way around, as in b). In e), f) and h) the types of the variables are not derived from one another and thus are incompatible. All these errors are detected at compile time.

5.3 Static and Dynamic Type

In languages with type extension, record and pointer variables have a *dynamic type* in addition to their *static type*. The static type is the type with which the variable is declared. The dynamic type is the type of the *object* that the variable holds at run time; it can be an extension of the static type. The static type is used by the compiler for type checking, while the dynamic type is used for the selection of methods at run time (see Chapter 6).

  Dynamic type

 Thus objects must contain type information at run time. This is typical of object-oriented languages and does not occur in conventional languages. When the object *rectangle^* is created with NEW(*rectangle*), it has the dynamic type *RectangleDesc*, which it retains during its whole life. The variable *rectangle* thus has the dynamic type *Rectangle* (POINTER TO *RectangleDesc*).

 After the assignment *figure := rectangle*, *figure* also points to an object of type *RectangleDesc*. The dynamic type of *figure* is thus *Rectangle* (Fig. 5.5), but its static type remains *Figure*.

  Pointer assignment

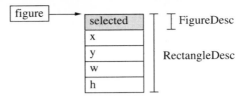

Fig. 5.5 The static type of *figure* is *Figure*;
the dynamic type of *figure* is *Rectangle*

*Record
assignment*

In the record assignment *figureDesc := rectangleDesc*, only those fields of *RectangleDesc* are transferred that also belong to *FigureDesc*. *figureDesc* does not contain the complete value of *rectangleDesc*; thus its dynamic type is not *RectangleDesc*, but only *FigureDesc*. For record variables the static and dynamic types are always the same.

*Records as
variable
parameters*

One exception is records that are passed as variable parameters. A formal variable parameter has the same address as the respective actual parameter. Thus it behaves as with pointers: its dynamic type can be an extension of its static type.

In the following procedure *P*, assume that *f* has the dynamic type *RectangleDesc*.

```
PROCEDURE P (VAR f: FigureDesc);
    VAR g: FigureDesc;
BEGIN
  f := g
END P;
```

What happens in the assignment *f := g*? Both variables have the same (static) type, thus the assignment should be possible. However, since *f* has the dynamic type *RectangleDesc* and *g* only the dynamic type *FigureDesc*, the fields *x*, *y*, *w* and *h* in the actual parameter corresponding to *f* would remain undefined.

Oberon-2 solves this problem by permitting the assignment to a variable parameter record only if its dynamic type is the same as its static type. The dynamic type of *f* is *RectangleDesc*; its static type is *FigureDesc*; thus the assignment *f := g* is not permitted. This check is done at run time.

Let us summarize:

- A variable of a record type *T* can only contain values of type *T*.

- A formal variable parameter of a record type T can contain values of type T or an extension thereof.
- A variable of type POINTER TO T can contain pointers to values of type T or an extension thereof.

The concept of dynamic type is central to object-oriented languages and distinguishes them from conventional languages. The static type is needed for static type checking (i.e., type checking at compile time), while the dynamic type is needed for the interpretation of messages.

Conventional languages with static type checking (e.g., Pascal) have only static types. In object-oriented languages without static type checking (e.g., Smalltalk), there are only dynamic types: variables are declared without type. Object-oriented languages with static type checking (e.g., Oberon-2, C++, Eiffel) employ both static and dynamic types.

5.4 Run-Time Type Checking

The dynamic type of a record or pointer variable can be tested at run time. The *type test*

Type test

    figure IS Rectangle

returns TRUE if *figure* has the dynamic type *Rectangle* (or an extension thereof), otherwise FALSE.

If *figure* has the dynamic type *Rectangle*, it should be possible to assign it to *rectangle*. This is possible if a *type guard* is specified for *figure*. The type guard

Type guard

    figure (Rectangle)

checks at run time whether *figure* has the dynamic type *Rectangle*. If so, the variable *figure* is treated within this designator as if its static type were *Rectangle*; if not, there is a run-time error. The following examples show uses for a type guard.

    rectangle := figure(Rectangle)   (*establishes assignment compatibility*)
    figure(Rectangle).x := 0   (*field x can be referenced*)
    figure(Rectangle).Fill(pat)   (*method Fill can be referenced*)

The type guard *figure(Rectangle)* plays a double role: It checks whether *figure* has the dynamic type *Rectangle*, and it temporarily changes the static type of *figure* to *Rectangle* (it widens it to *Rectangle*, as seen in Fig. 5.6). The type guard is thus a kind of type conversion. However, Oberon-2 checks at run time whether the conversion is legal, in contrast to many other languages in which types can be converted without type checking.

Fig. 5.6 *figure(Rectangle)* widens the static type of *figure* to *Rectangle*

A run-time error due to a failed type guard can be avoided by preceding the type guard by a type test:

    IF figure IS Rectangle THEN rectangle := figure(Rectangle) END

To improve the understanding of run-time type tests, we will look at a few examples. Which of the following statements are correct (see the type hierarchy in Fig. 5.2)?

    a) textBox := rectangle (TextBox)
    b) rectangle := figure (TextBox)
    c) rectangle := circle (Rectangle)
    d) figure := circle; rectangle := figure (Rectangle)

Statement a) is correct if the dynamic type of *rectangle* is *TextBox* or an extension thereof. If not, the type guard causes a run-time error. For b) the same applies as for a): If *figure* is at least of dynamic type *TextBox*, the designator *figure(TextBox)* is treated as if it were of static type *TextBox*. Thus it can be assigned to the variable *rectangle*. Statement c) is illegal because the dynamic type of *circle* can never be *Rectangle*. This error is detected by the compiler. Case d) is interesting: Here we attempt to smuggle *circle* to *rectangle* via *figure*. *figure := circle* is correct; *rectangle := figure (Rectangle)* is also correct as far as the compiler is concerned, but the type guard causes a run-time error because *figure* is of dynamic type *Circle* and not *Rectangle*.

Which of the following type tests return TRUE if *figure* is of dynamic type *TextBox*?

    a) figure IS Figure
    b) figure IS Rectangle
    c) figure IS TextBox

All three type tests return TRUE: *figure* contains a *TextBox* object, which is also a(n extended) *Rectangle* and *Figure* object.

Sometimes we want to apply a type guard to multiple occurrences of a variable, but we do not want to write it each time. In this case we can use the *with* statement: If f is a formal variable parameter of static type *FigureDesc*, then instead of writing

With statement

```
f(RectangleDesc).x := ...;
f(RectangleDesc).y := ...;
f(RectangleDesc).Fill(...)
```

we can write

```
WITH f: RectangleDesc DO
    f.x := ...;
    f.y := ...;
    f.Fill(...)
END
```

The meaning of this with statement is: if f is of dynamic type *RectangleDesc*, it is handled in the with statement as if its static type were also *RectangleDesc*. Thus the fields and methods of *RectangleDesc* can be referenced as $f.x$, $f.y$ and $f.Fill$. If f is not of dynamic type *RectangleDesc*, a run-time error results. A with statement is a regional type guard. The type test is performed only once, when the with statement is entered. With statements can also be applied to pointers, e.g.:

```
WITH figure: Rectangle DO
    figure.x := ...;
    figure.y := ...
END
```

5.5 Extensibility in an Object-Oriented Sense

At first glance it seems that extensibility of software is not something made possible only by object-oriented programming. In practice software systems were always extended and modified. So what is special about object-oriented extensibility? The special aspect is that object-oriented programming makes it possible to extend systems in such a way that existing program parts are not affected.

Open and closed modules

Meyer [Mey87] explains the open/closed principle in terms of *open* and *closed* modules. A module is open if it is still being developed. Its interface is still immature and subject to frequent correction. It is used by few clients, which means that a modification in the interface does not have dramatic consequences: few clients are affected by these changes. At some point, however, every module must be closed. Its interface is frozen then and the module is released for general use. Now a modification in the interface would have more serious consequences since the module is used by many clients.

The dilemma is that project management requires both properties: A module should remain open as long as possible so that it can mature; on the other hand, at some point clients must be able to rely on a stable interface. The goal would be to have a module closed for its current clients, yet open for new clients (Fig. 5.7).

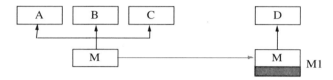

Fig. 5.7 *M* remains closed for *A*, *B* and *C* and is reopened for *D*.

How can this be achieved? There are four basic ways to extend the module *M*:

Modify the original

(1) The source code of *M* is changed. This causes problems for various reasons: First, it assumes the availability of the source code. Second, if the changes affect the interface, all clients have to be recompiled. Third, the clients are bogged down with the extension even though only a few actually use it.

Modify a duplicate

(2) The source code of *M* is copied and changes are made on the copy *M1*. This spares the trouble of recompiling existing clients and avoids bogging them down with unnecessary functionality. The drawback is its redundancy. The module now exists in two variants. Whenever an error is detected, it must be corrected at two locations. In addition, the source code of *M* is again required.

Embedding in another module

(3) *M* is embedded in *M1* in the sense that *M* is used by *M1*. Assume that *M* is a module:

```
MODULE M;
    ...
    PROCEDURE P (x: INTEGER);
    ...
END M.
```

It is now simple to implement a new module *M1* that has the same interface and imports *M*:

```
MODULE M1;

    IMPORT M;

    PROCEDURE P (x: INTEGER);
    BEGIN
        ... (*new functionality*) ...
        M.P(x)
    END P;
    ...
END M1.
```

This solution does not require the source code of M. The existing clients can continue to use M and are not troubled with the extensions of *M1*. However, one small problem remains: The clients of M cannot optionally use *M1* because they are statically bound to M. Each invocation of $M.P$ in their source code would have to be replaced with $M1.P$. But even that would not allow the substitution of M1 for M at run time.

(4) If M is a class, it can be extended by creating the subclass *M1*, in which the inherited methods can be overridden. As with embedding, the source code of M is not needed; M's clients do not need to be recompiled and are not bothered with the extensions in *M1*. In addition, programs that work with M can automatically also work with *M1*; their source code need not be modified, and M can be replaced with *M1* at run time. Clients are dynamically bound to M or *M1* (see Chapter 6).

Extension by inheritance

Extensibility in an object-oriented sense thus means: a class is reused in the form of object code, but it can still be extended in such a way that existing clients can also work with the extension without having to be modified.

However, inheritance is not intended to correct poor design. If a method of a class really was forgotten, there is no option but to reopen the class and to add the forgotten method.

5.6   Common Questions

Q: Why is it not possible to override inherited data fields in a
    subclass?

A: If it were permitted that a field f of an object a were of type
    INTEGER in the superclass A and of type CHAR in its sub-
    class B, then the compiler would not be able to perform a type
    check for $a.f := a.f + 1$. If a were of dynamic type A, then $a.f$
    would be of type INTEGER and the addition would be legal;
    but if a were of dynamic type B, then $a.f$ would be of type
    CHAR and the addition would be illegal. The type check
    could only be carried out at run time.

Q: Can a class be derived from more than one base class?

A: This is not possible in Oberon-2. In languages like C++ and
    Eiffel, such multiple inheritance is possible. Section 8.6
    explains why multiple inheritance is not permitted in Oberon-
    2 and how to survive without it.

Q: Can a subclass access fields and methods of its superclass if
    these are declared in another module and not exported?

A: No. In Oberon-2 it is the module, not the class, that is
    responsible for information hiding. Even subclasses cannot
    break through the module wall.

Q: Must an exported method be reexported each time it is
    overridden?

A: When it is overridden, an exported method must be provided
    with an export mark if the subclass to which it belongs is also
    exported.

6 Dynamic Binding

In Chapter 5 we saw that a subclass inherits code from its base class. However, code reuse is not the primary goal of inheritance. More important is the fact that a subclass inherits the *interface*, i.e., that it understands the same messages as its base class, although it may implement them differently. The compatibility between a subclass and its base class makes it possible for a variable at run time to contain objects of various types that react differently to a message.

6.1 Messages

A variable of static type *Figure* can assume various dynamic types, e.g., *Rectangle*, *Circle*, *Button*, etc. If it is of dynamic type *Rectangle*, the message *Draw* causes the invocation of the *Draw* method from *Rectangle*; if it is of dynamic type *Circle*, the same message causes the invocation of the *Draw* method from *Circle*. This mechanism is called *dynamic binding*: A message *obj.M* causes the invocation of the method *M* that belongs to the dynamic type of *obj*. The message is dynamically bound to a certain method (i.e., at the time it is sent).

Dynamic binding

Dynamic or late binding contrasts with static or early binding, which happens in conventional procedure invocations. With static binding, the compiler knows the address of the procedure to be invoked and generates a direct call. With dynamic binding, the compiler does not know the address of the corresponding method. This address must be determined at run time using the dynamic type of the receiver. Message sending is thus somewhat slower than calling a procedure. Over an entire program, however, this difference is hardly measurable.

Static binding

Clients do not need to distinguish object variants

Dynamic binding is central to object-oriented programming. It makes it possible to work with variables whose dynamic type is unknown and irrelevant at compile time. If an operation is to be applied to such a variable, one does not have to care about its actual dynamic type. One simply sends a message to the variable and lets the object interpret it. The message tells *what* is to be done. The object determines *how* it is done, i.e., which method is to be invoked.

Example

Let us look at an example. A class *Terminal* includes methods for printing characters, strings, and numbers on the screen:

```
TYPE
    Terminal = POINTER TO TerminalDesc;
    TerminalDesc = RECORD
        PROCEDURE (t: Terminal) Write (ch: CHAR);
        PROCEDURE (t: Terminal) WriteString (a: ARRAY OF CHAR);
        PROCEDURE (t: Terminal) WriteInt (value, width: INTEGER);
    END;
```

Assume that we need a variant of *Terminal* that converts all lower-case letters to upper-case letters before printing them. We implement a subclass *CapTerminal* in which we override the method *Write* so that it makes the required conversion using the predefined function CAP. *WriteString* and *WriteInt* are implemented in terms of *Write*; thus they do not have to be overridden for our purpose.

```
TYPE
    CapTerminal = POINTER TO CapTerminalDesc;
    CapTerminalDesc = RECORD (TerminalDesc) END;

PROCEDURE (t: CapTerminal) Write (ch: CHAR);
BEGIN
    IF (ch >= "a") OR (ch <= "z") THEN ch := CAP(ch) END;
    t.Write^ (ch)
END Write;
```

Every algorithm that works with *Terminal* can now also work with *CapTerminal*. For example, if *terminal* is a variable of type *Terminal* and *capTerminal* a variable of type *CapTerminal*, then the following procedure

```
PROCEDURE WriteOn (t: Terminal);
BEGIN
    ... t.Write(ch) ...
END WriteOn;
```

can be invoked not only as

```
WriteOn (terminal)
```

but also as

WriteOn (capTerminal)

The procedure does not need to know whether *t* is of dynamic type *Terminal* or *CapTerminal*. It need only know that *Terminal* objects understand a *Write* message. Due to dynamic binding, this message is handled either by the *Write* method of *Terminal* or by that of *CapTerminal*, depending on the current dynamic type of *t*.

6.2 Abstract Classes

Assume that there are other output classes beside *Terminal*: one for hard disk files, one for floppy disk files, and one for the network. These classes are similar: they all write data to some medium. It should be possible to exchange objects of these classes, that is, to use a hard disk file instead of a floppy disk file or vice versa. To achieve this, the classes must be compatible in the sense of type extension. But which class should serve as base class and which as subclass? Actually they are all at the same level.

A clean solution is to factor out the common behavior of all classes and to create a new base class *Stream*, from which all the other classes are derived (Fig. 6.1). Since there are no objects of type *Stream*, but only objects of type *Terminal*, *DiskFile*, *FloppyFile* or *NetFile*, we call *Stream* an *abstract class*.

Factoring out common behavior

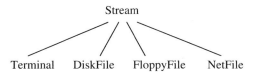

Fig. 6.1 Abstract class *Stream* and several concrete subclasses

What should the abstract class *Stream* look like? It certainly must contain methods like *Write*, *WriteString* and *WriteInt*. But how should these methods be implemented? *Write* cannot be implemented yet, because it differs from subclass to subclass; its implementation in *Stream* can only be empty. An empty method is called an *abstract method*, and classes that contain abstract methods are called *abstract classes*. The abstract class *Stream* is thus implemented as follows:

Implementing abstract classes

```
TYPE
    Stream = POINTER TO StreamDesc;
    StreamDesc = RECORD END; (*abstract*)

PROCEDURE (s: Stream) Write (ch: CHAR);  (*abstract*)
END Write;

PROCEDURE (s: Stream) WriteString (a: ARRAY OF CHAR);
    VAR i: INTEGER;
BEGIN
    i := 0;
    WHILE a[i] # 0X DO s.Write(a[i]); i := i + 1 END
END WriteString;

PROCEDURE (s: Stream) WriteInt (value, width: INTEGER);
    VAR n: LONGINT; i, k: INTEGER; neg: BOOLEAN; d: ARRAY 5 OF
CHAR;
BEGIN
    n := value; neg := n < 0; i := 0;
    IF neg THEN n := - n; width := width - 1 END;
    REPEAT
        d[i] := CHR(ORD("0") + n MOD 10);
        n := n DIV 10; i := i + 1
    UNTIL n = 0;
    FOR k := i TO width DO s.Write(" ") END;
    IF neg THEN s.Write("-") END;
    REPEAT i := i - 1; s.Write(d[i]) UNTIL i = 0
END WriteInt;
```

Stream includes one abstract method, *Write*, and two concrete methods, *WriteString* and *WriteInt*, whose implementation is based on *Write*. Thus *Stream* is only partially abstract. In *WriteString* and *WriteInt*, standard behavior is implemented that is inherited by subclasses, but can be overridden.

Abstract methods such as *Write must* be overridden in subclasses. It is good practice not to leave them empty but to implement them with a HALT statement (see Appendix A) that terminates execution. In case the programmer forgets to override them, the HALT statement reveals that error.

One concrete subclass of *Stream* is *DiskFile*. It is implemented as follows:

```
TYPE
    DiskFile = POINTER TO DiskFileDesc;
    DiskFileDesc = RECORD (StreamDesc) ... END;

PROCEDURE (f: DiskFile) Write (ch: CHAR);
BEGIN
    ... (*code to write ch to file f *)
END Write;
```

Write is the only method to override because *WriteString* and *WriteInt* are based on it.

If abstract methods have to be overridden anyway, what is the sense of declaring them already in the base class? Could they not be omitted in the base class and implemented only in the subclasses?

Interfaces of abstract classes

Abstract methods must not be omitted in the base class. The purpose of an abstract class is not to provide code that can be inherited, but to establish a common interface for all future subclasses. Establishing this interface in the base class is necessary to make dynamic binding work. A *Stream* variable can contain a *DiskFile* object at run time. If this object is to be sent an *Open* message, this is possible only if the interface of *Stream* permits an *Open* message.

Establishing a common interface is more important than inheriting code. Classes are often implemented as extensions of an abstract class. In these cases an interface is inherited, but no code. Code reuse is not important here; the common interface, however, is necessary in order to work with multiple subclasses without having to distinguish them in the program.

It does not make sense to create objects of an abstract class *Stream*. Nothing could be done with such objects. It does, however, make sense to work with variables whose static type is *Stream* and whose dynamic type is some extension of *Stream*. In many object-oriented programs, this is the normal case.

An abstract class is the design of its subclasses—a template that indicates which methods must be provided in the subclasses. This can be helpful. If a new *Stream* variant is to be implemented, most of its methods are already known.

Abstract classes are design

While we recommend moving as many methods as possible from the subclasses to the abstract class, it is usually unwise to do the same with data fields. Which fields are needed in a subclass depends on its implementation. The fields of the base class usually cannot be reused in subclasses. They often even impede extensibility [WiW89].

6.3　Examples

Let us recall the declaration of the class *Stream* from Section 6.2:

```
TYPE
    Stream = POINTER TO StreamDesc;
```

```
StreamDesc = RECORD END;  (*abstract*)

PROCEDURE (s: Stream) Write (ch: CHAR);  (*abstract*)
BEGIN
    HALT(99) (*this method should be overridden*)
END Write;

PROCEDURE (s: Stream) WriteString (a: ARRAY OF CHAR);
    VAR i: INTEGER;
BEGIN
    i := 0;
    WHILE a[i] # 0X DO s.Write(a[i]); i := i + 1 END
END WriteString;
```

The subclass *DiskFile* was derived from *Stream*:

```
TYPE
    DiskFile = POINTER TO DiskFileDesc;
    DiskFileDesc = RECORD (StreamDesc) ... END;

PROCEDURE (f: DiskFile) Write (ch: CHAR);
BEGIN
    ... (*write ch to file f*) ...
END Write;
```

What are the results of the following statements? Compare your answers with those in the right column. The notation *Stream.Write* means the invocation of the method *Write* in the class *Stream*.

```
VAR stream: Stream; file: DiskFile;

      NEW(stream); ...
(*a*) stream.Write(ch);            (*Stream.Write*)
(*b*) stream.WriteString("abc");   (*Stream.WriteString  -> Stream.Write*)

      NEW(file); ...
(*c*) file.Write(ch);              (*DiskFile.Write*)
(*d*) file.WriteString("abc");     (*Stream.WriteString  -> DiskFile.Write*)

      stream := file;
(*e*) stream.Write(ch);            (*DiskFile.Write*)
(*f*) stream.WriteString("abc");   (*Stream.WriteString  -> DiskFile.Write*)
```

Cases a and b are clear. Since *stream* is of dynamic type *Stream*, *Write* and *WriteString* are invoked from *Stream*. *WriteString* itself invokes *Write*.

Case c is also clear. The dynamic type of *file* is *DiskFile*, so *DiskFile.Write* is invoked. Case d is more interesting. The dynamic type of *file* is *DiskFile*, but the *WriteString* method was not overridden there. Thus the inherited method from *Stream* is invoked, which in turn sends a *Write* message to its receiver. Since the receiver is of dynamic type *DiskFile*, *DiskFile.Write* is invoked.

Cases e and f are textually the same as a and b, but they yield the same results as c and d because *stream* is now of dynamic type *DiskFile*. Here we clearly see the dynamic binding.

Let us consider another example. A class *CryptFile* is to be implemented to encrypt an output before writing it to a file. This class is derived from *DiskFile* and the method *WriteString* is overridden.

```
TYPE
    CryptFile = POINTER TO CryptFileDesc;
    CryptFileDesc = RECORD (DiskFileDesc) END;

PROCEDURE (crypt: CryptFile) WriteString (a: ARRAY OF CHAR);
    VAR b: ARRAY 256 OF CHAR;
BEGIN
    Encrypt(a, b);  (*b is an encryption of a*)
    crypt.WriteString^ (b) (*call WriteString from the base class*)
END WriteString;
```

What are the results of the following statements?

```
VAR crypt: CryptFile;
...
NEW(crypt);
stream := crypt;
stream.WriteString("abc");
(*  CryptFile.WriteString -> Stream.WriteString -> DiskFile.Write*)
```

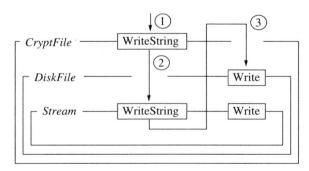

Fig. 6.2 Effects of the statement *stream.WriteString("abc")*

Figure 6.2 shows the results. Since *stream* is of dynamic type *CryptFile*, *CryptFile.WriteString* is invoked (1). This method calls the method with the same name in the base class of *CryptFile*, i.e., *DiskFile*. This is the inherited method *Stream.WriteString* (2). There the receiver is sent the message *Write*. The receiver is still of dynamic type *CryptFile*; thus the respective *Write* is invoked, i.e., the *Write* method inherited from *DiskFile* (3).

6.4   Message Records

Message records

Methods are only *one* possibility to handle messages. Another possibility is to take the expression "sending a message" literally. Then a message is a data package (a *message record*) that is passed to an object for handling. All we need for that is various message records, as well as one method per class that interprets the message records.

Let us return to our example with figures, rectangles and circles from Chapter 5. Figures can be sent the messages *Draw*, *Store* or *Move*. If these messages are implemented as records, we have:

```
TYPE
    Message = RECORD END; (*base type of all messages*)

    DrawMsg = RECORD (Message) END;
    StoreMsg = RECORD (Message) rider: OS.Rider END;
    MoveMsg = RECORD (Message) dx, dy: INTEGER END;
```

The concrete message types are extensions of the empty type *Message* and contain their parameters as record fields. Records of this type can be passed to a *message handler*, which is a method as in the following:

```
TYPE
    Figure = POINTER TO FigureDesc;
    FigureDesc = RECORD
        selected: BOOLEAN;
        PROCEDURE (f: Figure) Handle (VAR m: Message);
    END;
```

Message handler

The message handler interprets message records based on their dynamic type and reacts accordingly. It has to be overridden in every class. For the class *Rectangle* it takes the following form:

```
TYPE
    Rectangle = POINTER TO RectangleDesc;
    RectangleDesc = RECORD (FigureDesc)
        x, y, w, h: INTEGER
    END;
```

```
PROCEDURE (r: Rectangle) Handle (VAR m: Message);
BEGIN
    WITH
        m: DrawMsg DO ... (*draw rectangle r*)
    |   m: MoveMsg DO ... (*move rectangle r by m.dx, m.dy*)
    |   m: StoreMsg DO ... (*store rectangle r on m.rider*)
    |   ...
    ELSE (*ignore m*)
    END
END HandleRectangle;
```

The message m is analyzed using a with statement with variants (see Appendix A). The above with statement is to be read as follows: If m is of dynamic type $DrawMsg$, the statement sequence after the first DO symbol is executed and m is handled as a variable with static type $DrawMsg$; if m is of dynamic type $MoveMsg$, the statement sequence after the second DO symbol is executed and m is handled as a variable with static type $MoveMsg$ (hence access to $m.dx$ and $m.dy$ is permitted); if none of the variants applies, the else branch is executed, and if there is no else branch, a run-time error results.

With statement with variants

In this example, $Handle$ ignores unknown messages: the else branch of the with statement is empty. It would also be possible to react to unknown messages with an error message or to forward them to the handler of the base type.

To send a message to an object, an appropriate message record is filled and is passed to the handler of the object:

Using message records

```
VAR f: Figure; move: MoveMsg;
...
move.dx := 10; move.dy := 20;
f.Handle(move)
```

Depending on the dynamic type of f, a different message handler will be invoked that reacts to the *move* message in its own way.

Result parameters of a message are returned in the message record. To compute the area of a figure, say, the figure can be sent a message $getArea$. The message handler returns the area in $getArea.value$:

```
TYPE
    GetAreaMsg = RECORD (Message) value: LONGINT END;
VAR
    getArea: GetAreaMsg;
    area: LONGINT;

f.Handle(getArea);
area := getArea.value
```

Message records are similar to Smalltalk messages, which are also analyzed at run time by a handler that invokes the appropriate method. In Smalltalk, however, the message handler is built into the system, while in Oberon it is implemented by the programmer.

The Oberon system itself was implemented with message records. Likewise the Oberon0 system described in Chapter 11 uses message records in connection with viewers (windows).

Advantages

Message records have several advantages over methods:

- Messages are data packages that can be stored and sent later.

- A message can easily be distributed to more than one object. This is called a *broadcast*. Consider a list of figures that have to be moved on the screen. With methods, the caller would have to traverse the list and send a *Move* message to every figure:

    ```
    f := firstFigure; WHILE f # NIL DO f.Move(dx, dy); f := f.next END
    ```

    The structure of the list must be known to the caller (which is not always the case) and the code for the traversal is duplicated in every client. With message records one can implement the list traversal in a procedure *Broadcast* to which the message is passed as a parameter:

    ```
    PROCEDURE Broadcast (VAR m: Message);
        VAR f: Figure;
    BEGIN
        f := firstFigure; WHILE f # NIL DO f.Handle(m); f := f.next END
    END Broadcast;
    ```

    This allows hiding the list structure and keeping the code for the list traversal localized.

- An object can be sent a message that it does not understand. It may ignore the message or forward it to another object. For example, a *fill* message can be broadcast to all figures although only rectangles and circles understand it, but not lines. With methods this is not possible because the compiler checks if a message is understood by the receiver.

- It is possible to implement the message handler as a procedure variable rather than as a method. Then it can be exchanged at run time to dynamically change the behavior of an object.

Message records also have some disadvantages: *Drawbacks*

- It is not immediately clear which operations belong to a class, i.e., which messages an object understands. To find that out, one has to look at the implementation of the message handler.

- Messages are interpreted at run time using a with statement whose variants are processed sequentially. This is slower than a method invocation, which can be implemented with a single table lookup (see Appendix A.12.4).

- Message sending is somewhat clumsy. First the input parameters have to be packaged in the record, then the message handler has to be invoked, and finally the output parameters can be obtained from the record:

```
msg.inPar := ...;
obj.Handle(msg);
... := msg.outPar
```

- What was considered an advantage above can also be a drawback: the compiler cannot check whether an object understands a message. For example, the following program would be correct for the compiler:

```
TYPE
    NonsenseMsg = RECORD (Message) END;
VAR
    f: Figure;
    nonsense: NonsenseMsg;
...
f.Handle(nonsense)
```

At run time f would not understand *nonsense*. The object would ignore the message or the program would be terminated with a run-time error. The error might arise only after months and is difficult to find then.

Thus message records have advantages and disadvantages. In general, methods are preferable because they are more efficient, safer, and more readable. To implement broadcasts, however, it makes sense to employ the greater flexibility of message records (see also Chapter 8.7).

6.5   Common Questions

Q: Can a class be restricted rather than extended, i.e., can inherited methods and fields be removed in a subclass?

A: No. If a method M inherited from class A were removed from a subclass B, it would still be possible to send M to a B object stored in a variable of type A. What would that message yield? However, to prevent the invocation of M for B, one can override B with a method that generates an error message.

Q: In overriding a method, can the parameter types be an extension of the parameter types in the base method; i.e., if B is a subclass of A, are the following declarations permitted?

```
PROCEDURE (x: A) M (y: A); ...
PROCEDURE (x: B) M (y: B); ...
```

A: No. The types of the formal parameters in the two methods must match (except for the receiver). Otherwise the following could occur:

```
VAR a, a1: A;
...
a.M(a1)
```

If a is of dynamic type B, method M of B is invoked, which requires a parameter that is at least of type B. If the dynamic type of the actual parameter $a1$ is only A rather than B, M is invoked with a parameter of the wrong type. The compiler would have to generate a run-time test in M that would report an error if the parameter were not of type B. This would be costly.

Q: Does $obj.M\hat{}$ invoke the method M from the base class of the static or the dynamic type of obj?

A: The method from the base class of the *static* type of the receiver is invoked.

7 Typical Applications

Object-oriented programming yields very elegant solutions in some cases; in others it is of almost no use and can even add complexity. Applications that profit from object-oriented programming are the following:

- abstract data types
- generic components
- heterogeneous data structures
- replaceable behavior
- adaptable components
- semifinished products

Whenever a situation requires generic components, heterogeneous data structures or replaceable behavior, classes are the approach of choice. An experienced programmer recognizes such situations and employs classes then (and only then).

7.1 Abstract Data Types

Classes are an excellent structuring medium. They group associated data and operations and bring order to programs. They help to hide unimportant details from clients and thus reduce the complexity of software.

Classes as a structuring medium

Even if inheritance and dynamic binding are not used, it can make sense to implement a data type as a class in order to make it an identifiable, self-contained entity. An example is a class to control an RS232 interface. Details such as interface registers, handshake protocol and signals, can be hidden behind the following interface:

```
TYPE
   RS232 = RECORD
      PROCEDURE (VAR x: RS232) Init (address, bitRate, dataBits,
         stopBits, parity: LONGINT);
      PROCEDURE (VAR x: RS232) Send (ch: CHAR);
      PROCEDURE (VAR x: RS232) Receive (VAR ch: CHAR);
   END;
```

This interface is simple, hardware independent, and stable with regard to modifications of the implementation. However, it should be considered whether the component is really needed as a type. If not, a module like the following is the simpler and more efficient solution:

```
DEFINITION RS232;
   PROCEDURE Init (bitRate, dataBits, stopBits, parity: INTEGER);
   PROCEDURE Send (ch: CHAR);
   PROCEDURE Receive (VAR ch: CHAR);
END RS232.
```

The cost of data abstraction

Data abstraction is not for free. Although a class usually eliminates complexity, it also adds a certain amount of new complexity. After all, a new component is defined with operations whose syntax and semantics must be kept in mind. Data abstraction is only justified if the simplification is substantially higher that the newly introduced complexity. For example, it would not make sense to define the following class for a person's salary:

```
TYPE
   Salary = RECORD
      amount: INTEGER;
      PROCEDURE (s: Salary) Set (value: INTEGER);
      PROCEDURE (s: Salary) Get (VAR value: INTEGER);
      PROCEDURE (s: Salary) Increment (value: INTEGER);
   END;
```

The class *Salary* introduces more complexity than it eliminates. Instead, the standard type INTEGER would be perfectly adequate. The example may be exaggerated, but such errors occur frequently among programmers who feel the need to express *everything* with classes.

Among all features of object-oriented programming, data abstraction is the one that is least novel, yet most frequently applicable. Inheritance and dynamic binding are applicable in *some* programs; data abstraction is useful in almost all.

Data abstraction and the structuring possibilities that it provides are a major reason for the popularity of object-oriented languages. For Modula-2 programmers, data abstraction is a well-known technique. For Cobol or C programmers it constitutes substantial progress. This also explains why some view object-oriented programming as revolutionary, while others find it less spectacular.

7.2 Generic Components

A component is called *generic* if it can work with various types of objects. Languages like Ada [DoD83] and Eiffel [Mey87] offer genericity as a language construct. Genericity can also be simulated with inheritance, as we will see in this section.

Consider a generic binary tree. The algorithms for inserting or searching for objects in the tree are independent of whether the objects are numbers, character strings, or more complex data. It is wise to implement them so that they are not tailored to a certain type of object, but work with generalized objects that can later be replaced with numbers, character strings, etc. Such a binary tree could have the following interface:

A generic binary tree

```
TYPE
  Tree = RECORD
    PROCEDURE (VAR t: Tree) Init;
    PROCEDURE (VAR t: Tree) Insert (x: Node);
    PROCEDURE (VAR t: Tree) Delete (x: Node);
    PROCEDURE (VAR t: Tree) Search (x: Node): Node;
  END;
```

Instead of numbers or character strings, this tree handles objects of the abstract type *Node*. Although the structure of the nodes is unknown, the tree must make certain assumptions about them: Every node must have a left and a right child, and it must be possible to compare nodes in order to locate them in the tree. These assumptions are expressed in the following interface of *Node*:

```
TYPE
  Node = POINTER TO NodeDesc;
  NodeDesc = RECORD
    left, right: Node;
    PROCEDURE (x: Node) EqualTo (y: Node): BOOLEAN;
    PROCEDURE (x: Node) LessThan (y: Node): BOOLEAN;
  END;
```

These assumptions suffice for implementing the methods of class *Tree*.

```
TYPE
   Tree = RECORD
      root: Node
   END;

PROCEDURE (VAR t: Tree) Init;
BEGIN root := NIL
END Init;

PROCEDURE (VAR t: Tree) Insert (x: Node);
   VAR this, parent: Node;
BEGIN
   this := t.root; x.left := NIL; x.right := NIL;
   WHILE this # NIL DO
      parent := this;
      IF x.EqualTo(this) THEN RETURN (*don't insert duplicates*) END;
      IF x.LessThan(this) THEN this := this.left ELSE this := this.right END
   END;
   IF t.root = NIL THEN t.root := x
   ELSIF x.LessThan(parent) THEN parent.left := x
   ELSE parent.right := x
   END
END Insert;

PROCEDURE (VAR t: Tree) Search (x: Node): Node;
   VAR this: Node;
BEGIN
   this := t.root;
   WHILE (this # NIL) & ~ x.EqualTo(this) DO
      IF x.LessThan(this) THEN this := this.left ELSE this := this.right END
   END;
   RETURN this
END Search;

PROCEDURE (VAR t: Tree) Delete (x: Node);
   VAR this, parent, p, q: Node;
BEGIN
   this := t.root;
   WHILE (this # NIL) & ~ x.EqualTo(this) DO
      parent := this;
      IF x.LessThan(this) THEN this := this.left ELSE this := this.right END
   END;
   IF this # NIL THEN (*x.EqualTo(this); find a node p that can replace this*)
      IF this.right = NIL THEN p := this.left
      ELSIF this.right.left = NIL THEN p := this.right; p.left := this.left
      ELSE (*p := smallest node greater than this*)
         p := this.right; WHILE p.left # NIL DO q := p; p := p.left END;
         q.left := p.right; p.left := this.left; p.right := this.right
      END;
      IF this = t.root THEN t.root := p
      ELSIF this.LessThan(parent) THEN parent.left := p
      ELSE parent.right := p
      END
   END
END Delete;
```

How can a binary tree that handles objects of type *Node* be used to store character strings? This is simple if character strings are made compatible to *Node*. In order to do that, a subclass *StringNode* is derived from *Node* containing a character string as data field and overriding the methods *EqualTo* and *LessThan*:

Storing character strings in the binary tree

```
TYPE
    StringNode = POINTER TO StringNodeDesc;
    StringNodeDesc = RECORD (NodeDesc)
        s: POINTER TO ARRAY OF CHAR
    END;

PROCEDURE (x: StringNode) EqualTo (y: Node): BOOLEAN;
BEGIN RETURN x.s^ = y(StringNode).s^
END EqualTo;

PROCEDURE (x: StringNode) LessThan (y: Node): BOOLEAN;
BEGIN RETURN x.s^ < y(StringNode).s^
END LessThan;
```

Note that parameter y of both methods is of type *Node* (overridden methods must have the same parameter types as the respective method of the base class). Thus a type guard $y(StringNode)$ is necessary in order to access $y.s$. Character strings are inserted in the tree as follows:

```
VAR t: Tree; s: StringNode;
...
NEW(s); ... t.Insert(s);
```

The method *Insert* compares nodes using the messages *EqualTo* and *LessThan*, which are dynamically bound to the respective methods of *StringNode*. In a similar way, it is possible to store numbers in the tree by deriving a type *IntegerNode* and overriding the methods *EqualTo* and *LessThan*. What have we achieved with the generic type *Tree*?

- *Tree* can work with all objects whose type is derived from *Node* and that can be compared with *EqualTo* and *LessThan*.
- *Node* serves as a design pattern for future node classes.
- *Tree* can be reused without modification or recompilation.

Languages like Ada, C++ and Eiffel include genericity as a language construct. In Eiffel, for example, a class can be parameterized with a type T that follows the class name in square brackets. A generic stack in Eiffel takes the following form:

Genericity as a language construct

```
class Stack [T]
   ...
   Push (x: T) is do ... end;
   Pop: T is do ... end;
end
```

The operations *Push* and *Pop* work with objects of type *T*. In the declaration of a stack variable, *T* can be replaced with a concrete type such as INTEGER, resulting in a stack of integer numbers:

```
intStack: Stack[INTEGER];
i: INTEGER;
...
intStack.Push(3); ... i := intStack.Pop
```

Stack can be used for any types of elements without needing an element base class such as *Node*. This kind of genericity, however, is suited only for simple data structures that make no assumptions about the elements they maintain, e.g., stacks, queues or unsorted lists. Most useful data structures such as trees, sets or sorted lists require at least that their elements can be compared. Eiffel thus permits a more detailed specification of the generic class *Tree*, called constrained genericity. The class declaration

```
class Tree [T -> Node]
   ...
end
```

specifies that the concrete type corresponding to *T* must be a *Node* or an extension thereof. Here, too, an abstract class *Node* has to be used to define the required behavior of all future nodes.

An important aspect of genericity in Eiffel is that the compiler enforces that all objects managed by *Stack* have the same type, i.e., that they are homogeneous. Inheritance, on the other hand, allows *Stack* to manage a heterogeneous set of elements, e.g., numbers mixed with character strings. This might or might not be desirable (see Section 7.3), but with inheritance the homogeneity of the element set can only be checked at run time.

With genericity we can write $i := intStack.Pop$. If *Stack* is parameterized with INTEGER, then *Pop* always returns INTEGER objects. Type checks can be done at compile time. However, if the stack is implemented using inheritance from an abstract class *Node*, then *Pop* returns *Node* objects that must first be converted to *IntegerNode* objects with a type guard. The type guard requires a type check at run time.

Note that inheritance can be used to simulate genericity, but not vice versa. Genericity cannot replace inheritance [Mey86]. Inheritance is the more powerful and more fundamental concept.

The example of the class *Tree* calls attention to another important fact: Many classes have not only an interface to their clients, but usually also one or more interfaces to their components, in this case to *Node* (Fig. 7.1). A programmer using the class *Tree* must also know the interface of *Node*, because an extension of *Node* must be implemented.

Classes usually have multiple interfaces

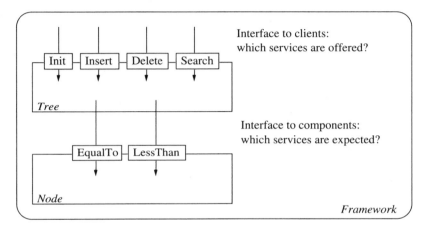

Fig. 7.1 Interfaces of a class to its clients and components

When a class like *Tree* is designed, it is not enough to consider just the services that the class itself will offer. It is equally important to decide which objects the class needs in order to do its job and which services are expected from these objects. This leads to a set of classes that work together to carry out a certain task. Such a system of classes is called a *framework* (see Chapter 10). *Tree* and *Node* form a framework for binary trees. A framework represents a semifinished product that can later be extended for various purposes.

Genericity is applicable whenever an object has to manage a set of components. If this object is to be kept so general that it can work with various component types, an implementation with classes is appropriate. One proceeds as follows:

Summary

(1) Consider which services are expected from the components.
(2) Design one or more abstract classes that offer these services.
(3) Implement the generic object using the abstract component class(es).

7.3 Heterogeneous Data Structures

One of the most useful applications of object-oriented programming is the management of heterogeneous data structures. Situation of this kind have the following characteristics:

(1) Objects occur in variants.
(2) The program using the objects does not want to distinguish the variants.
(3) The number of future variants is unknown; new ones can be added later.

Table 7.2 gives examples of such situations.

Variants	Operations
Objects in a graphics editor (lines, rectangles, circles, …)	draw, move, click, …
Objects on a screen (windows, icons, menus, …)	draw, move, click, …
Objects in a dialog window (buttons, texts, scroll bars, …)	draw, move, click, …
Objects in a game (hunter, prey, walls, …)	draw, move, collide, …
Objects in a simulation (cars, persons, traffic lights, …)	activate, delay, …

Table 7.2 Examples of objects that occur in variants

Conventional implementation of a graphics editor

Let us examine a graphics editor that supports the drawing, selection and moving of lines, rectangles and circles. In conventional languages like Modula-2, the various kinds of figures would be implemented as a variant record:

```
TYPE
    Figure = POINTER TO FigureDesc;
    FigureDesc = RECORD
        next: Figure;
        CASE kind: FigureKind OF
            line: x0, y0, x1, y1: INTEGER
        |   rect: x, y, w, h: INTEGER
        |   circle: mx, my, radius: INTEGER
        END
    END;
```

Using this record type, a list can be created that contains figures of various kinds:

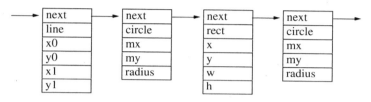

Fig. 7.3 Heterogeneous data structure with variant records

Variant records are dangerous, however, because most compilers do not generate code to check whether the program uses the correct variant of an object at run time. Furthermore, whenever an operation is applied to a figure, its possible variants must be distinguished in the program code. In order to draw all the figures in a list, say, we would have to write:

```
figure := firstFigure;
WHILE figure # NIL DO (*draw all figures*)
    CASE figure^.kind OF
        line: ... (*draw line*)
    |   rect: ... (*draw rectangle*)
    |   circle: ... (*draw circle*)
    END;
    figure := figure^.next
END
```

The places requiring case analysis are usually scattered over the whole program. What is even worse is that the introduction of a new kind of figure (e.g., splines) requires the modification of the data type *Figure* which can in turn require the recompilation of client modules. Furthermore, each case statement must be modified to accommodate spline objects as well. This is tedious and error-prone. Software of this sort tends to be messy and difficult to extend.

Object-oriented implementation of a graphics editor

Object-oriented languages permit a more elegant approach. Figures are viewed as abstract objects (black boxes) about which certain assumptions are made: they can be linked into a list, and they can be drawn, moved, read and stored. This is all the editor has to know in order to be able to work with figures. It need not know that there are rectangles, circles, lines, and all the other concrete figure kinds; and it need not know *how* to draw, move and store them.

Abstract figures

These considerations lead to the declaration of the abstract class *Figure* below. (The module *OS* used in this declaration is described in Appendix B).

```
TYPE
    Figure = POINTER TO FigureDesc;
    FigureDesc = RECORD (*abstract*)
        next: Figure;
        selected: BOOLEAN;
        PROCEDURE (f: Figure) Draw;
        PROCEDURE (f: Figure) Move (dx, dy: BOOLEAN);
        PROCEDURE (f: Figure) HandleMouse (x, y: INTEGER;
            buttons:SET);
        PROCEDURE (f: Figure) Load (VAR r: OS.Rider);
        PROCEDURE (f: Figure) Store (VAR r: OS.Rider);
        ...
    END
```

Concrete figures

The concrete figure types are subclasses of *Figure*. They include additional fields and override the abstract methods of *Figure*.

```
TYPE
    Line = POINTER TO LineDesc;
    LineDesc = RECORD (FigureDesc)
        x0, y0, x1, y1: INTEGER;
        PROCEDURE (ln: Line) Draw;
        PROCEDURE (ln: Line) Move (dx, dy: BOOLEAN);
        ...
    END;

    Rectangle = POINTER TO RectangleDesc;
    RectangleDesc = RECORD (FigureDesc)
        x, y, w, h: INTEGER
        PROCEDURE (r: Rectangle) Draw;
        PROCEDURE (r: Rectangle) Move (dx, dy: BOOLEAN);
        ...
    END;

    Circle = POINTER TO CircleDesc;
    CircleDesc = RECORD (FigureDesc)
        mx, my, radius: INTEGER
        PROCEDURE (c: Circle) Draw;
        PROCEDURE (c: Circle) Move (dx, dy: BOOLEAN);
```

```
      ...
END;
```

Objects of this kind again permit the construction of a heterogeneous list (Fig. 7.4).

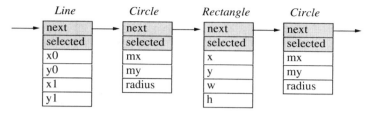

Fig. 7.4 Heterogeneous data structure composed of objects

For the editor, all the figures in the list are of static type *Figure*; i.e., the editor sees only the fields and methods of class *Figure* (the shaded parts in Fig. 7.4). Actually, however, behind each object there is a line, a rectangle or a circle. To draw all figures, the editor need only do the following:

```
figure := firstFigure;
WHILE figure # NIL DO
    figure.Draw;
    figure := figure.next
END
```

The editor no longer has to distinguish the variants. It simply sends each figure a *Draw* message, trusting that the figure, regardless of its type, will correctly handle the message. The introduction of a new figure type *Spline* does not affect the editor. It is able to store spline objects like all the other figures in its data structure, and if the object to which it sends a *Draw* message happens to be a spline object, then a spline is drawn without the editor being aware of it.

No more case distinctions

The operations on objects are no longer scattered over the whole program, but collected in the figure classes. This simplifies maintenance. The introduction of a spline class requires only the implementation of this single class; the rest of the program remains unchanged.

Better localization

Note that two kinds of extensions occur in this example. First, the class *Figure* was extended to *Line, Rectangle* and *Circle*. Second, the entire editor was extended. Originally it could only work with abstract figures; now it can draw lines, rectangles and circles. It can be extended at any time to draw new types of figures.

Extensibility

Input/output of figures

The graphics editor will have to store the figures to a file occasionally. The input/output of heterogeneous data structures is a nontrivial problem. The editor itself cannot load and store figures because it does not know their data fields. It must leave this task to the figures, which override the methods *Load* and *Store* inherited from *Figure*. But before the editor can send a figure a *Load* message it must first create the figure object. How does the editor know what type the object must be? This is a tricky problem and we will come back to it in Section 8.3.

Loading extensions at run time

A remarkable feature of the Oberon system is that progams can be extended at run time. Assume that the kernel of the editor consists of a module *Figures* defining the abstract class *Figure*, and a module *Editor* that handles windows and contains general editing commands. Each subclass of *Figure* is implemented in its own module (i.e, modules *Lines*, *Rectangles*, *Circles*, etc.). Now, the editor can be loaded so that at first only the kernel modules *Editor* and *Figures* are in memory. This makes for a compact program and short loading times. In this configuration, the editor does not know about any concrete kinds of figure.

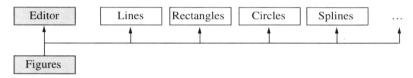

Fig. 7.5 Extensibility of programs by dynamic loading of modules

While the editor is running, the user can decide to load *Lines* or *Circles*. These modules are linked to the already loaded modules then and give the editor the ability to draw lines or circles. Each user can load those modules as needed. It is not necessary to always use the editor with its full functionality. Each user can load customized functionality without bothering others (see Section 8.2).

Actually, a system is really extensible only if *anyone* (not just the author) can extend a program at *any time* (even while it is loaded). This is the case in Oberon. New modules, and thus new classes, can be implemented and loaded whose existence is unknown to the program, yet the program can still use them. The graphics editor knows nothing of a *Splines* module; still, this module can be added—without modifying or relinking the editor. In interpretative object-oriented systems like Smalltalk, this is also possible, but not so in most compilative systems. Oberon is an exception: it is a compilative system that offers a degree of extensibility similar to that of Smalltalk.

In summary, if a program is to work with multiple variants of a class, it should not distinguish them, but view them as various extensions of an abstract class. The procedure is similar to that for generic components:

Summary

(1) Consider which operations and data are common to all variants.
(2) Define an abstract class with these features and a subclass for each variant.
(3) Work with variables of the abstract class without considering which object variants might be stored in them at run time.

7.4 Replaceable Behavior

If an object or an algorithm is to change its behavior at run time, this can also be implemented elegantly with classes.

Let us look at an example: Editors normally display data in *frames* on the screen. A frame is a rectangular area into which text and graphics can be drawn. It provides operations such as *DrawLine* or *DrawChar* causing a line or a character to be drawn on the screen. To output the frame contents to a printer, we have to use print operations instead of display operation for every piece of text or graphics displayed in the frame.

Uniform output on screen and printer

Of course, we would like to avoid having different output operations for the screen and for the printer, and choosing between them every time a figure has to be drawn. Therefore, a frame should not direct output immediately to the screen or to the printer, but to an abstract output medium that we call *Port*. At run time the abstract port can be replaced with a screen port, a printer port, or any other concrete output medium. The interface of the abstract class *Port* takes the following form:

```
TYPE
    Port = POINTER TO PortDesc;
    PortDesc = RECORD
        x, y, w, h: INTEGER; (*clipping rectangle*)
        PROCEDURE (p: Port) DrawLine (x0, y0, x1, y1: INTEGER);
        PROCEDURE (p: Port) DrawChar (ch: CHAR);
        ...
    END;
```

The screen port and the printer port are subclasses of *Port* that override the abstract methods so that output appears on the screen or on the printer, repetively.

```
TYPE
    ScreenPort = POINTER TO ScreenPortDesc;
    ScreenPortDesc = RECORD (PortDesc)
        PROCEDURE (p: ScreenPort) DrawLine (x0, y0, x1, y1: INTEGER);
        PROCEDURE (p: ScreenPort) DrawChar (ch: CHAR);
        ...
    END;

    Printer Port = POINTER TO PrinterPortDesc;
    PrinterPortDesc = RECORD (PortDesc)
        PROCEDURE (p: PrinterPort) DrawLine (x0, y0, x1, y1: INTEGER);
        PROCEDURE (p: PrinterPort) DrawChar (ch: CHAR);
        ...
    END;
```

Every frame has a data field of type *Port* to which all output operations are directed by the frame's methods (e.g., *DrawLine*). The clients of the frame are usually unaware of this redirection.

```
TYPE
    Frame = POINTER TO FrameDesc;
    FrameDesc = RECORD
        port: Port;
        ...
    END;

PROCEDURE (f: Frame) DrawLine (x0, y0, x1, y1: INTEGER);
BEGIN
    f.port.DrawLine(x0, y0, x1, y1)
END DrawLine;
    ...
```

Depending on which concrete port is installed in *f.port*, output goes to the screen or to the printer. The port can be changed at run time, thus changing the behavior of the frame. All clients of *f* that output to the screen can now print as well without having to be modified.

Note that the screen and the printer usually have different coordinate systems and different resolutions. The normal approach to handle this problem is to use a virtual coordinate system with a very high resolution in the interface of *Port* and to convert it in the methods of the respective port to the screen or printer coordinate system with the resolution of the respective device.

Other examples   Another example of replaceable behavior is a parameterized process scheduler. Parallel processes can be handled in chronological order (first in, first out, FIFO) or by priority. In order to be able to change the strategy at run time, it is useful to implement the scheduler as a variable of an abstract class *Scheduler*; at run time the variable could contain an object of the concrete class *FIFOScheduler* or *PriorityScheduler*.

In summary, to change behavior at run time, proceed as follows: *Summary*

(1) Consider which operations make up the replaceable behavior.
(2) Define an abstract class that provides these operations as methods. Implement concrete behavior in subclasses.
(3) Work with variables of the abstract class; these can contain objects of concrete subclasses with differing behavior at run time.

7.5 Adaptable Components

The reuse of components such as procedures or modules is often prevented by the lack of a proper fit. We all know the situation where we have a component with certain functionality, but we cannot use it because slightly different functionality is needed. Object-oriented programming offers a solution: If the component is a class, it can be extended and adapted by deriving a subclass, possibly with new data fields, and overriding inherited methods. Neither the original class nor its existing clients need to be adapted.

Consider the example of a text class: Assume that we need texts with various fonts and the usual operations such as insertion and deletion of characters. We have a class *Text* that meets most of the requirements, but does not support fonts: *Extending a text class*

```
TYPE
    Text = POINTER TO TextDesc;
    TextDesc = RECORD
        ... (*data*)
        PROCEDURE (t: Text) Length (): LONGINT;
        PROCEDURE (t: Text) Insert (pos: LONGINT; s: ARRAY OF CHAR);
        PROCEDURE (t: Text) Delete (from, to: LONGINT);
        ... (*other methods*)
    END;
```

Although we cannot use *Text* directly, it is certainly an advantage to not have to write the required text class from scratch, but to base it on *Text*. This reduces the implementation and testing effort.

In order to support fonts, *Text* is extended to a new class *StyledText*. The text is considered to consist of a sequence of segments. A segment is a sequence of characters of the same font and is represented by a node of type *Style* that contains the length and font of the respective segment. The fonts of the whole text are stored in a list of *Style* nodes (also see Fig. 7.6):

```
TYPE
    Style = POINTER TO StyleDesc;
    StyleDesc = RECORD
        font: OS.Font;    (*font of text segment*)
        len: LONGINT;     (*length of text segment*)
        next: Style
    END;

    StyledText = POINTER TO StyledTextDesc;
    StyledTextDesc = RECORD (TextDesc)
        styles: Style;
        PROCEDURE (t: StyledText) Insert (pos: LONGINT;
            s: ARRAY OF CHAR);
        PROCEDURE (t: StyledText) Delete (from, to: LONGINT);
        PROCEDURE (t: StyledText) SetStyle (from, to: LONGINT;
            font: OS.Font);
        ...
    END;
```

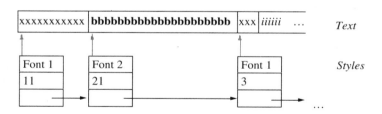

Fig. 7.6 Data structures of *StyledText*

The methods *Insert* and *Delete* must also update the style list now, so they are overridden:

```
PROCEDURE (t: StyledText) Insert (pos: LONGINT; s: ARRAY OF CHAR);
BEGIN
    ... (*update style list*)
    t.Insert^ (pos, s)  (*call Insert method from the base class*)
END Insert;

PROCEDURE (t: StyledText) Delete (from, to: LONGINT);
BEGIN
    ... (*update style list*)
    t.Delete^ (from, to)  (*call Delete method from the base class*)
END Delete;
```

The method *Length* is independent of the fonts and does not need to be modified. A new method, *SetStyle*, is necessary to modify the font of a text segment.

What has been achieved with this extension? The existing class *Text* was adapted to special needs by adding a new layer, *StyledText* (Fig. 7.7).

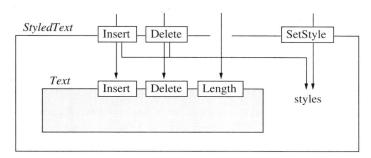

Fig. 7.7 *StyledText* as a new layer around *Text*

From the outside the class maintains the appearance of a *Text*. Thus all existing clients of *Text* can also work with *StyledText*. An editor designed for *Text* does not notice the difference if *StyledText* is substituted for *Text*, but it now automatically manipulates fonts when *Insert* or *Delete* are invoked.

Figure 7.7 should not be confused with a set diagram, which would reflect the is-a relationship between classes and would have the opposite appearance: Here *StyledText* is enclosed in *Text* because every *StyledText* object is also a *Text* object (Fig. 7.8).

Fig. 7.8 Set diagram to represent the is-a relationship

While so far we have only considered the extension of *abstract* classes, *StyledText* represents the extension of a concrete class. The extension of concrete classes normally occurs when extensibility was not planned from the beginning. We must warn the reader: Although reasonable in certain situations, ad hoc extensions can lead to unclean solutions, particularly when extension is abused to add forgotten features to a class.

Extending concrete classes

Extensibility should be planned from the beginning. This does not mean that all kinds of future extensions must be foreseen. It simply means that extensibility *in a particular direction* should be planned by working not with concrete objects, but with variables of abstract classes that can later contain arbitrary concrete objects.

7.6   Semifinished Products

A class can deliberately be kept in a raw state. Avoiding application-specific features increases the chances of reusing the class in other programs. Such a class contains only those parts that are needed in all foreseeable contexts. It is a semifinished product that can be extended to a finished product by adding application-specific features.

Frames as semifinished products

An example of a semifinished product is the class *Frame* that we encountered in Section 7.4. In Oberon a frame is a rectangular drawing plane for the representation of text, graphics, or other data. It is also responsible for interpreting user input such as mouse clicks or keyboard input.

Concrete frame classes are application-specific; i.e., they can often be used only in a certain context: a text frame can be used for representing text, but not for drawing graphics. Likewise graphic frames are inappropriate in a spreadsheet program. The generally reusable parts of frames are only those that appear in all contexts in which a frame can be used, i.e.:

(1)   A frame can be installed in a viewer (window), moved on the screen, and resized.

(2)   A frame can be told to redraw its contents, regardless of what the contents might be.

(3)   A frame can be given mouse clicks or keyboard input for processing, although it is left open how this input is processed by a concrete frame.

Such a general frame can be extended to a text frame, a graphic frame, or a spreadsheet frame. It is a *semifinished product* that factors out the application-independent aspects of various concrete frames and specifies a common interface for all future frame variants. The interface of an abstract class *Frame* could take the following form:

```
TYPE
    Frame = POINTER TO FrameDesc;
    FrameDesc = RECORD
        x, y, w, h: INTEGER;  (*position on screen*)
        ...
        PROCEDURE (f: Frame) MoveBy (dx, dy: INTEGER);
        PROCEDURE (f: Frame) Resize (dw, dh: INTEGER);
        PROCEDURE (f: Frame) Redraw (x, y, w, h: INTEGER);
        PROCEDURE (f: Frame) HandleMouse
            (x, y: INTEGER; buttons: SET);
        PROCEDURE (f: Frame) HandleKey (ch: CHAR);
        ...
    END;
```

MoveBy is a concrete method. Its implementation is the same for all frame variants and thus can already be given in the class *Frame*. *Redraw* is an abstract method: since an abstract frame does not yet know what it is to display, it remains empty. *HandleMouse* and *HandleKey* are also abstract, for an abstract frame does not know how to handle user input. *Resize* is a semiabstract method: it moves the lower right corner of a frame and invokes *Redraw* in order to redraw frame parts that have not been visible before. Although *Resize* does not need to be overridden in subclasses, it is only operational after *Redraw* has been overridden.

Now let us examine how to make a finished product *TextFrame* out of the semifinished product *Frame*. We have to declare *TextFrame* as a subclass of *Frame* and include fields and methods necessary for displaying text; the abstract methods of *Frame* have to be overridden.

Extending a frame to a text frame

```
TYPE
    TextFrame = POINTER TO TextFrameDesc;
    TextFrameDesc = RECORD (FrameDesc)
        text: Text;
        origin: LONGINT;
        ...
        (*overridden methods*)
        PROCEDURE (f: TextFrame) Redraw (x, y, w, h: INTEGER);
        PROCEDURE (f: TextFrame) HandleMouse
            (x, y: INTEGER; buttons: SET);
        PROCEDURE (f: TextFrame) HandleKey (ch: CHAR);

        (*text-specific methods*)
        PROCEDURE (f: TextFrame) Init (t: Text; origin: LONGINT);
        PROCEDURE (f: TextFrame) Scroll (newOrigin: LONGINT);
    END;
```

Text frames inherit all the behavior of frames: they can be installed in a viewer, redraw themselves upon request, and handle user input.

In the same way as *TextFrame*, a class *GraphicFrame* or *TableFrame* could be created. Rather than starting from scratch, the design and implementation of *Frame* could be reused. When extending a semifinished product, however, it is important to have documentation that tells which methods must be made concrete and which not.

7.7　Summary

This chapter has shown situations in which classes are useful. The reader should remember these situations and their solutions. They represent reusable design.

To know such design patterns is more important than to use a specific design method or notation. Design requires experience and skill. It cannot be canned in a single method. Examples are the best teachers, and giving examples was the purpose of this chapter. Almost all of these design patterns can be found again in the case study in Chapter 11.

In summary, we can say that object-oriented programming is best suited when the problem involves complex objects, especially when these occur in variants that should be operated upon without distinguishing them.

Object-oriented programming is also suited to systems that demand a high degree of extensibility. In a graphics editor, it must be possible at any time to add a new kind of figure whose instances are displayed and moved like all other figures—without modifying existing software.

Finally, object-oriented programming is suited to implementing library components. If components are being collected in a library, it can only be an advantage if these are made extensible and adaptable in the form of classes.

The goal of object-oriented programming is not to produce customized components for a specific application, but classes or frameworks for repeated reuse. It is especially important to find good abstractions from which many concrete classes can be derived.

8 Useful Techniques

This chapter shows several techniques that are useful for writing object-oriented programs:

- initialization of objects
- extension of a system at run time
- persistent objects
- embedding classes in other classes
- extension of a class in multiple directions
- handling multiple inheritance
- models and views
- iterators
- modifying inherited methods

8.1 Initialization of Objects

Most objects must be initialized before they can be used. Their data fields need to obtain values, and auxiliary objects must often be created that the new object needs for its work.

Oberon-2 does not have a special language construct for the initialization of objects; ordinary procedures are used instead. For every class T a procedure $InitT$ is written that handles all initialization tasks for T objects. If T is declared as:

Initialization procedures

```
TYPE
    T = POINTER TO TDesc;
    TDesc = RECORD
        x: INTEGER;
        y: REAL
    END;
```

its initialization procedure could be:

```
PROCEDURE InitT (t: T; x: INTEGER; y: REAL);
BEGIN
  t.x := x; t.y := y
END T;
```

Every newly created *T* object must be initialized with *InitT*:

```
NEW(t); InitT(t, x, y);
```

Initialization procedures are better than initialization methods

We recommend implementing *InitT* as a procedure rather than as a method. Assume the following subclass *T1*:

```
TYPE
  T1 = POINTER TO TDesc1;
  TDesc1 = RECORD (TDesc)
    z: CHAR
  END;
```

If *InitT* were a method, it would have to be overridden in *T1*, and with an additional parameter to initialize *z*. However, this is not permitted, for overriding methods does not allow adding parameters. If the initialization is implemented as a procedure, there is no problem with additional parameters:

```
PROCEDURE InitT1 (t: T1; x: INTEGER; y: REAL; z: CHAR);
BEGIN
  InitT(t, x, y); t.z := z
END InitT1;
```

The fields of the base class *T* are initialized by invoking *InitT*.

Initialization procedures should not create the objects to be initialized

It is tempting to implement the initialization so that the object to be initialized is created in the process, as in the following example:

```
PROCEDURE NewT (x: INTEGER; y: REAL): T;
  VAR t: T;
BEGIN
  NEW(t); t.x := x; t.y := y; RETURN t
END NewT;
```

This is not recommended, however, because *NewT* can no longer be used as above in a procedure *NewT1* in order to initialize *T* objects.

```
PROCEDURE NewT1(x: INTEGER; y: REAL; z: CHAR): T1;
  VAR t1: T1;
BEGIN
  t1 := NewT(x, y);  (*error: NewT returns a T object and not a T1 object*)
  t1.z := z
  RETURN t1
END NewT1;
```

8.2 Extending a System at Run Time

Section 7.3 showed that a graphics editor could be extended at run time with new objects (rectangles, circles, lines) that were not known when the editor was implemented. This section explains how to do this.

Let us review the graphics editor example: The editor does not work directly with rectangles or circles, but with variables of the abstract class *Figure*, which is declared in the module *Figures* and establishes the interface of all future figure classes:

Extending a graphics editor

```
DEFINITION Figures;
    TYPE
        Figure = POINTER TO FigureDesc;
        FigureDesc = RECORD
            selected: BOOLEAN;
            PROCEDURE (f: Figure) Draw;
            PROCEDURE (f: Figure) Move (dx, dy: INTEGER);
            ...
        END;
    ...
END Figures.
```

Another module of the editor is *FigureFrames*, which contains the class *Frame* for displaying figures and reacting to user input. *Frame* holds a list of all figures displayed in it; new figures can be inserted with the message *Install*:

```
DEFINITION FigureFrames;
    IMPORT Figures, Viewers;

    TYPE
        Frame = POINTER TO FrameDesc;
        FrameDesc = RECORD (Viewers.FrameDesc)
            figures: Figures.Figure;  (*list of all figures in this frame*)
            ...
            PROCEDURE (f: Frame) Install (x: Figures.Figure);
            ...
        END;

    VAR
        currentFrame: Frame;  (*currently edited Frame*)
    ...
END FigureFrames.
```

This is the kernel of the editor. During its implementation it is not necessary to know which figures will exist later. The editor can work with any subclass of *Figure*.

Adding ellipses

In order to extend the editor to accommodate ellipses, the following steps are taken:

(1) Define a class *Ellipse* as a subclass of *Figure*.

```
TYPE
    Ellipse = POINTER TO EllipseDesc;
    EllipseDesc = RECORD (Figures.Figure)
        x, y: INTEGER; (*center*)
        a, b: INTEGER  (*axes*)
    END;
```

(2) Override the abstract methods inherited from *Figure*.

```
PROCEDURE (e: Ellipse) Draw;
BEGIN ... (*draw ellipse e*)
END Draw;
    ...
```

(3) Implement a command *New* that creates an ellipse object and adds it to the list of figures in the current frame, *FigureFrames.currentFrame*.

```
PROCEDURE New;
    VAR e: Ellipse;
BEGIN
    NEW(e);
    ... (*get e.x, e.y, e.a, and e.b as arguments of the command New*) ...
    FigureFrames.currentFrame.Install(e)
END New;
```

All this is packaged in a new module *Ellipses*. Existing modules of the editor are not touched. In order to draw a new ellipse object, the command *Ellipses.New* is invoked. The following occurs:

(1) If the module *Ellipses* is not already loaded, it is loaded and linked to the editor.
(2) The command *New* is executed. It creates an ellipse object and installs it in the list of figures in the current frame.
(3) The frame sends a *Draw* message to the newly inserted figure (without knowing its type); this causes the ellipse to be drawn.

Figure 8.1 shows the relationship between the modules and the data structures they contain.

Dynamic loading of the module Ellipses

Note that the module *Ellipses* is loaded and linked to the editor only on demand. Neither *Figures* nor *FigureFrames* know (i.e., import) *Ellipses*. They can thus be compiled and used long before

Ellipses exists. *Ellipses*, on the other hand, imports the modules *Figures* and *FigureFrames* and uses them.

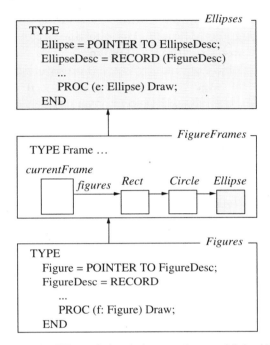

Fig. 8.1 The module *Ellipses* is loaded at run time and linked to the kernel of the editor. It installs ellipse objects in the editor kernel.

The editor kernel can work with ellipses due to dynamic binding. In the ellipse object the editor sees an instance of the abstract class *Figure* and communicates with it via messages that invoke methods from the class *Ellipse*, which is higher in the import hierarchy. Such invocations are therefore termed *up-calls*. The editor invokes methods that it does not know. Only the user, who executes the command *Ellipses.New*, is aware of them.

Up-calls

8.3 Persistent Objects

An object is termed persistent if it survives the program that created it. Later invocations of the program or other programs (possibly on other computers) find the object in the same state in which the creating program left it.

One way to make objects persistent is to write them to a file and to read them as needed. This is simple as long as the structure of the objects is known. However, if the structure of the objects is unknown to the writing or reading program, as in Section 8.2, matters are more complicated. The question is how to load and store objects whose structure is unknown.

Input/output of objects of unknown type

To *store* an object of unknown type is pretty easy: The object is sent a *Store* message and reacts by writing its data to the designated file. After all, each object knows its own structure.

In order to *load* an object, however, it cannot simply be sent a *Load* message. The object does not exist yet; it must first be created. But in order to do so its type must be known. How can this be done?

The solution is to store not only the *value* of an object, but also the name of its *type*. Fig. 8.2 shows an example of two figures in memory and their representation in a file. The linking of the objects results implicitly from their order in the file.

Representation in memory

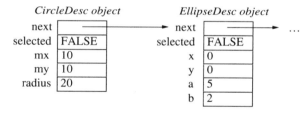

Representation in a file

Circles.CircleDesc FALSE 10 10 20   Ellipses.EllipseDesc FALSE 0 0 5 2 ...

Type name   Value

Fig. 8.2 Representation of objects in memory and in a file

Now we only need a way to extract the type name of an object in order to store it to the file and, given a type name, to create an object of this type.

Type descriptors

In Oberon each object contains a pointer to its *type descriptor*, which is invisible to the ordinary programmer. The type descriptor holds run-time type information such as the name of the object's type (Fig. 8.3). All objects of a class have the same type descriptor.

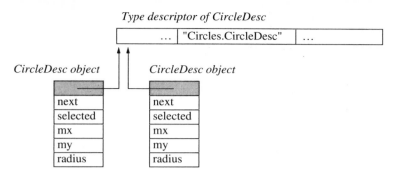

Fig. 8.3 Objects and their type descriptors (with type names)

With the help of the type descriptors, we can implement a procedure *ObjToName* to retrieve the type name of a given object and a procedure *NameToObj* to create an object of a given type name. (Module *OS*, which is used in the following interface, is described in Appendix B.)

```
DEFINITION Objects;

    TYPE
        Object = POINTER TO ObjectDesc;
        ObjectDesc = RECORD
            PROCEDURE (x: Object) Load  (VAR r: OS.Rider); (*abstract*)
            PROCEDURE (x: Object) Store  (VAR r: OS.Rider); (*abstract*)
        END;

        PROCEDURE ObjToName  (x: Object; VAR name: ARRAY OF CHAR);
        PROCEDURE NameToObj  (name: ARRAY OF CHAR; VAR x: Object);

    END Objects.
```

Figure must be derived from *Object* so that *ObjToName* and *NameToObj* can be applied to *Figure* objects and *Load* and *Store* messages can be sent to them.

```
    TYPE
        Figure = POINTER TO FigureDesc;
        FigureDesc = RECORD (Objects.Object.Object)
            next: Figure;
            ...
            PROCEDURE (f: Figure) Load (VAR r: OS.Rider);
            PROCEDURE (f: Figure) Store (VAR r: OS.Rider);
            ...
        END;
```

*Input/output
procedures for
figures*

Now we are ready to write figures to a file and to read them again. The following procedures handle these tasks:

```
PROCEDURE WriteFigure (VAR r: OS.Rider; x: Figure);
    VAR name: ARRAY 64 OF CHAR;
BEGIN
    IF x = NIL THEN r.WriteString("")    (*NIL = empty type name, no value*)
    ELSE Objects.ObjToName(x, name); r.WriteString(name); x.Store(r)
    END
END WriteFigure;

PROCEDURE ReadFigure (VAR r: OS.Rider; VAR x: Figure);
    VAR name: ARRAY 64 OF CHAR; y: Objects.Objects
BEGIN
    r.ReadString(name);
    IF name = "" THEN x := NIL
    ELSE Objects.NameToObj(name, x); x.Load(r)
    END
END ReadFigure;
```

If x is the head of a list of figures, the whole list is stored as follows:

```
WHILE x # NIL DO WriteFigure(r, x); x := x.next END;
WriteFigure(r, NIL)
```

The following statements read a list of figures with the head *head*.

```
ReadFigure(r, x); head := x;
WHILE x # NIL DO ReadFigure(r, x.next); x := x.next END
```

The input and output of figures is now symmetrical and completely generic [PHT91]. Any future extension of figures can be stored with *WriteFigure* and loaded with *ReadFigure* without changing anything in these procedures. In new *Figure* classes only the methods *Load* and *Store* have to be overridden.

In systems in which accessing type names is not possible at run time, the following option remains: Before an object is stored, it is sent a message *GetTypeName*. The object returns its type name. This name can now be stored with the object's value. For loading objects, a table is created with type names and a prototype object of each type. When a type name is read from the file, it is located in the table and a copy of the corresponding prototype object is created. For each type, its name and a prototype object must be entered in the table at the start of the program.

If the name of a type is read that is declared in a module that has not yet been loaded, *nameToObj* causes this module to be loaded. If a type table with prototype objects is used, loading of modules should also be built in if the operating system permits it.

Type names can consume quite a bit of space in a file. It is therefore reasonable to store them in compressed form. This can be implemented as follows: With the first occurrence of a type name, it is written in full length and entered at the end of a table. For further occurrences the index in the table is written instead of the full name. Reading takes place in the opposite order: With the first occurrence the full name is read and entered at the end of a table. For further occurrences only the index is read, which is used to extract the name from the table. The methods *WriteString* and *ReadString* of the class *OS.Rider* (see Appendix B) read and write character strings in compressed form. The table for converting character strings to indices and vice verse is a data field of *Rider*. At the start of input/output, the *Rider* object is initialized with *InitRider*.

Compressed storage of type names

```
TYPE
    String = ARRAY 32 OF CHAR;
    Rider = RECORD
        ...
        tab: ARRAY maxnames OF String;  (*tab[0] = "" (for NIL)*)
        end: INTEGER  (*tab[0..end-1] are filled*)
    END;

PROCEDURE InitRider (VAR r: Rider);
BEGIN r.tab[0] := ""; r.end := 1
END InitRider;

PROCEDURE (VAR r: Rider) WriteString (s: ARRAY OF CHAR);
    VAR i: INTEGER;
BEGIN i := 0;
    LOOP (*search s in r.tab*)
        IF i = r.end THEN (*not found -> first occurrence of s*)
            r.Write(CHR(i));
            i := -1; REPEAT INC(i); r.Write(s[i]) UNTIL s[i] = 0X;
            COPY(s, r.tab[r.end]); INC(r.end); EXIT
        ELSIF s = r.tab[i] THEN r.Write(CHR(i)); EXIT
        ELSE INC(i)
        END
    END
END WriteString;

PROCEDURE (VAR r: Rider) ReadString (VAR s: ARRAY OF CHAR);
    VAR i: INTEGER; ch: CHAR;
BEGIN r.Read(ch);
    IF ORD(ch) = r.end THEN (*full text follows*)
        i := -1; REPEAT INC(i); r.Read(s[i]) UNTIL s[i] = 0X;
        COPY(s, r.tab[r.end]); INC(r.end)
    ELSE COPY(r.tab[ORD(ch)], s)
    END
END ReadString;
```

Figure 8.4 shows a text with and without type name compression .

Full text
CircleDesc...EllipseDesc...EllipseDesc...CircleDesc...EllipseDesc...

Compressed text
1CircleDesc...2EllipseDesc...2...1...2...

Fig. 8.4 Text with and without compression of type names

8.4   Wrapping Classes in Other Classes

Consider two classes A and B that are not compatible. We want to use B wherever A is currently used. However, B cannot become a subclass of A because it already exists and we cannot or do not want to change the existing class hierarchy.

For example, our graphics editor from Section 8.2 is to be extended to handle text pieces like figures, allowing them to be moved, selected, and deleted. Using class *Text* for this would be fine, but the problem is that *Text* already exists and thus cannot be made a subclass of *Figure*. Furthermore, this would violate the is-a relationship, for a text is not a figure.

The solution is to wrap *Text* in a new class *TextFigure* that is a subclass of *Figure*. Wrapping means that the text becomes a field of class *TextFigure*:

```
TYPE
    TextFigure = POINTER TO TextFigureDesc;
    TextFigureDesc = RECORD (FigureDesc)
        t: Text;
        ...
    END;
```

Now the graphics editor can handle *TextFigure* objects like rectangles, circles and other figures. It can add them to the list of figures and send them any messages that figures understand (*Draw, Store*, etc.). *TextFigure* objects must translate these messages into *Text* messages and forward them to their field *t*. The following example assumes that texts understand a *Store* message.

```
PROCEDURE (f: TextFigures) Store (VAR r: OS.Rider);
BEGIN
    f.Store^ (r);  (*store fields of base class Figures*)
    f.t.Store (r)  (*store text of this figure*)
END Store;
```

This simple technique is useful in many situations: If B must be compatible with A, but cannot become a subclass, it is wrapped in a new subclass of A that forwards all A messages to B.

8.5 Extensibility in Multiple Dimensions

In Section 6.2 the abstract class *Stream* was described; it was extended to various subclasses like *DiskFile*, *FloppyFile* and *NetFile*, which were variants with respect to the output medium. Variants could also be created with respect to another criterion such as the encryption technique: there could be a plain character stream, a stream encrypted with the DES method (e.g., see [Sed88]), and a stream encrypted with the RSA method. Thus the class *Stream* can be extended in multiple dimensions (Fig. 8.5).

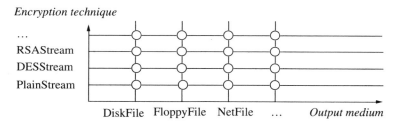

Fig. 8.5 Extension of the class *Stream* in two dimensions

Each variant of the output medium should be combinable with each variant of the encryption technique, giving a *DESDiskFile*, a *DESFloppyFile*, etc. With n variants of the output medium and m variants of the encryption technique, we obtain $n*m$ classes (Fig. 8.6).

Cartesian product of two attributes

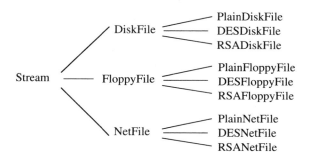

Fig. 8.6 Subclasses of *Stream*

How can this explosion of the number of classes be avoided without sacrificing the possibility to combine the output medium and the encryption technique? There is a simple method based on wrapping classes: Define a new class *EncryptionStream* as a subclass of *Stream*; give it a data field of type *Stream* containing one particular variant of the output medium (*DiskFile, FloppyFile*, etc.). *EncryptionStream* can now be extended to cover the various encryption techniques. By plugging a certain output medium into the desired encryption technique, the two dimensions can be combined, resulting in only $n+m+1$ (instead of $n*m$) classes (Fig. 8.7).

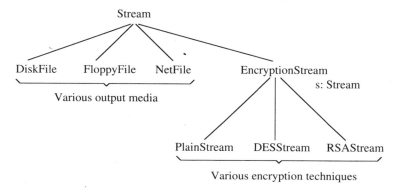

Fig. 8.7 Field *s* of *EncryptionStream* can contain *DiskFile, FloppyFile* or *NetFile*

Implementing
EncryptionStream

The method *Write* in *EncryptionStream* is overridden so that the *Write* message is forwarded to field *s*:

```
TYPE
    EncryptionStream = POINTER TO EncryptionStreamDesc;
    EncryptionStreamDesc = RECORD (StreamDesc)
      s: Stream  (*DiskFile, FloppyFile, NetFile*)
    END;

PROCEDURE (e: EncryptionStream) Write (ch: CHAR);
BEGIN  ·
    e.s.Write(ch)
END Write;
```

In the subclasses of *EncryptionStream* the *Write* method is also overridden and the respective encryption algorithm is implemented:

```
TYPE
    DESStream = POINTER TO DESStreamDesc;
    DESStreamDesc = RECORD (EncryptionStreamDesc) ... END;
```

```
PROCEDURE (d: DESStream) Write (ch: CHAR);
    VAR ch1: CHAR;
BEGIN
    ... (*enccrypt ch giving ch1*)
    d.Write^ (ch1)
END Write;
```

To combine DES encryption with output to disk, a variable d is created as follows:

Combining DES encryption with output to disk

```
VAR d: DESStream; f: DiskFile;
...
NEW(d); NEW(f); d.s := f
```

The message $d.WriteString(string)$ is now processed as follows (Fig. 8.8):

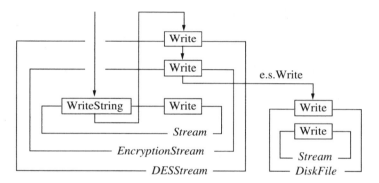

Fig. 8.8 Processing the message *d.WriteString(string)*

WriteString is sent to d and handled by the *WriteString* method inherited from *Stream*. This method sends its receiver a *Write* message for every character in *string* (see Section 6.2). Since the dynamic type of the receiver is *DESStream*, the *Write* method of *DESStream* is invoked; there the character is encrypted and forwarded to the *Write* method of the base class *EncryptionStream*. This forwards the message to its field *e.s*, which invokes the *Write* method of *DiskFile*, where the character is output.

The programmer does not need to keep this message sequence in mind. How the messages are forwarded is an implementation detail. The programmer, who in this case is the user of *DESStream*, only needs to know the interface and the specification the class. It suffices to know that all output to d finally reaches the correct output medium in encrypted form.

Every program that can work with *Stream* can also work with *DESStream, RSAStream* or any other encryption variant. Every encryption technique can be combined with every output medium.

Extensibility in multiple dimensions only works if the abstract base class (here *Stream*) already establishes the entire interface of the subclasses. Every message to an encryption variant must be mapable onto a message with the same name in the output medium variant. In addition, an output medium variant cannot send itself messages because the dynamic type of its receiver is no longer *EncryptionStream* but, for example, *DiskFile*.

Despite this constraint, the technique of extending a class in multiple dimensions is useful in some situations.

8.6   Multiple Inheritance

If it is possible to derive a class from *one* superclass, why should it not be possible to derive it from two or more superclasses? If a class has more than one superclass, we call this *multiple inheritance*.

Multiple inheritance is not supported in Oberon-2. This section explains why and shows how multiple inheritance can be attained with single inheritance.

Fig. 8.9 Multiple inheritance: *C* inherits from *A* and *B*

In Fig. 8.9 class *C* is derived from both *A* and *B*. *C* inherits all fields and methods from *A and B*. Every *C* object is both an *A* object and a *B* object; thus it is compatible with both.

At first glance multiple inheritance seems simple and natural. On closer inspection, however, it suffers from various problems:

Name clashes

- If *A* and *B* contain fields or methods with identical names, a *name clash* results in *C*: the names are inherited from both superclasses and become ambiguous. Languages that support multiple inheritance must provide a means to resolve such name clashes.

Diamond structure

- If *A* and *B* are extensions of a class *D*, the repeated inheritance results in a diamond structure (Fig. 8.10).

Fig. 8.10 Diamond structure

All methods of D are inherited from both A and B. This inevitably leads to name clashes in C. But worse yet, all data fields of D are present in both A objects and B objects. Should they be present twice in C objects, or only once?

- Multiple inheritance leads to class libraries that are not trees, but directed acyclic graphs. This results in more complex dependencies in the library and makes it less comprehensible. *Complex class libraries*

- Multiple inheritance also leads to less efficient code. For example, in C++ a method invocation causes additional run-time costs because of the overhead involved with multiple inheritance—even if the program uses only single inheritance [Str89]. *Run-time costs*

Most well-known class libraries (e.g., Smalltalk's) do without multiple inheritance. For this reason, and because of the problems mentioned above, Oberon-2 was designed without multiple inheritance.

If multiple inheritance is not available, how can we make a class C compatible with both A and B? Fortunately the classes can often be reorganized to avoid the need for multiple inheritance. *Avoiding multiple inheritance*

In the simplest case the class hierarchy can be designed so that A is derived from B or vice versa (Fig. 8.11). This is possible especially if A and B do not exist yet, but are designed along with C. In Fig. 8.11 C objects are both A objects and B objects.

Fig. 8.11 One superclass of C is derived from the other

If this does not work, we can attempt to wrap B in C and to inherit only from A or vice versa (Fig. 8.12). The fields and methods of B can now be used in C objects via the field b. However, we lose the compatibility of C objects with B objects.

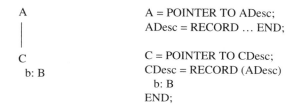

```
A                        A = POINTER TO ADesc;
|                        ADesc = RECORD ... END;
|
C                        C = POINTER TO CDesc;
  b: B                   CDesc = RECORD (ADesc)
                           b: B
                         END;
```

Fig. 8.12 One superclass becomes a component of the subclass

An entirely satisfactory solution can be found by extending A and B to subclasses CA and CB and to link these via data fields (Fig. 8.13).

CA and CB must be viewed as a twin class with two ends. The CA end is compatible with A, the CB end with B. For example, a CA object can be inserted in a list of A objects, a CB object in a list of B objects. CA objects handle A messages and forward B messages to their field b. CB objects do exactly the opposite. Note that in this solution no name clashes occur and the problems of the diamond structure disappear.

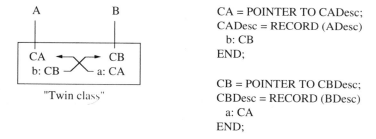

```
                         CA = POINTER TO CADesc;
                         CADesc = RECORD (ADesc)
                           b: CB
                         END;

                         CB = POINTER TO CBDesc;
                         CBDesc = RECORD (BDesc)
                           a: CA
                         END;
```

"Twin class"

Fig. 8.13 Resolving multiple inheritance with a twin class

Example

Let us look at a concrete example: a computer game in which balls move on a playing field and thereby bounce off surrounding walls. Balls and walls are displayable game objects derived from a common base class *Item*. Balls are also active objects (processes) that gain control every few milliseconds to move themselves a bit on the playing field. Assume the existence of a class *Process* from which all classes of active objects are derived (Fig. 8.14).

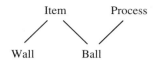

Fig. 8.14 Class hierarchy of a computer game

Ball must be compatible with *Item* so that balls can be inserted in a
list of game objects; *Ball* must also be compatible with *Process* so
that the operating system can handle balls like other processes.

Using the technique described above, *Ball* is implemented as a
twin class *BallItem* and *BallProcess* (Fig. 8.15):

```
TYPE
    BallItem = POINTER TO BallItemDesc;
    BallItemDesc = RECORD (ItemDesc)
        process: BallProcess;
        ...
        PROCEDURE (f: BallItem) Draw;
        PROCEDURE (f: BallItem) Move (dx, dy: INTEGER);
        ...
    END;

    BallProcess = POINTER TO BallProcessDesc;
    BallProcessDesc = RECORD (ProcessDesc)
        item: BallItem;
        ...
        PROCEDURE (p: BallProcess) Activate;
        PROCEDURE (p: BallProcess) Passivate;
        ...
    END;
```

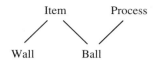

Fig. 8.15 Balls are modelled as a twin class *BallItem/BallProcess*.

A new ball is created and initialized as follows:

```
VAR ball: BallItem; ballProcess: BallProcess;

NEW(ball); NEW(ballProcess);
ball.process := ballProcess; ballProcess.item := ball;
...
```

The variable *ball* can be inserted into the list of game objects, the variable *ballProcess* into the list of processes. If a ball process p becomes active and wants to move its ball, it calls *p.item.Move*. If the program wants to stop a moving ball b, it invokes *b.process.Passivate*.

8.7   Models and Views

Interactive programs usually consist of three parts:

MVC concept

(1) The *Model* maintains the central data structure, e.g., text, graphics, tables, etc.
(2) The *View* is responsible for displaying the data on the screen.
(3) The *Controller* handles user input such as mouse clicks or keyboard input.

How the three parts interact in order to manipulate and display data is called the *Model/View/Controller* (MVC) concept [KrP88]. This is a reusable pattern that occurs in almost all interactive programs. Figure 8.16 shows the interaction of the three parts.

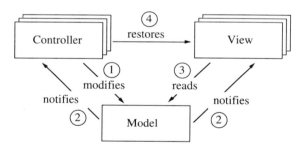

Fig. 8.16 The MVC concept: Arrows indicate the flow of messages. The numbers are explained below.

A model may be shown in multiple views. For example, there could be two views of a text showing different portions of it; or a sequence of numbers could have one view that shows it as a text and another that shows it as a chart. All views show the same model. If the model changes, all views must be updated.

Views and controllers occur pairwise; each view has its own controller since the same input directed to various views can have different effects. A mouse click in the text view of a number sequence might cause selection of the text, while a mouse click in the chart view might cause the chart to be moved.

The following messages flow between model, view and controller (numbers refer to Fig. 8.16): *Messages in the MVC concept*

(1) The controller reacts to keyboard input or mouse clicks by modifying the model (e.g., inserting characters in a text).

(2) The model notifies its views that it has been modified and thus its views must be updated. Even controllers are notified, for it is possible that the modification of the model requires different interpretation of subsequent input.

(3) The view was instructed to update the model (e.g., to draw an inserted text stretch). It acquires the necessary data from the model and displays them on the screen.

(4) Sometimes the controller accesses the view directly, for example, if the contents of the view are to be scrolled. Here the model is not modified, but only one particular view is shifted.

The program that modifies the model must not simultaneously update the view because then only this particular view would be up to date. Other views of the same model would be inconsistent. The correct way is to modify only the model, which tells all its views to update themselves.

View and model need to be clearly separate. If they are combined to a single class, there can be only *one* view of the model. Usually this is an unnecessary restriction.

The Oberon System also employs the MVC concept, but in a somewhat different form. View and controller are combined to a single class *Frame* (Fig. 8.17), which makes sense because view and controller always occur pairwise. This combination reduces the number of messages for updating views and controllers. *Implementation in the Oberon System*

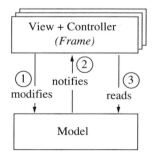

Fig. 8.17 The MVC concept in Oberon

In the original MVC concept the model knows its views and controllers. It maintains a list of these objects and sends them notify messages whenever it is modified. In the Oberon System the model does not know its views. When the model is modified, it broadcasts a notify message to *all* frames on the screen. The frames themselves know whether they belong to the broadcasting model and thus whether they need to react to the message. In this way, more messages are sent than necessary, but the handling of dependent views becomes easier.

Example of the MVC concept

Let us look at an example that shows how model, view and controller interact in the Oberon System. Assume that an insertion mark (caret) is in a text frame and the user presses a key. What happens? The Oberon System determines the frame containing the insertion mark and sends it the message *HandleKey* along with the value of the pressed key. This invokes the following method:

```
PROCEDURE (f: Frame) HandleKey (ch: CHAR);
BEGIN
    IF ch = DEL THEN ... (*delete character to the left of the caret*)
    ELSE f.text.Write(ch) ... (*insert ch into the text*)
    END
END HandleKey;
```

The frame plays the role of the controller. It does not directly display *ch* on the screen, but only modifies the model (the text). The text must then notify all frames in which it is displayed. It sends a message record of type *NotifyInsMsg* to the viewer system (module *Viewers*), which broadcasts it to all viewers on the screen, which in turn broadcast it to all frames they contain.

```
TYPE
    NotifyInsMsg = RECORD (OS.Message)
        t: Text;
        beg, end: LONGINT
    END;

PROCEDURE (t: Text) Write (ch: CHAR);
    VAR msg: NotifyInsMsg;
BEGIN
    ... (*insert ch at t.pos; t.pos := t.pos + 1*)
    msg.t := t; msg.beg := t.pos-1; msg.end := t.pos;
    Viewers.Broadcast(msg)
END Write;
```

Viewers and frames have a message handler (in the sense of Section 6.4) that analyzes the message at run time and either reacts to it or ignores it. The message handler for text frames looks like this:

```
PROCEDURE (f: Frame) Handle (VAR m: OS.Message);
BEGIN
    WITH
        m: Texts.NotifyInsMsg DO
            IF m.t = f.text THEN (*frame shows the modified text*)
                ... (*read m.t from m.beg to m.end*)
                ... (*and draw it on the screen*)
            END
    |   m: Texts.NotifyDelMsg DO
        ...
        ELSE (*ignore the message*)
    END
END Handle;
```

Only if the message handler understands the *NotifyInsMsg* message and only if the frame is displaying the modified model (i.e., if $m.t = f.text$) is the update made on the screen. In all other cases the message is ignored. Fig. 8.18 shows this process. There are two viewers, each containing two frames. The shaded frames are those that belong to the modified model and react to *NotifyInsMsg*.

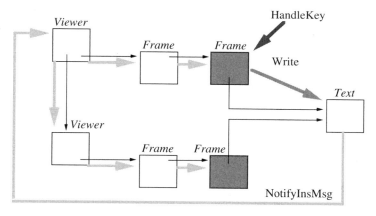

Fig. 8.18 Message distribution in the MVC concept

Broadcasts like this are the most important application of message records. Since the sender does not know the receivers, the message is simply sent to all possible receivers. Only those for which the message is intended react. A broadcast of this type would hardly be possible without message records.

8.8 Iterators

We often have a number of objects and want to carry out an operation on each of them, but we do not know how to access the objects. Because of data abstraction, the implementation of the data structure containing the objects is hidden; it could be an array, a linear list, or a tree. Consider the following class *Dictionary*, whose interface looks like this:

```
DEFINITION Dictionaries;
TYPE
    Elem = POINTER TO ElemDesc;
    ElemDesc = RECORD
        PROCEDURE (x: Elem) EqualTo (y: Elem): BOOLEAN;
        PROCEDURE (x: Elem) LessThan (y: Elem): BOOLEAN;
        PROCEDURE (x: Elem) Print;
    END;

    Dictionary = RECORD
        PROCEDURE (VAR d: Dictionary) Enter (x: Elem);
        PROCEDURE (VAR d: Dictionary) Retrieve (x: Elem; VAR y: Elem);
    END;

PROCEDURE Init (VAR d: Dictionary);
END Dictionaries;
```

The implementation of *Dictionary* is hidden. Assume that we want to print a list of all elements of *Dictionary*. What possibilities do we have?

A separate method for each operation

The simplest possibility is to provide a method *PrintAll* that prints all elements:

```
PROCEDURE (VAR d: Dictionary) PrintAll;
    VAR e: Elem;
BEGIN
    e := d.firstElem;
    WHILE e # NIL DO e.Print; e := e.next END
END PrintAll;
```

This solution is unsatisfactory. Each operation on *Element* requires a method in *Dictionary*, for example, *StoreAll* to write all elements to a file or *SelectAll* to find all elements whose key matches a certain criterion. Furthermore, the implementation of *Dictionary* requires the knowledge of which operations will later be applied to the elements or extensions thereof (e.g., *e.Print*, *e.Store*, *e.Select*, etc.).

Iterator class

Another possibility is to declare an iterator class in the same module as *Dictionary* as follows:

```
TYPE
    Iterator = RECORD
        PROCEDURE (VAR it: Iterator) SetTo (d: Dictionary);
        PROCEDURE (VAR it: Iterator) Next(): Elem;
    END;
```

An iterator is an object that moves over a data structure. *SetTo* sets the iterator to the beginning of the dictionary; *Next* returns the next element. The iterator makes it possible to traverse the elements of *Dictionary* sequentially and to apply some operation to them:

```
iterator.SetTo(d); e := iterator.Next();
WHILE e # NIL DO e.Print; e := iterator.Next() END
```

This solution is general enough, but requires that the code for traversing the elements be present in each client. Besides, if the data structure is a tree, which can best be traversed recursively, *Next* cannot be implemented efficiently.

The result type of *Next* is *Elem*, but the actual type of the returned objects can be an extension thereof (e.g., *MyElem*). Using a type guard makes it possible to send the object returned by *Next* a *MyElem* message that is not accommodated in *Elem*:

```
iterator.SetTo(d); e := iterator.Next();
WHILE e # NIL DO
    IF e IS MyElem THEN e(MyElem).Store(rider) END;
    e := iterator.Next()
END
```

A third possibility is to work with message records. A message record is passed to *Dictionary*, which broadcasts it to all elements. Every element must have a message handler that reacts to the message record. However, for simple tasks like printing *Dictionary* elements, this solution is too heavy-duty.

Operations as message records

Finally, *Dictionary* can provide a universal method *ForAll* that takes a procedure as parameter and calls it for all elements:

Operations as procedure variables

```
PROCEDURE (VAR d: Dictionary) ForAll (P: PROCEDURE (e: Elem));
BEGIN
    e := d.firstElem;
    WHILE e # NIL DO P(e); e := e.next END
END ForAll;
```

The method could be invoked as

```
d.ForAll(Print)
```

where *Print* is a client's procedure:

```
PROCEDURE Print (e: Elem);
BEGIN
    e.Print
END Print;
```

In Oberon-2 this solution is usually the simplest and most readable. Several other languages have special iterator constructs or block objects that permit a more comfortable implementation of iterators.

8.9 Modifying Inherited Methods

In order to modify an inherited method in a subclass, it must be overridden there. Assume a class *Frame* containing a method *TrackMouse* that tracks mouse movements and moves the cursor accordingly:

```
PROCEDURE (f: Frame) TrackMouse;
    VAR x, y: INTEGER; buttons: SET;
BEGIN
    LOOP
        OS.GetMouse(x, y, buttons);  (*get mouse position and buttons*)
        IF buttons = {} THEN EXIT END;
        OS.DrawCursor(x, y)  (*move cursor to new position *)
    END
END TrackMouse;
```

In a subclass *MyFrame* we want the mouse pointer (cursor) to change its form as long as a mouse button is pressed. This is easy to implement by overriding *TrackMouse* in *MyFrame* and changing the cursor form before and after the invocation of the inherited method (see also Fig. 8.19):

```
PROCEDURE (f: MyFrame) TrackMouse;
BEGIN
    SaveCursor;
    ChangeCursorTo(crossHair);
    f.TrackMouse ^;  (*calls TrackMouse from Frame*)
    RestoreCursor
END TrackMouse;
```

MyFrame.TrackMouse

Frame.TrackMouse

Fig. 8.19 Overriding allows adding behavior to the beginning and the end of an inherited method

It is easy to add behavior to the beginning and the end of an inherited method. But how can we add something to the middle of such a method, e.g., how can we modify *TrackMouse* so that the cursor moves on a grid instead of continuously? We can do so by letting the *TrackMouse* method of the base class pass control to the programmer immediately before the cursor is drawn. More specifically, *TrackMouse* calls an empty method *Constrain* (a hook) that can be overridden to add new behavior:

```
PROCEDURE (f: Frame) TrackMouse;
    VAR x, y: INTEGER; buttons: SET;
BEGIN
    LOOP
        OS.GetMouse(x, y, buttons);
        IF buttons = {} THEN EXIT END;
        f.Constrain(x, y);
        OS.DrawCursor(x, y)
    END
END TrackMouse;

PROCEDURE (f: Frame) Constrain (VAR x, y: INTEGER);
END Constrain;
```

If a subclass like *MyFrame* does not override *Constrain*, the empty method is invoked with no effect. But if *Constrain* is overridden, it is called every time before the cursor is drawn, thus giving control to the subclass (Fig. 8.20).

```
PROCEDURE (f: MyFrame) Constrain (VAR x, y: INTEGER);
BEGIN
    x := (x + grid DIV 2) DIV grid * grid;
    y := (y + grid DIV 2) DIV grid * grid
END Constrain;
```

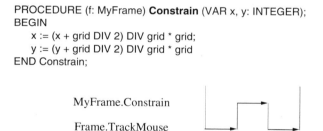

MyFrame.Constrain

Frame.TrackMouse

Fig. 8.20 Adding behavior to an inherited method
by overriding a hook method

By invoking hook methods, the superclass allows the subclass to intervene in the algorithm. This technique is often used to make algorithms more adaptable. Sometimes a complete algorithm consists solely of invocations of such empty hook methods. The redrawing of a frame, for example, could consist of the removal of the selection, the setting of a clipping rectangle, and the proper drawing of the frame.

```
PROCEDURE (f: Frame) Redraw;
BEGIN
    f.RemoveSelection;
    f.SetClippingRect(f.X, f.Y, f.W, f.H);
    f.Draw
END Redraw;
```

The operations *RemoveSelection, SetClippingRect* and *Draw* are different in graphic frames and text frames. Thus the methods cannot be implemented in the abstract class *Frame*. But *Redraw* establishes the right order of the operations and thus provides the outline of an algorithm that can be filled out in subclasses.

9 Object-Oriented Design

Designing a program means decomposing it into smaller, more comprehensible parts and describing their interactions. The parts can be modules, procedures, files, or classes. In object-oriented design we are interested primarily in classes. Our question is thus: How can we find the classes required for the implementation of a system?

9.1 Functional Design

Conventional program design begins with the question: *What* is the program supposed to do? The orientation is towards the *tasks* that are to be solved. We begin with the overall task and decompose it into subtasks, then reduce the subtasks to smaller subtasks, and so on until the subtasks are so simple that they can be formulated directly in a programming language.

This approach is called *stepwise refinement* [Wir71]. We advance from the abstract to the concrete, from the overall task to the details. Stepwise refinement is a *top-down* method that leads to an hierarchy of procedures or functions (Fig. 9.1). It is therefore also called functional decomposition.

Stepwise refinement

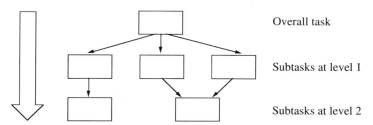

Fig. 9.1 Program hierarchy in functional design: Arrows indicate the *uses* relationship.

Advantages

Stepwise refinement has many advantages: It is easy to use and systematic, and it leads to well-structured programs. Important parts (e.g., the top-level logic) are designed first and less important details later; the design of the control logic shapes the rest of the program.

Drawbacks

But stepwise refinement also has drawbacks: It is precisely the control logic that is the most sensitive part of a program. In the early stages of design, the form of the control logic is often still in the dark. In fact, sometimes it is not even clear whether there should be a single main function or multiple functions at the same level. In an operating system, for example, it is difficult to tell which part is the main function. Where should refinement begin? Of course, each part can be refined independently, but this leads to separate program hierarchies without common parts at the base.

Stepwise refinement does not promote software reuse. All subtasks are tailored to the requirements of the main function, so the resulting program is a customized work of craftsmanship. Its parts are hardly usable in other programs.

Finally, software designed by stepwise refinement is sensitive to modifications. If the requirements on the main function change, the decomposition often has to be rethought, which can render large parts of the program design disposable.

Although stepwise refinement is a technique that works perfectly for the design of small programs or algorithms, it is less suitable for the design of large systems.

9.2   Object-Oriented Design

Concentration on abstractions

In object-oriented design the main question is not *what* the system is to do, but *with which objects* it is to work. This approach concentrates on the data and the operations applied to them. Since the objects can hardly be viewed as the top of the system, object-oriented design is more of a *bottom-up* technique.

The system is organized as a set of objects that can be operated like independent machines via clearly defined operations. The control logic can later be built on these objects in such a way that the resulting system can have multiple functions at the top (Fig. 9.2).

Object-oriented design has at least the following advantages: The resulting classes reflect the entities in the respective application; programs thus become more problem-oriented and more comprehensible. Object-oriented design permits systems with multiple functions at the top. New software components are easier to add than in task-oriented design. The classes at the base were not tailored to one specific application and can more readily be reused in other programs.

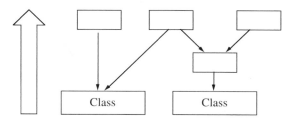

Fig. 9.2 Program hierarchy in object-oriented design. Arrows indicate the uses relationship.

A drawback of object-oriented design is that the classes at the base are often too general. If an application needs binary trees that provide only insertion and searching, then operations like storing, reading and merging of trees are superfluous. The extra functionality has to be carried along although it is not needed. This is the price paid for reusability.

Advantages
Drawbacks

Object-oriented design is mainly a bottom-up technique. However, this does not mean that programs should be designed exclusively bottom-up. In practice, design is both bottom-up and top-down, depending on which technique is most suitable at the moment. For example, if we are designing software for the control of a computer network, we first design the basic classes that model the network, its layers, and its protocols. Then we build on these classes to design the control logic of the system top-down. At some point, we might observe that we need an address service. We go back and design a class at the base to offer this service. Then we continue the top-down design process.

In practice, design is a mixture of top-down and bottom-up

Some authors recommend that object-oriented design be neither top-down nor bottom-up, but from the known to the unknown parts of a system [Bud91].

9.3   Identifying the Classes

The starting point for every design is a requirements definition that specifies what requirements the program is to fulfill. Since it is

Requirements definition

independent of any later implementation, classes, methods and other object-oriented aspects do not need to be considered yet. Any familiar notation is suitable.

We use the requirements definition to identify the classes of the system. Although it would be naive to believe that a certain method can automatically lead to good designs, the ever recurring question is how we should proceed when trying to identify the classes. We cannot prescribe a mechanical technique for that; designing a system requires experience and skill. The only advice we can give is to use the following considerations as a guideline in the design process.

9.3.1 Basic Design Considerations

Classes model real-world entities

The goal of object-oriented design is to establish a one-to-one relationship between the real-world entities and the classes in the program. In the design of a text editor, for example, texts should be represented by a class *Text* and windows by a class *Window*. In a traffic simulation system the objects should be cars, roads and traffic lights. We therefore start the design process with the following three questions:

Identifying classes

(1) *What are the physical and logical entities of the real-world system?*
This question leads to the classes. Physical entities could be switches, sensors or displays. Logical entities could be a process, a measurement, or a command. Any concept that is central to the system, represents important data, or can assume various states is a candidate for a class.

Identifying methods

(2) *Which operations can be carried out with these objects?*
This question leads to the methods. The operations of a class *Sensor*, for example, could be turning it on, turning it off, reading its value, etc. The search for methods should not be restricted by the current requirements, but should be carried out with the reusability of the class in mind. Any reasonable operation is a candidate for a method.

One approach that has proved useful is to simulate various scenarios in which the class appears and to ask: Which events could occur? Which objects will react to these events and how? Which other actions or events are triggered?

(3) *Which data must be stored in an object to allow the operations to do* *Identifying data*
their tasks? *fields*

This question leads to the data fields of a class. The data fields
represent the state of an object, which can be modified and
read via methods. They form the concrete data structure that is
hidden from the clients of the class. The data of a class *Sensor*,
for example, could be its current value and the sampling
interval.

These three questions help to find the classes and to specify their
interfaces. For example, by applying these questions we might
create a class *Sensor* that looks like this:

```
TYPE
    Sensor = RECORD
        value, interval: REAL;
        ...
        PROCEDURE (VAR s: Sensor) Switch (on: BOOLEAN);
        PROCEDURE (VAR s: Sensor) Value (): REAL;
        ...
    END;
```

What has been achieved so far? With each class, some behavior has *Concentrating*
been extracted from the program and has been concentrated in one *behavior*
place. The remaining program is leaner and less complex. It can
work with the classes at a higher level. Once sufficiently many
classes have been created in this way, the remaining control logic is
often relatively simple.

However, there is a danger of creating too many classes. This *Mistakes*
makes the program complex, not because of its inpenetrable
control structure, but because of its many (and often irrelevant)
components and their interactions.

Another mistake is to build *everything* with classes, forgetting
about modules and abstract data types, which are not extensible,
but somewhat simpler and more efficient than classes. Whenever
we use a class, we should consider whether a module or an
abstract data type might not be adequate instead.

9.3.2 Additional Design Considerations

In addition to the three basic questions above, the following considerations are useful for identifying the classes of a system:

Typical patterns

Are there situations that particularly lend themselves to being solved with classes?

Are there objects that occur in variants? Are variants to be added later? Is there some behavior to be exchanged for another at run time? Situations of this kind were described in Chapter 7. They particularly lend themselves to an object-oriented implementation because extensibility and dynamic binding can be exploited.

Information hiding

Which system-specific parts should be hidden from clients?

Programs often contain system-specific details that are difficult to understand and are among the first things that must be modified when the system is ported. Such details should be encapsulated in modules or in classes so that modifications in them remain local and clients can use them without knowing their implementation.

Modifications

Which parts of the software are likely to change? How can the effects of such changes be limited?

Often future modifications of a program are already indicated during its construction, because a more efficient solution is sought, because the program is to be ported, or because external conditions change. The affected parts should be hidden in a class and provided with an interface that remains stable even if the implementation behind it changes.

Basic services

Can we identify generally useful services that are also needed in other programs?

Studies have shown that more than half of all code also occurs in similar form in other programs. Examples include code for list handling, for text and graphics operations, and for input/output formatting. It makes sense to decouple such basic services from the program where they were initially used and to make them available to other programs in the form of reusable classes.

How others do it

What decomposition is used in similar systems?

Good design is learned by experience rather than by rules. Editors are always constructed in a similar way, as are bookkeeping programs and simulation systems. Studying existing systems helps to collect a repertoire of design patterns and to learn how to use them. In this sense we refer the reader to Chapter 11, which contains the complete implementation of a window system with an extensible text and graphics editor.

9.3.3 Deriving Classes from a Verbal Specification

R. Abbott suggests a method by which classes, methods, and data fields can be almost mechanically derived from a verbal specification [Abb83]. He advises observing the nouns, verbs and adjectives that occur in the text.

Abbott's method

The *nouns* in the text are candidates for classes or data fields. They describe the objects that are handled or the properties of an object. The *verbs* in the text are candidates for methods. They describe the operations that are executed with the objects. The *adjectives* in the text suggest data fields. They describe a property or a state of an object.

If a specification contains the phrase "The editor must be able to draw and erase figures and change their size", then *editor, figure* and *size* are the occurring nouns. *Editor* and *figure* are central objects and suggest classes, while *size* indicates only a property of a figure and is thus a data field. The size of a figure is not complex enough to make it worth implementing as a class. It can be expressed simply in two numbers that specify the height and width of the figure. The verbs of the specification are *draw, delete*, and *modify*. They suggest methods of the class *Figure*. Adjectives do not exist in this part of the specification.

We readily see that this method cannot provide the complete design of classes; it can only be used as a starting point. The reasons are clear: On the one hand, the results can only be as good as the specification. An incomplete specification does not contain all necessary nouns, verbs and adjectives and thus does not lead to the required classes. On the other hand, not *every* noun is a class and not *every* verb is a method. The *relevant* words have to be filtered out, which is not always easy.

Shortcomings

It is a common mistake to create too many classes, i.e., to include ones that do not have complex data or interesting methods.

9.3.4 CRC Cards

The literature on object-oriented analysis and design describes CRC cards (Class/Responsibilities/Collaborators cards), which are recommended as an aid for identifying classes [BeC89]. CRC cards are simple file cards on which we note the responsibilities and collaborators of classes.

CRC cards

For each class there is a card labeled with the name of the class. In the left column of the card we list what the class is responsible for; in the right column we write the names of the other classes with which it collaborates (Fig. 9.3).

Class Drawing	
Responsibilities	**Collaborators**
Knows which figures it contains Draws figures Can find the figure at a certain location …	List Figure

Fig. 9.3 CRC cards for a class *Drawing*

The responsibilities need not yet correspond to the methods. A responsibility such as "knows which figures it contains" can consist of several methods, e.g., *Insert, Delete, Broadcast*. Inversely, a method can assume several responsibilities. The data of the class can be specified on the back of the card. Since data are hidden to clients, this is the right place to write them down. Of course it is also possible to use the card for specifying the class interface in a certain syntactical notation (e.g., a programming language) if this is desired.

Advantages   CRC cards have various advantages: They are easy to understand, to produce, and to discard. Multiple cards can be laid out on a large table and arranged by various criteria, giving a good overview of the system. The limited size of the cards helps to keep the size of classes small. If abstract classes are to be distinguished from their concrete subclasses, a stack of cards can be created with the abstract class at the top and the concrete classes underneath.

9.4   Designing the Interface of a Class

Interfaces   The interface of a class consists of the fields and methods that are visible to clients. The interface of a class *File*, for example, could look like this:

```
TYPE
    File = POINTER TO FileDesc;
    FileDesc = RECORD
        name-: ARRAY 64 OF CHAR;
        pos-, len-, result-: LONGINT;
        PROCEDURE (f: File) Open (name: ARRAY OF CHAR);
        PROCEDURE (f: File) Close;
        PROCEDURE (f: File) SetTo (pos: LONGINT);
        PROCEDURE (f: File) Read (VAR ch: CHAR);
        PROCEDURE (f: File) Write (ch: CHAR);
    END;
```

The interface should be designed so that the class can be used in as many contexts as possible with as few and as simple operations as possible. A good indication for the value of a class is to what degree other programmers are willing to use it. Class interfaces should be designed according to the following criteria [Hof90]:

The goal of interface design

(1) *Consistency*
    Set up your own rules (based on standard guidelines) and stick to them. The rules can apply to parameter passing (input parameters before output parameters), to naming (consistent use of verbs, nouns and adjectives), or to the use of upper and lower case in names. Consistent interfaces make it easier to understand the rest of a system if part of it is already known.

Interface criteria

(2) *Simplicity*
    Avoid needless features. The smaller the interface, the easier it is to use the class.

(3) *No redundancy*
    Avoid offering the same service in more than one way; eliminate redundant features.

(4) *Atomicity*
    Do not combine several operations if they are also needed individually. Keep independent features separate.

(5) *Reusability*
    Do not customize classes to specific clients, but make them general enough to be reusable in other contexts.

(6) *Robustness with respect to modifications*
    Design the interface of a class so that it remains stable even if the implementation of the class changes.

Naming conventions

The following examples serve to clarify these criteria. Let us start with naming conventions which significantly contribute to the readability of programs. Since such conventions are seldom explicitly described, we give some rules here that have proven useful over time (Table 9.4).

Names for	Start with	Examples
Constants, variables	Lower-case noun Lower-case adjective	version, wordSize full
Types	Upper-case noun	File, TextFrame
Procedures	Upper-case verb	WriteString
Functions	Upper- case noun Upper-case adjective	Position Empty, Equal
Modules	Upper-case noun	Files, TextFrames

Table 9.4 Proven naming conventions

In names consisting of several words, every word (except possibly the first one) should start with a capital letter. Data and methods with similar semantics should be named identically. An operation that draws a window, a frame or a figure should bear the same name in each case. This simplifies learning and understanding new classes.

Avoiding redundancy

Consider a message *text.Search(pattern, pos)*, which searches for a pattern in a text beginning at position *pos*. Another message *text.SearchNext* looks for the next occurrence of the same pattern starting at the position where the pattern was last found. *SearchNext* should be omitted since it can easily be expressed with *Search*.

Atomicity

The message *file.Open(name, pos)* opens a file and sets the reading position to *pos*. This operation is not atomic. It should be decomposed into two operations that can be used individually: *file.Open(name)* and *file.SetTo(pos)*.

Conflicts

The above criteria can conflict with each other: On the one hand, a class should be held as general as possible to increase its chances of reuse; on the other hand, unnecessary features are to be avoided. How can this be resolved? Or: Only atomic operations should be provided that can be combined in a flexible way; on the other hand, this makes client code consist of many individual operations that have to be invoked in the correct order. In such cases we have to decide according to our priorities by selecting one criterion over another.

Good interface design requires skill. With classes we are able to create virtual languages that contain new data types and new operations. Thus interface design is actually language design! Since it is difficult to design a good language, it is not surprizing that the design of good classes proves challenging. Whether a class is good in the sense of the above criteria can only be evaluated when it is used by persons other than its author.

9.5 Abstract Classes

Abstract classes were introduced in Chapter 6. They contain empty methods that must be overridden in subclasses. In the construction of extensible software systems, abstract classes play an important role: they are the design of their subclasses, a common pattern that establishes the behavior of all future extensions.

Abstract classes are the design of their subclasses

For example, in the implementation of a graphical user interface, an abstract class *InterfaceItem* might specify that all its subclasses (*Button*, *CheckBox*, *ScrollBar*, etc.) must understand the messages *Draw*, *Move* and *Resize*.

```
TYPE
    InterfaceItem = POINTER TO InterfaceDesc;
    InterfaceDesc = RECORD
        PROCEDURE (x: InterfaceItem) Draw;
        PROCEDURE (x: InterfaceItem) Move (dx, dy: INTEGER);
        PROCEDURE (x: InterfaceItem) Resize (dx, dy: INTEGER);
        ...
    END;
```

Concrete subclasses like *Button* inherit this interface. They understand the same messages and can thus be used wherever an *InterfaceItem* is expected.

The purpose of an abstract class is to serve as a pattern from which other classes can be derived; the purpose of a concrete class is to create objects from it. Abstract classes are thus reusable: *InterfaceItem* can be seen as a pattern for new interface items. Concrete classes are often tailored to a specific purpose and thus not so readily usable in a different context; it is also harder to derive new classes from concrete ones. We should therefore try to identify as many abstract classes as possible in our application domain. The more abstract classes we design, the more reusable abstractions we obtain.

Finding abstract classes

How can we find abstract classes? One possibility is to observe from the beginning that there are variants of a class from which we can factor out common behavior. This is the case with generic components (Section 7.2), heterogeneous data structures (Section 7.3), and replaceable behavior (Section 7.4).

The other possibility is to start with a concrete class that has proven useful and to attempt to devise a reusable abstraction from it. Assume the existence of a class *BarChart*. The reusable abstraction here is not the bar chart, but a more general diagram. The common properties of diagrams can be isolated and defined as an abstract class *Chart*, of which *BarChart* is a special case. Note that the goal is to make the *interface* reusable rather than the code.

Making classes reusable

Reuse does not happen by accident. In order to make classes really reusable, the designer must not rest with the first design. It must be reworked to increase its value. Just as important as designing a new class is revising an existing one to make it simpler and more reusable. Experienced programmers spend as much time on simplifying existing classes as on writing new ones. Useful abstractions are usually created by persons with an obsession for simplicity, who are willing to rewrite code several times to achieve comprehensible and reusable classes [JoF88].

Whether a class is reusable or not can be evaluated only after it has actually been reused. A class that has not been reused repeatedly and by different persons cannot be called reusable.

9.6   Relationships between Classes

Contracts

Classes do not exist in isolation, but interact with other classes to perform a certain task. When two classes cooperate, one takes the role of a *server* that offers some services; the other takes the role of a *client* that uses these services. The two classes are said to be linked by a *contract*. A contract is a set of services (methods) that a class offers. For the description of classes and contracts, the notation used in Fig. 9.5 is recommended in [WWW90].

Contracts are depicted by an arrow from the client to the server. The arrow leads into a numbered semicircle; the corresponding note explains the contract. Although a contract usually consists of multiple methods, only one arrow is drawn to keep the picture simple.

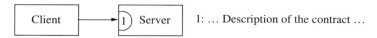

Fig.9.5 A contract between a client and a server.
The arrow indicates the flow of messages.

A class can support multiple contracts. A frame in Oberon, for example, supports the following two contracts (Fig. 9.6).

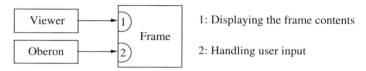

Fig. 9.6 Class *Frame* with two contracts

A viewer sends messages that cause the frame to change its size and to display its contents. Oberon sends messages that pass mouse clicks and keyboard input to the frame.

A contract is only one way in which classes can interact. Altogether there are three possible relationships between two classes A and B:

Relationships between classes

(1) *A has a B*: An A object has n data fields of type B.

(2) *A uses a B*: An A object uses (a contract of) a B object.

(3) *A is a B*: A is a subclass of B.

A *uses-a* relationship is normally based on a *has-a* relationship, which is often not drawn.

These relationships make it possible to graphically represent the interplay of classes. Such representations are called *collaboration graphs* [WWW90].

Collaboration graphs

Figure 9.7 shows such a graph that describes a traffic control system. A crossing has n roads. Each road has a sensor and a traffic light. The sensor can be a contact sensor or an induction sensor. The sensor and the light are managed by a controller that inspects the sensor and uses the acquired data to control the light.

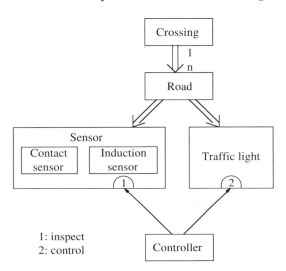

Fig. 9.7 Collaboration graph for a traffic control system

The components of a collaboration graph can, of course, also be modules or abstract data types rather than classes. There are also various other notations that have been suggested for describing classes and their relationships (e.g., [Boo91], [CoY90], [RBP91], [ShM88]).

The value of a graphical notation

A graphical notation can be useful to capture the ideas in the minds of the designers and to make them tactile. It serves as a documentation and as the basis for discussions between designers. However, a notation is only a means to an end and not the end itself. Even the best notation cannot guarantee good designs. CASE tools also need to be seen in this light, as they are often good documentation tools, but cannot replace the work of the designer. Designing is creative work and requires experience and insight. Notation is the mechanical part of the job. If the design is simple and clear, it is less important *which* notation is used or whether a particular notation is used at all.

9.7 When to Use Classes

Languages like Smalltalk offer no data types except classes and no operations except methods. In hybrid languages like Oberon-2, one has the choice to use other constructs beside classes and methods. There are basic types (INTEGER, CHAR, etc.), structured types (arrays, records, etc.), modules, and abstract data types. Often an array is more natural than a class, and a procedure simpler than a method.

This raises the question: When should classes be used and when not? We believe that classes are only justified if at least one of the following conditions is met:

(1) *If the data is sufficiently complex to justify encapsulation*: Classes should abstract from complex data by hiding details. The abstract view that a class offers must be significantly simpler than the concrete data structure that it encapsulates. A class *Speed* would hardly make sense because speed can be expressed more simply as an integer. A class *File*, by contrast, is useful because it hides unnecessary details, such as a data buffer, a position, or access rights. Using the abstraction *File* is simpler than using its concrete data structure.

Sufficiently complex data

(2) *If there are sufficiently many useful operations with the data*: If accessing and modifying data fields seem to be the only operations, then generally a record is the more suitable construct. For a class *Speed* there are no interesting operations: A value can be stored in it and retrieved again, and possibly speeds can be added, but this can be done with integers as well. A method *Add* is no easier to understand than the standard operation + (quite the contrary). A class *File*, on the other hand, has many useful operations: opening, closing, reading, writing, etc.

Sufficiently many useful operations

Classes with only a single method are suspect. In exceptional cases they might be practical, especially in situations where an operation is associated with a state (as in a random number generator). Usually, however, for a single method, a procedure is the better construct.

(3) *If the data exist in variants*: The most useful applications of object-oriented programming come from heterogeneous data structures. If a program has to

Variants

work with variants of data that should be handled in a uniform way, then these data are candidates for classes. Making them classes enables dynamic binding and allows new variants to be added later without having to change the algorithms that work with existing variants.

The uniform treatment of variants is perhaps the most important incentive for using classes, because without classes it is hardly possible to add new variants to a program without modifying or at least recompiling it.

Reusability

(4) *If there is a chance of extension and reuse*:
Some data are so general that they can be used not only in the program in which they were conceived, but also in other programs. Pop-up menus, for example, are application-independent, reusable and extensible (e.g., nested menus). Thus it makes sense to implement them as a class.

When not to use classes

In most other cases, classes are impractical: If the data are simple, arrays, records or sets suffice. They are at least as comprehensible as classes and are more efficient. An array for which the number and type of its elements is fixed should not be implemented as a class.

If data are application-specific and used only locally to an algorithm, then classes usually do not pay off. For example, converting an integer to a digit string requires an intermediate data structure to store the individual digits. An array is sufficient for that.

Via data abstraction, classes help to reduce the complexity of programs. However, we have to be aware that each class also introduces a certain amount of new complexity: The semantics of its operations must be understood and remembered; its implementation requires code that increases the size of a program and thus the possibility of errors. The benefits of data abstraction must be substantially higher than its overhead in order to justify the introduction of a class.

Choosing the right construct for data abstraction

Classes are only one possible construct among many. They often permit elegant solutions, but this is no reason to express *everything* in classes. Compare this with recursion: Recursion allows a very elegant implementation of certain algorithms; but this does not mean that *all* algorithms should be implemented recursively. Often ordinary loops are more natural and more efficient.

The Oberon system itself consists only in part of classes. The major part consists of modules, abstract data types, and ordinary procedures. Nevertheless, it is modular and extensible.

Figure 9.8 shows how to select a suitable construct for data abstraction.

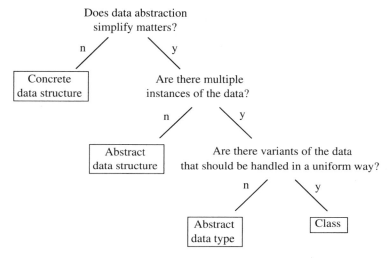

Fig. 9.8 Choosing the right construct for data abstraction

The bottom line is: Classes should not be used at any price, but only if they make a program more comprehensible and extensible, and if this extensibility is required. Flexibility has its price, and who would pay for something that is not used? It is the craft of an experienced programmer to know when to use classes.

Classes—not at any price

9.8 Common Design Errors

Teaching good design is difficult if not impossible. In fact, it is sometimes easier to show how *not* to design programs. This information can also be useful. Avoiding the worst mistakes already leads to quite acceptable designs. This section describes some of the most frequent design errors:

- too many trivial classes
- mixing up *is-a* and *has-a* relationships
- mixing up superclass and subclass
- identical variants

- methods associated with the wrong class
- too deep or too flat class hierarchy

These errors can even be found in some books on object-oriented programming.

9.8.1 Too Many Trivial Classes

Too many trivial classes

The previous section showed that classes do not always pay off. It is a common mistake (especially among beginners) to create a class for every concept, no matter how simple. Classes like *Salary* or *Amount* inflate a program without reducing its complexity or contributing significantly to its flexibility.

In such cases it is clear that classes are not the proper construct. Other cases are less obvious, e.g., time. Should an ordinary record be used:

```
TYPE
    Time = RECORD
        hours: INTEGER;
        minutes: INTEGER;
        seconds: INTEGER
    END
```

or rather a class:

```
TYPE
    Time = RECORD
        PROCEDURE (VAR t: Time) Get (VAR h, m, s: INTEGER);
        PROCEDURE (VAR t: Time) Set (h, m, s: INTEGER);
        PROCEDURE (VAR t: Time) Add (t1: Time);
        PROCEDURE (VAR t: Time) Subtract (t1: Time);
        PROCEDURE (VAR t: Time) LessThan (t1: Time);
    END
```

This depends on what is to be done with times. If they are used only locally in a program without carrying out calculations on them, a record suffices. A record is easy enough to understand and allows efficient access. If time is viewed as a reusable component that is also needed in other programs, and if times are to be added and subtracted, then an abstract data type or a class is appropriate. A class also makes it possible to change the implementation of time without affecting the clients. Thus it depends on what we want to do with the data.

9.8.2 Mixing up Is-a and Has-a Relationships

Inheritance establishes an *is-a relationship* between a subclass and its superclass. *B* should only be derived from *A* if it *is* an extension or refinement of *A*. Instead, inheritance is often abused to represent a *has-a relationship*, e.g.:

Mixing up is-a and has-a relationships

```
TYPE
    Point = RECORD x, y: INTEGER END;
    Line = RECORD (Point) x1, y1: INTEGER END;
```

The idea is that a line can be described by its two endpoints. The coordinates of one point are inherited; those of the other are added in *Line*. This is wrong! A line *is* not a point. It *has* two points. The declaration should read:

```
TYPE
    Line = RECORD p0, p1: Point END;
```

This error sometimes occurs also in a more subtle form:

```
TYPE
    Rectangle = RECORD ... END;
    Window = RECORD (Rectangle) ... END;
```

Although it is true that a window could be viewed as a refinement of a rectangle, the is-a relationship limits the flexibility of *Window*. Oval windows might be introduced in the future; then a window *is* no longer a rectangle, but *has* a certain shape, which could be rectangular or oval. A better design would be:

```
TYPE
    Form = POINTER TO FormDesc;
    FormDesc = RECORD (*abstract*) END;

    Rectangle = POINTER TO RectangleDesc;
    RectangleDesc = RECORD (FormDesc) ... END;

    Window = RECORD
        form: Form;
        ...
    END;
```

If *Window* were derived from *Rectangle*, this would have the further drawback that it could not be derived from another class without using multiple inheritance. It might be necessary, for example, to derive *Window* from a class *ListNode* in order to link various windows in a list.

9.8.3 Mixing up Superclass and Subclass

Mixing up superclass and subclass

Sometimes it is difficult to say which of two classes should be the superclass and which the subclass. Fig. 9.9 shows an example.

Fig. 9.9 Is *Square* a subclass of *Rectangle* or vice versa?

It could be argued that a rectangle is an extension of a square, for while a square requires a corner and a dimension, a rectangle requires the same data and an additional dimension.

This argument is wrong because not every rectangle is a square. The opposite is true: every square is a rectangle! The subclass must be a *specialization* of the superclass. The relationship between classes must be selected so as to yield an is-a relationship. Only then can objects of the subclass be used wherever objects of the superclass are expected.

9.8.4 Identical Variants

Identical variants

Some programmers tend to distinguish between objects that have the same structure and behavior, but differ in the value of a data field. For example, they view red and blue rectangles as belonging to different classes (Fig. 9.10).

Fig. 9.10 Subclasses with identical structure and behavior

This class hierarchy is generally incorrect. If red and blue rectangles have the same kind of data and methods, they should belong to the same class *Rectangle*. They differ only in the value of a data field that specifies their color:

```
TYPE
    Rectangle = POINTER TO RectangleDesc;
    RectangleDesc = RECORD
        color: Color;
        ...
    END
```

Deriving separate subclasses would, however, be justified if red and blue rectangles would react differently to a message.

9.8.5 Methods Associated with the Wrong Class

Sometimes it is not clear to which class an operation should be assigned. Removing elements from a list, for example, requires a method *Remove*. Should this method belong to lists or to elements? Should we write

Methods associated with the wrong class

    list.Remove(element)

or

    element.RemoveFrom(list)

It can be argued that elements should be autonomous and thus responsible to remove themselves from a list. This argumentation is wrong. The removal of elements is a list operation.

The receiver of a message must always be the object whose data are changed by the operation. In this example the list, not the element, is changed. The state of a list must only be modified by its own operations; anything else would violate information hiding, and invariants on the state of the list could no longer be guaranteed.

But what happens when a method modifies the data of multiple classes? To which class should this method be assigned? Such a situation usually indicates a design error. The method should be decomposed into several methods that each modify only the data of their receiver.

9.8.6 Too Deep or too Flat Class Hierarchy

Although it is difficult to say *how* deep a class hierarchy should be, class hierarchies that are too deep or too flat are generally undesirable.

Too deep or too flat class hierarchy

Excessively deep hierarchies occur when concrete classes are frequently extended with the goal of reusing code. This is a particularly common practice in Smalltalk, where the source code of every class is available and invites reuse. The problem with too deep hierarchies is that each method scarcely does any work before passing the message to the superclass. An operation is thus spread over numerous methods. This can impede maintenance and error localization.

Overly flat hierarchies occur when subclasses reuse little or nothing from their superclasses. The extreme case would be a single abstract class *Object* from which all other classes are derived. This is certainly wrong, for it sacrifices almost all the advantages of object-orientedness.

A class hierarchy should be balanced. The inner nodes should represent abstract classes, the leaves concrete ones. When many concrete classes are derived from an abstract class, this extends the class tree in its width. When abstract classes are derived from other abstract classes, this usually extends the tree in depth (Fig. 9.11).

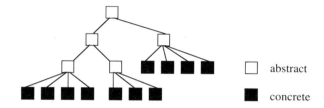

Fig. 9.11 Class hierarchies should be neither too deep nor too flat

10 Frameworks

Object-oriented systems are seldom written from scratch, but are usually built on existing systems. Object-oriented programming normally means extending a given system. This extensibility is one of the great advantages of OOP. Only when new programs can build on existing ones, can the productivity of programmers be increased.

If one class can be derived from another, programmers already save a lot of work. If, however, a whole set of classes can be reused together, the advantage is even greater. A set of cooperating classes is called a *framework* [Deu89]. We will first examine the idea of frameworks and then look at some examples.

10.1 Subsystems and Frameworks

Large systems generally consist of several subsystems, where each subsystem is composed of a set of objects or other components that cooperate to perform a certain task. A subsystem itself can be viewed as a single component with an interface to the outside (Fig. 10.1).

Subsystems

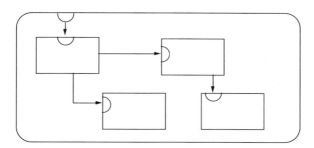

Fig. 10.1 Subsystem consisting of four classes

A subsystem like this is usually designed for a particular application, which makes it application-specific and scarcely reusable. In order to achieve reusability, the application-independent parts have to be isolated. They form the *framework* of the subsystem (Fig. 10.2). Application-specific tasks are left to later extensions of the framework.

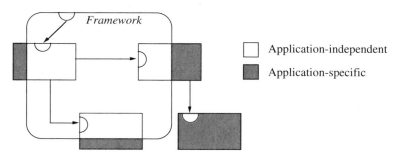

Fig. 10.2 Framework of a subsystem

A frameworks is the design of subsystems

A framework is a set of abstract and concrete classes that cooperate in order to handle the application-independent aspects of a task. By extending its classes, the framework can be developed into various concrete subsystems.

In the same way as an abstract class is the design of its concrete subclasses, a framework is the design of the subsystems to which it can be extended. As an abstract class is the generalization of a concrete class, a framework is the generalization of a system of classes.

Domains

Although frameworks are not tailored to a specific application, they are designed for certain application *domains*. Examples include frameworks for graphical user interfaces, for simulation tasks, and for operating systems. The design of a framework requires a great deal of experience and expert knowledge in the respective domain. Only then can a designer factor out the commonalities of all programs in that domain and implement them in a framework that can easily be extended to concrete applications.

Frameworks and procedure libraries

A framework of classes is significantly more useful than a loose collection of procedures or modules. Procedure libraries offer only individual operations, but give no clue as to how these operations can be assembled to a practical system. The toolbox of the Apple Macintosh is such an example. Anyone who has ever used this library knows how difficult it is to find the procedures required for a certain task and to invoke them in the proper order.

Menu selection, for example, requires the following individual operations:

A framework for menus

(1)   display the menu
(2)   track mouse movement and invert contacted menu items
(3)   determine the item at which the mouse button was released
(4)   handle the respective menu item

The first three operations are the same for all menus; only the last one is application-specific. A major part of menu selection can be programmed once and for all. Only the handling of the individual menu item must be left to the application. Thus menu selection can be implemented as a reusable framework consisting of a concrete class *Menu* and an abstract class *MenuItem* (Fig. 10.3):

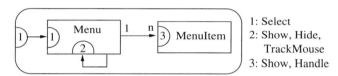

1: Select
2: Show, Hide, TrackMouse
3: Show, Handle

Fig. 10.3 Framework for menu selection (notation see Section 9.6)

Menu holds a list of menu items and has a method *Show* that displays the whole menu, a method *Hide* that removes it from the screen, and a method *TrackMouse* that tracks mouse movement, inverts contacted menu items, and returns the selected item. A method *Select* controls the whole menu selection:

```
PROCEDURE (menu: Menu) Select;
    VAR item: MenuItem;
BEGIN
    menu.Show;
    menu.TrackMouse(item);
    menu.Hide;
    IF item # NIL THEN item.Handle END
END Select;
```

Menu items are initially represented by the abstract class *MenuItem*, whose methods are empty, e.g.:

```
PROCEDURE (item: MenuItem) Handle;  (*abstract*)
END Handle;
```

Handle is overridden in subclasses, and objects of these subclasses are used in *Menu* to fill out the framework. During menu selection the *Handle* method of the subclasses is invoked and the respective menu item is handled. The application-independent framework is thus parameterized via subclasses of *MenuItem*.

Instead of implementing *Handle* as a method, it is better to make it a procedure variable. In this way we avoid having a subclass for each menu item and get by with only a few item kinds (e.g., *TextItem* and *PictureItem*) in which an appropriate *Handle* procedure is installed.

Inverted control flow

In frameworks the flow of control is exactly opposite to that in conventional programs using procedure libraries (Fig. 10.4).

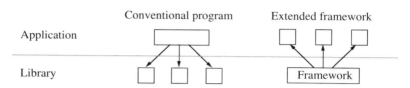

Fig. 10.4 Control flow in conventional programs and frameworks

In conventional programs the programmer writes a main program that invokes procedures from the library. With frameworks it is the other way round: Here the actual main program (the framework) comes from a library and invokes methods that the programmer provides. It is not the application that invokes library routines, but library routines that invoke parts of the application. This is called the Hollywood principle, "Don't call us, we'll call you" [Swe85].

10.2 The MVC Framework

One frequently used framework was already introduced in Section 8.7: the Model/View/Controller framework (MVC). It consists of three abstract classes: a model, its views, and its controllers (Fig. 10.5).

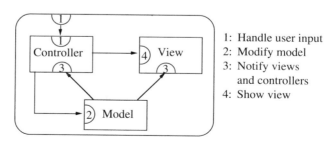

1: Handle user input
2: Modify model
3: Notify views
   and controllers
4: Show view

Fig. 10.5 The MVC framework

This framework forms the application-independent part of many interactive programs. By extending the three classes, it can be developed into various editors, such as a text editor or a graphics editor (Fig. 10.6).

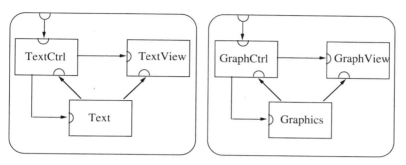

Fig. 10.6 Extension of the MVC framework to a text editor and a graphics editor

10.3 A Framework for Objects in Texts

Many document editors process text that contains not only characters but also other objects such as pictures, tables, and formulas that flow with the text (Fig. 10.7).

Texts

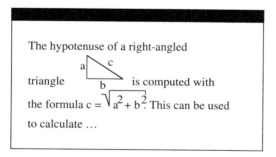

Fig.10.7 Text with floating objects

The document editor *Write* [Szy92] provided with the Oberon System is based on such texts. They have proven very useful and flexible, primarily because the kinds of objects in a text are not fixed in advance. The programmer can implement any kind of new objects (e.g., hypertext buttons) and let them float in the text without modifying the editor. The objects react to mouse clicks:

Elements

pictures go into editing mode, hypertext buttons follow a link into another text, etc.

We call objects floating in the text *elements*. Together with texts and text frames they form a framework for many useful applications such as document editors, spreadsheet programs, hypertext systems, or other programs that manage, display and edit some kind of objects.

The framework consists of the classes *Text*, *TextFrame* and *Element*. The classes *Text* and *TextFrame* are concrete, while *Element* is abstract (Fig. 10.8).

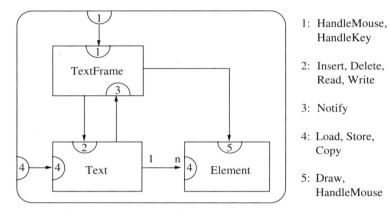

1: HandleMouse, HandleKey

2: Insert, Delete, Read, Write

3: Notify

4: Load, Store, Copy

5: Draw, HandleMouse

Fig.10.8 Framework for texts and included elements

Operations on elements

How do texts and elements interact? A text holds a list of elements and their positions. When it is loaded from or stored in a file, the elements also have to be loaded or stored. In order to do so, the text sends the elements *Load* or *Store* messages that each element interprets in its own way. If a piece of text is to be copied, all elements in it get a *Copy* message. Beside this, a text does not need to know anything about elements.

How does a text frame interact with elements? When the contents of a frame are redrawn, the elements get a *Draw* message that causes them to display themselves at a certain position in the frame. If the user clicks on an element with the mouse, the frame sends the element a *HandleMouse* message. Again, a text frame need not know what kinds of elements exist. It communicates with them only via messages and thus can work with any kind of element.

Class Element

The necessary assumptions about elements are expressed in the interface of the abstract class *Element*:

```
TYPE
    Element = POINTER TO ElementDesc;
    ElementDesc = RECORD
        PROCEDURE (e: Element) Load (VAR r: OS.Rider);
        PROCEDURE (e: Element) Store (VAR r: OS.Rider);
        PROCEDURE (e: Element) Copy (): Element;
        PROCEDURE (e: Element) Draw (x, y: INTEGER);
        PROCEDURE (e: Element) HandleMouse
            (x, y : INTEGER; buttons: SET);
    END;
```

The framework can be extended by deriving concrete subclasses from *Element*, e.g., *GraphicElement*, *FormulaElement* or *HypertextElement*. While the editor is running, these classes can be dynamically added to the editor and objects of these classes (pictures, formulas, hypertext buttons, etc.) can be inserted in the text. They increase the functionality of the editor according to the needs of the user.

Concrete elements

We cannot overemphasize how important it is to have a system that allows adding modules to a running program. Only in such systems are programs truly extensible without recompilation or relinking.

Dynamic extensibility

Compare this to editors in other systems. In most systems an editor must be loaded with its full functionality. This leads to long loading times and large memory consumption, and overwhelms the user with an abundance of functions that are hardly ever used. In the Oberon System the run-time extensibility of programs allows each user to keep in memory only the core of the editor plus the few functions that are actually needed.

Chapter 11 contains a complete implementation of texts with elements.

10.4 Application Frameworks

If frameworks can be extracted from subsystems, why should it not be possible to extract the common behavior of *whole applications*? Old-style batch programs scarcely have such common parts, but many interactive applications do. Commonalities can be found that can be isolated and collected into an application framework.

Dialog programs of the first generation mimic the behavior of batch programs. Data and commands have to be entered in a fixed order. Mistyped input often cannot be taken back because the program already expects the next input. The program has control over the user, who cannot make inputs in arbitrary order.

Dialog programs

The next generation of dialog programs uses *menus* that permit input in any order. However, menus are often hierarchically arranged with a main menu and several submenus that again can contain submenus. Each menu drives the program in a certain state (Fig. 10.9).

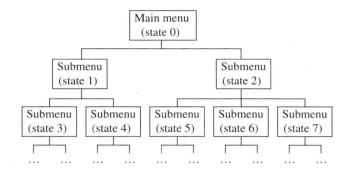

Fig.10.9 Hierarchical menus introduce states

Now the user can execute commands in any order, but must move up and down the menu tree until the proper state is attained that allows the desired command. States in which only certain input is permitted impair the user-friendliness of a program and should be avoided whenever possible.

Event-driven applications

Modern dialog programs are event-driven. They have only one state, in which *all* inputs are possible *in any order*. Each input (keyboard input, mouse click, etc.) is an event and causes a message to be sent to an object that handles the event. The core of such applications is a loop that waits for events and distributes them to the appropriate handler (Fig. 10.10). The program structure is inverted: the handlers belonging to the application are called by the framework belonging to the library

Event loop

In the Oberon System the event loop is implemented in the module *Oberon*. It need not be reimplemented in each program.

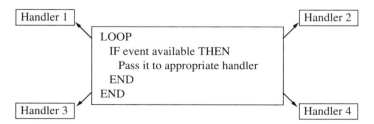

Fig.10.10 Event-driven program structure

This event-handling mechanism is reusable. It is common to all event-driven programs and thus a candidate for the framework. Interactive applications share still other commonalities: They often work with windows, moving and resizing them in a uniform way. These operations are independent of the window contents and thus can be included in the framework. Other common parts include frames, dialog buttons, and menus.

An application framework is thus a standard program that offers the basic functionality that is expected of any application: window management (without contents), menus, loading and storing documents, reading mouse clicks and keyboard input (without processing), etc. This functionality is achieved via a set of classes, some of which are concrete, thus implementing concrete behavior, and some of which are abstract and need to be made concrete in subclasses.

Application frameworks

Various application frameworks are commercially available that facilitate the writing of interactive applications. Some well-known ones include *MacApp* [Sch86], *NextStep* [Web89], and *ET++* [GWM88].

Let us take a brief look at MacApp, which is from the Apple company. It is implemented in Object Pascal and consists of a library of classes that are connected in a certain way to form an application framework (Fig. 10.11).

MacApp

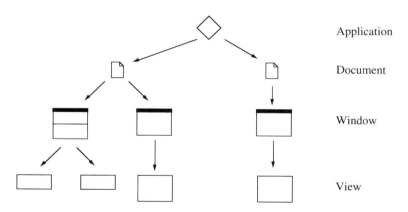

Fig.10.11 Application framework *MacApp*

Each MacApp program is an extension of the class *Application*. An application processes one or more documents that are displayed in one or more windows. A window contains one or more views that display text, graphics, or other data and react to user input. Note that MacApp uses somewhat different terminology from that in Oberon. *Window* is a *Viewer* in Oberon, and *View* is a *Frame*.

Each class of the MacApp framework already fulfills certain tasks. *Application* handles initialization tasks and distributes events, *Window* moves and resizes windows, and *View* adapts the view size to the surrounding window.

Programming by difference

A concrete application is made from the standard behavior of the framework by extending some of these classes and overriding certain methods. This is a good example of *programming by difference*: Only those parts are programmed that deviate from the standard behavior.

11 Oberon0 – A Case Study

In many books, object-oriented programming is taught with tiny examples like stacks, lists and queues. These examples are not representative at all; indeed, they give a completely inaccurate picture of the actual applications and advantages of this technique. Object-oriented programming is programming in the large and requires large, realistic examples. For this reason this chapter presents a realistic case study—a system of windows that can be moved and resized and in which text and graphics can be edited—in full source code.

Why a realistic case study?

By reading source code, we can learn a lot. In school we learn both to read and to write. We read good books to improve our style. Why then do we study so few good programs? Why do we not try to take up their style before writing our own programs? Perhaps because too few good programs are around as source code. Where source code is available, it is usually appreciatively read, as the Smalltalk class library has proven.

The system we describe in this chapter is called *Oberon0* because its functionality and implementation are close to the Oberon System [WiG92]. Several things were solved differently, however: In Oberon0 most messages were implemented with methods and not with message records as in Oberon. Details that would have inflated the source code without contributing to the object-oriented idea were omitted. Thus Oberon0 is less powerful and less efficient than Oberon. But it is a realistic system that can be used for simple editing tasks. The source code of Oberon0 is available along with the object code of the Oberon System (see Appendix D).

Oberon and Oberon0

Oberon0 was implemented under Oberon and uses procedures from Oberon's file system, mouse and screen control, etc. To avoid

Base module OS

describing all these Oberon modules, they were hidden beneath a module *OS*. The interface of *OS* is described in Appendix B.

Parts of Oberon0   Oberon0 consists of five parts:

(1) windows and frames
(2) user input handling
(3) text editing
(4) graphics editing
(5) integration of graphics and texts

The system has 1300 lines of code, 11 modules, and 11 classes. Each module and each class is first described in general, followed by an annotated program listing with explanations. All exported procedures can also be found in the index at the end of the book.

A large part of Oberon0 is written in conventional style. Not all data types are classes; not all operations are methods. This is not a shortcoming, but a conscious design decision. Classes are employed only where they make the program simpler or better extensible. One of the goals of this case study is to show the reader where classes make sense and where to do without them.

The reader should take time with this chapter. It cannot be read as a bed-time story, but needs to be studied with pencil and paper in hand. Only the study of complete examples provides the necessary experience to write object-oriented programs.

11.1 The Viewer System

We start with a description of the viewer system. The viewer system of Oberon0 handles rectangular regions of a raster display in which data can be viewed and edited. These regions are called windows or *viewers*.

Viewers   Viewers completely divide the screen into rectangles (tiling viewers). For the sake of simplicity, Oberon0 has only *one* column of viewers (Fig. 11.1) rather than two as in Oberon.

The black bar at the top of each viewer is the title bar containing the name of the viewer and a list of commands (the menu). Pressing the left mouse button while the mouse pointer is located on the bar permits resizing the viewer by moving the bar up or down with the mouse. Viewers can also be opened and closed by special commands.

Frames

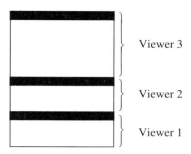

Fig. 11.1 Oberon0 screen with three viewers

Data are not directly drawn into a viewer, but into a rectangular area within the viewer called a *frame*. Frames have two responsibilities:

(1) They display data (text, graphics, etc.).
(2) They handle user input (mouse clicks and keyboard input).

These are also the tasks of a viewer: A viewer is responsible for drawing its border and for handling user input, although the input is usually passed on to the frames in the viewer. A viewer is therefore a subclass of frame. For the sake of simplicity, viewers in Oberon0 always contain exactly two frames: a menu frame with the name of the viewer and a list of Oberon commands, and a contents frame, in which the actual data appear (Fig. 11.2). Frames combine the responsibilities of views and controllers from the MVC concept (Section 8.7).

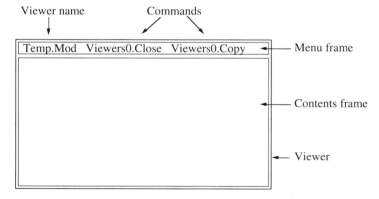

Fig. 11.2 Viewer with a menu frame and a contents frame

Viewers and frames are so closely related that it makes sense to package them together in a module *Viewers0*:

Interface of Viewers0

```
DEFINITION Viewers0;
IMPORT OS;

TYPE
```

Frame

```
  Frame = POINTER TO FrameDesc;
  FrameDesc = RECORD (OS.ObjectDesc)
    x, y: INTEGER;   (*left bottom in pixels relative to left bot. of screen*)
    w, h: INTEGER;   (*width, height in pixels*)
    PROCEDURE (f: Frame) Draw;
    PROCEDURE (f: Frame) Modify (dy: INTEGER);
    PROCEDURE (f: Frame) Move (dy: INTEGER);
    PROCEDURE (f: Frame) Copy (): Frame;
    PROCEDURE (f: Frame) HandleKey (ch: CHAR);
    PROCEDURE (f: Frame) HandleMouse (x, y: INTEGER; buttons: SET);
    PROCEDURE (f: Frame) Handle (VAR m: OS.Message);
    PROCEDURE (f: Frame) Neutralize;
    PROCEDURE (f: Frame) SetFocus;
    PROCEDURE (f: Frame) Defocus;
  END;
```

Viewer

```
  Viewer = POINTER TO ViewerDesc;
  ViewerDesc = RECORD (FrameDesc)
    menu-, cont-: Frame;
    next-: Viewer;
    PROCEDURE (v: Viewer) Close;
  END;

VAR
  focus-: Frame;   (*the frame that gets the keyboard input*)

PROCEDURE New (menu, cont: Frame): Viewer;
PROCEDURE ViewerAt (y: INTEGER): Viewer;
PROCEDURE Broadcast (VAR m: OS.Message);
```

Commands

```
PROCEDURE Close;
PROCEDURE Copy;

END Viewers0.
```

Frame coordinates

The position and size of a frame *f* is shown in Fig. 11.3. The coordinates $(f.x, f.y)$ are relative to the lower left corner of the screen. In this implementation of the viewer system, $f.x$ is always 0, but that can change, of course (see Section 11.5).

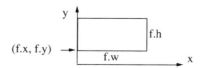

Fig. 11.3 Position and size of a frame *f*

Frame is an abstract class. It simply provides an *interface* without completely implementing it. Due to this interface, a viewer knows which operations it can apply to a frame. And since a viewer can work with general frames, it can also work with frame extensions, such as text frames (Section 11.3.3) and graphics frames (Section 11.4.2).

f.Draw

    requests frame f to redraw its contents.

f.Modify(dy)

    shifts the lower border of frame f by dy pixels up ($dy > 0$) or down ($dy < 0$).

f.Move(dy)

    moves frame f by dy pixels up ($dy > 0$) or down ($dy < 0$).

f1 := f.Copy()

    makes a copy of frame f.

f.HandleKey(ch)

    requests frame f to process character ch which was typed at the keyboard. This message is only sent to a frame if it is the focus frame (see below).

f.HandleMouse(x, y, b)

    requests frame f to react to mouse input. This message is repeatedly sent to the frame as long as it contains the mouse pointer. x and y are the mouse coordinates relative to the lower left corner of the screen, and b is the set of pressed mouse buttons (*OS.left, OS.middle, OS.right*).

f.Handle(m)

    analyzes the message record m and reacts to it. This is the message handler of frames.

f.Defocus

    is sent to the focus frame f immediately before another frame becomes the focus frame.

f.SetFocus

    makes f the focus frame.

f.Neutralize

    requests frame f to remove all marks (caret, selection, etc.) from the screen.

Messages to frames

A viewer inherits the interface from frames, but overrides some methods. For example, when a viewer is resized by a *Modify* message, part of its border needs to be redrawn. Viewers also understand a *Close* message.

Messages to viewers

v.Close

requests the viewer *v* to close itself.

One of the frames is the *focus frame*. All characters typed at the keyboard are sent to the focus frame via *HandleKey* messages. When the left mouse button is pressed in a frame, this frame becomes the new focus frame.

The procedure *New* creates a viewer and displays it on the screen. *ViewerAt(y)* returns the viewer containing the coordinate *y*. *Broadcast(m)* sends the message record *m* to all viewers on the screen.

Copy and *Close* are commands that are placed in the menu frame of a viewer. *Close* closes the viewer that contains the command, and *Copy* creates a copy of that viewer and displays it.

Viewer list

All viewers are linked via a field *next*. A global variable *viewers* points to the bottom viewer on the screen (Fig. 11.4).

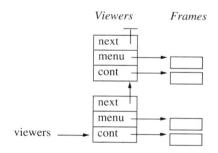

Fig. 11.4 List of all viewers on the screen

We now come to the implementation of the module *Viewers0*. Code that requires explanation is marked with a number in the margin (e.g., ①). This number refers to comments at the end of the code section (marked with the corresponding number in black, e.g., ❶). The imported module *OS* is described in Appendix B.

Implementation of Viewers0

```
MODULE Viewers0;
IMPORT OS;

CONST
    barH = 14;              (*default height of title bar*)
    minH = barH + 2;        (*minimal height of a viewer*)

TYPE
    Frame* = POINTER TO FrameDesc;
    FrameDesc* = RECORD (OS.ObjectDesc)
        x*, y*: INTEGER;    (*left bottom in pixels relative to left bot. of screen*)
```

```
    w*, h*: INTEGER    (*width, height in pixels*)
  END;
  Viewer* = POINTER TO ViewerDesc;
  ViewerDesc* = RECORD (FrameDesc)
    menu-, cont-: Frame;    (*menu frame, contents frame*)
    next-: Viewer;
  END;

VAR
  focus-: Frame;        (*the frame that gets the keyboard input*)
  viewers: Viewer;      (*root for list of viewers on the screen*)

PROCEDURE (f: Frame) Draw*;
END Draw;

PROCEDURE (f: Frame) Copy* (): Frame;
END Copy;

PROCEDURE (f: Frame) Neutralize*;
END Neutralize;

PROCEDURE (f: Frame) HandleKey* (ch: CHAR);
END HandleKey;

PROCEDURE (f: Frame) HandleMouse* (x, y: INTEGER; buttons: SET);
END HandleMouse;

PROCEDURE (f: Frame) Handle* (VAR m: OS.Message);
END Handle;

PROCEDURE (f: Frame) Modify* (dy: INTEGER);
BEGIN INC(f.y, dy); DEC(f.h, dy)
END Modify;

PROCEDURE (f: Frame) Move* (dy: INTEGER);
BEGIN INC(f.y, dy)
END Move;

PROCEDURE (f: Frame) Defocus*;
BEGIN focus := NIL
END Defocus;

PROCEDURE (f: Frame) SetFocus*;
BEGIN IF focus # NIL THEN focus.Defocus END; focus := f
END SetFocus;

PROCEDURE (v: Viewer) Erase (h: INTEGER);
BEGIN
  IF h > 0 THEN (*clear bottom block and draw left and right border*)
    OS.EraseBlock(v.x, v.y, v.w, h);
    OS.FillBlock(v.x, v.y, 1, h);
    OS.FillBlock(v.x+v.w-1, v.y, 1, h)
  END;
  OS.FillBlock(v.x, v.y, OS.screenW, 1)
END Erase;
```

Frame methods

Viewer methods

```
PROCEDURE (v: Viewer) FlipTitleBar;
BEGIN
    OS.InvertBlock(v.x+1, v.y+v.h-barH, OS.screenW-2, barH)
END FlipTitleBar;

PROCEDURE (v: Viewer) Neutralize*;
BEGIN v.menu.Neutralize; v.cont.Neutralize
END Neutralize;

PROCEDURE (v: Viewer) Modify* (dy: INTEGER);
BEGIN
    v.Neutralize;
    v.Modify^ (dy); v.Erase(-dy+1); v.cont.Modify(dy)
END Modify;

PROCEDURE (v: Viewer) Move* (dy: INTEGER);
BEGIN
    v.Neutralize; v.menu.Move(dy); v.cont.Move(dy);
    OS.CopyBlock(v.x, v.y+1, v.w, v.h-1, v.x, v.y+dy+1);
    INC(v.y, dy)
END Move;

PROCEDURE (v: Viewer) Draw*;
BEGIN
    OS.FadeCursor;
    v.Erase(v.h); v.menu.Draw; v.cont.Draw; v.FlipTitleBar
END Draw;

PROCEDURE (v: Viewer) HandleMouse* (x, y: INTEGER; buttons: SET);
    VAR b: SET; x1, y1: INTEGER; dy, maxUp, maxDown: INTEGER;
BEGIN
    OS.DrawCursor(x, y);
    IF y > v.menu.y THEN
        IF OS.left IN buttons THEN (*left click in menu bar => resize viewer*)
            (*----- track mouse movements*)
            v.FlipTitleBar;
            REPEAT
                OS.GetMouse(b, x1, y1); OS.DrawCursor(x1, y1)
            UNTIL b = {};
            v.FlipTitleBar;
            (*----- compute how far v can be moved up or down*)
            dy := y1 - y; maxDown := v.h - minH;
            IF v.next = NIL THEN maxUp := OS.screenH - v.y - v.h
            ELSE maxUp := v.next.h - minH; v.next.Neutralize
            END;
            IF dy < - maxDown THEN dy := - maxDown
            ELSIF dy > maxUp THEN dy := maxUp
            END;
            (*----- move v up or down and adjust neighbor viewers*)
            OS.FadeCursor; v.Neutralize;
            IF dy < 0 THEN (*move down*) v.Modify(-dy); v.Move(dy)
            ELSE (*move up*) v.Move(dy); v.Modify(-dy)
            END;
            IF v.next # NIL THEN v.next.Modify(dy)
            ELSE OS.EraseBlock(v.x, v.y+v.h, v.w, OS.screenH-v.y-v.h)
```

see ①

```
        END
      ELSE v.menu.HandleMouse(x, y, buttons)
      END
    ELSE v.cont.HandleMouse(x, y, buttons)
    END
END HandleMouse;

PROCEDURE (v: Viewer) Handle* (VAR m: OS.Message);
BEGIN
    v.menu.Handle(m); v.cont.Handle(m)
END Handle;

PROCEDURE (v: Viewer) Close*;
    VAR x: Viewer;
BEGIN
  OS.FadeCursor; v.Neutralize;
  IF v.next # NIL THEN v.next.Modify(-v.h)
  ELSE OS.EraseBlock(v.x, v.y, v.w, v.h)
  END;
  IF viewers = v THEN
    viewers := v.next
  ELSE
    x := viewers;
    WHILE x.next # v DO x := x.next END;
    x.next := v.next
  END
END Close;

PROCEDURE ViewerAt*(y: INTEGER): Viewer;
    VAR v: Viewer;
BEGIN
  v := viewers;
  WHILE (v # NIL) & (y > v.y + v.h) DO v := v.next END;
  RETURN v
END ViewerAt;

PROCEDURE New* (menu, cont: Frame): Viewer;
    VAR below, above, v, w: Viewer; top: INTEGER;
BEGIN
  (*----- compute position of new viewer*)
  IF ViewerAt(OS.screenH) = NIL THEN
    top := OS.screenH
  ELSE
    w := viewers; v := viewers.next;
    WHILE v # NIL DO
      IF v.h > w.h THEN w := v END;
      v := v.next
    END;
    top := w.y + w.h DIV 2
  END;
  (*----- generate new viewer and link it into viewer list*)
  above := viewers; below := NIL;
  WHILE (above # NIL) & (top > above.y + above.h) DO
    below := above; above := above.next
  END;
```

Other procedures

see ②

```
        NEW(v); v.x := 0; v.w := OS.screenW; v.next := above;
        IF below = NIL THEN v.y := 0; v.h := top
        ELSE v.y := below.y + below.h; v.h := top - v.y
        END;
        IF v.h < minH THEN RETURN NIL END;
        v.menu := menu; v.cont := cont;
        menu.x := v.x+1; menu.y := v.y+v.h-barH; menu.w := v.w-2; menu.h := barH-1;
        cont.x := v.x+1; cont.y := v.y+1; cont.w := v.w-2; cont.h := menu.y - v.y-1;
        IF below = NIL THEN viewers := v ELSE below.next := v END;
        IF above # NIL THEN above.Modify(v.h) END;
        v.Draw;
        RETURN v
    END New;

    PROCEDURE Broadcast* (VAR m: OS.Message);
        VAR v: Viewer;
    BEGIN
        v := viewers;
        WHILE v # NIL DO v.Handle(m); v := v.next END
    END Broadcast;
```

Commands

```
    PROCEDURE Close*;
        VAR x, y: INTEGER; buttons: SET; v: Viewer;
    BEGIN
        OS.GetMouse(buttons, x, y); v := ViewerAt(y); v.Close
    END Close;

    PROCEDURE Copy*;
        VAR v: Viewer; x, y: INTEGER; buttons: SET;
    BEGIN
        OS.GetMouse(buttons, x, y); v := ViewerAt(y);
        v := New(v.menu.Copy(), v.cont.Copy())
    END Copy;

BEGIN (*Viewers0*)
    viewers := NIL; focus := NIL
END Viewers0.
```

Explanations

Most methods of class *Frame* are empty and must be overridden in subclasses because abstract frames do not know what their contents are or how they should react to mouse clicks and keyboard input. The methods *Move*, *SetFocus* and *Defocus*, on the other hand, can already be implemented for abstract frames and usually do not need to be overridden. *Modify* can be implemented too, but it must be overridden in subclasses to redraw the part of the frame that becomes visible after a modification (see, e.g., Section 11.3.3).

❶   A viewer reacts to a mouse click in the title bar by allowing its upper border to be moved up or down. This process requires explanation (Fig. 11.5).

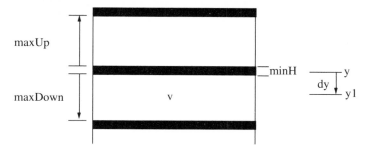

Fig. 11.5 Shifting the upper border of the viewer *v* by *dy* pixels

The mouse was pressed at position *y* and released at *y1*. The vertical shift vector is *dy = y1-y*. The viewer border can be shifted by at most *maxUp* pixels up or *maxDown* pixels down before bumping into the next viewer (viewers must maintain a minimum height *minH*). When the top of a viewer is shifted, the viewer above must be resized and thus receives a *Modify* message.

The position of a new viewer is determined so that its upper ❷ edge *top* is either at the very top of the screen (if there is no other viewer yet) or in the middle of the largest existing viewer. In the latter case the new viewer *v* is positioned between two other viewers *below* and *above* (Fig. 11.6). The viewer *above* is reduced in size and thus receives a *Modify* message.

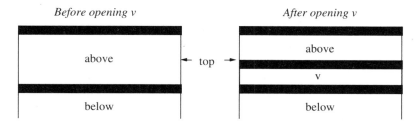

Fig. 11.6 Opening a new viewer with top edge *top*

Viewer and *Frame* are two components with complex data and useful operations. Thus it is justified to implement them as classes. Since viewers will display variants of frames (text frames, graphics frames, etc.), it makes sense to define the common behavior of all frames in an abstract class *Frame*. Viewers do not work with concrete frame variants, but with abstract frames; hence they do not need to know the variants. They are able to display any frame variant that might be developed in the future. This provides an

What can be learned?

example of heterogeneous, extensible data structures in the sense of Section 7.3. The classes *Viewer* and *Frame* can also be seen as a framework for an extensible viewer system.

Although it is also possible to extend a viewer by deriving subclasses from it, this is not planned and generally not necessary. In our implementation viewers are fixed containers for frames. Only their contents vary, but not the viewers themselves.

11.2 Handling User Input

Event loop

Viewers and frames can react to keyboard input and mouse clicks. But how are these events reported? This is the task of the *event loop*. Whenever the system is idle, it falls back to the event loop and polls the state of the input devices.

Keyboard input

As soon as a key is pressed, the event loop sends a message to the focus frame, which handles it appropriately. If the focus frame is a text frame, it might insert the character into its text at the position of the insertion mark (caret). If it is a graphics frame, it might interpret the character as a command. After having handled the event the frame returns control to the event loop.

Mouse clicks

As long as no key is pressed, the frame that contains the mouse pointer is requested to react to the mouse. Normally the frame does nothing except draw the mouse pointer. If a mouse button is pressed, the reaction might be the placement of the caret, text or graphics selection, or some kind of drawing. Then control is returned to the event loop again.

Multiprogramming

Since viewers can react to events in any order, and since they return control after a short time, the impression arises that all programs corresponding to the viewers run in parallel. In reality there is only one process that alternately gives control to the programs for a short amount of time.

In the same way as in Oberon0 user input is also handled in the Oberon System. The event loop in Oberon is located in the module *Oberon*, so we also wrap it in a module *Oberon0*, which has a very simple interface:

Interface of Oberon0

```
DEFINITION Oberon0;
    PROCEDURE Loop;
END Oberon0.
```

The Oberon0 system is started by invoking *Loop* (the event loop). It can be stopped by pressing the escape key. The source code of

Oberon0 should be comprehensible without explanation. The modules *Texts0* and *TextFrames0* are discussed in the next section.

```
MODULE Oberon0;
IMPORT OS, Viewers0, Texts0, TextFrames0;
CONST ESC = 1BX;

PROCEDURE Loop*;
   VAR ch: CHAR; x, y: INTEGER; buttons: SET;
      v: Viewers0.Viewer; t: Texts0.Text;
BEGIN
   NEW(t); t.Clear;
   v := Viewers0.New(TextFrames0.NewMenu("LOG", "Viewers0.Close"),
      TextFrames0.New(t)); (*open the log viewer*)
   LOOP  (*wait for events*)
      IF OS.AvailChars() > 0 THEN OS.ReadKey(ch);
         IF ch = ESC THEN EXIT
         ELSIF Viewers0.focus # NIL THEN Viewers0.focus.HandleKey(ch)
         END
      ELSE OS.GetMouse(buttons, x, y);
         v := Viewers0.ViewerAt(y);
         IF v # NIL THEN v.HandleMouse(x, y, buttons)
         ELSE OS.DrawCursor(x, y)
         END
      END
   END
END Loop;

END Oberon0.
```

Implementation of Oberon0

11.3 A Text Editor

The most frequent kind of data to be displayed in viewers is text. Thus we shall design and implement classes that permit displaying and editing text in an Oberon0 viewer.

Which classes and modules are necessary? Recall Section 8.7, in which the MVC concept was introduced as a useful technique in designing interactive programs (Fig. 11.7).

MVC structure

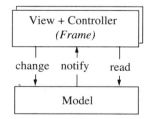

Fig. 11.7 The MVC concept

According to the MVC concept, an interactive program consists of a model and several views and controllers. How can we transpose this onto a text editor?

Our model is the text; thus we need a class that manages text. The view and controller part is handled by frames, so we need a class *TextFrame*, a subclass of *Frame*, that displays a text on the screen and handles keyboard input and mouse clicks. Text frames are installed in viewers; we can use the class *Viewer* from Section 11.1 for that. Finally, we need a module that has commands to open and close a text viewer; we call it *Edit0*. Each of these classes is implemented in its own module; the resulting hierarchy of modules and classes is shown in Fig. 11.8.

Viewers work with text frames by sending them messages and thus requesting them to change their size or to display their contents. However, *Viewers0* does not import *TextFrames0*, but regards all kinds of frames (including text frames) as extensions of the class *Viewers0.Frame*. A text frame is installed in a viewer with *Viewers0.New* without the viewer needing to know this *Frame* extension.

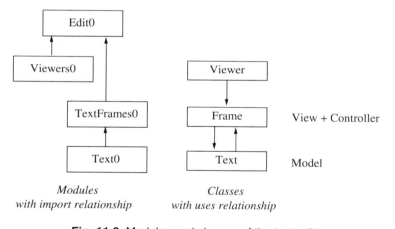

Modules
with import relationship

Classes
with uses relationship

Fig. 11.8 Modules and classes of the text editor

The class *Text* actually has two responsibilities: It handles ASCII text and it adds various fonts. In order to be able to describe these two tasks independently, we model them as a class *AsciiText*, which handles plain text, and a subclass *Text*, which adds the fonts.

Note that a text editor is no trivial program; its implementation imposes many details, although here we have avoided as much detail as possible by sacrificing efficiency and generality.

11.3.1   Plain Texts (AsciiTexts)

The class *AsciiTexts.Text* handles a text as a sequence of ASCII characters. Operations on texts include insertion, deletion, reading, writing, loading, and storing. This leads to the following interface:

```
DEFINITION AsciiTexts;
IMPORT OS;

TYPE
  Text = POINTER TO TextDesc;
  TextDesc = RECORD (OS.ObjectDesc)
    len-: LONGINT;      (*text length*)
    pos-: LONGINT;      (*read/write position*)
    PROCEDURE (t: Text) Clear;
    PROCEDURE (t: Text) Insert (at: LONGINT; t1: Text; beg, end: LONGINT);
    PROCEDURE (t: Text) Delete (beg, end: LONGINT);
    PROCEDURE (t: Text) SetPos (pos: LONGINT);
    PROCEDURE (t: Text) Read (VAR ch: CHAR);
    PROCEDURE (t: Text) Write (ch: CHAR);
    PROCEDURE (t: Text) Load (VAR r: OS.Rider);
    PROCEDURE (t: Text) Store (VAR r: OS.Rider);
  END;

  NotifyInsMsg = RECORD (OS.Message) t: Text;  beg, end: LONGINT END;
  NotifyDelMsg = RECORD (OS.Message) t: Text;  beg, end: LONGINT END;

END AsciiTexts.
```

Interface of AsciiTexts

A text t is a sequence of characters at positions 0 to $t.len$-1. It has a read/write position $t.pos$ where characters can be read and written with *Read* and *Write*. In the following explanation the open interval $[a..b[$ indicates a text segment beginning with the character at position a and ending with the character at position b-1.

Messages to ASCII texts

$t.Clear$
> clears the text t.

$t.Insert(p, t1, a, b)$
> inserts the text segment $[a..b[$ of $t1$ at position p in t.

$t.Delete(a, b)$
> deletes the segment $[a..b[$ in t.

$t.SetPos(p)$
> sets the read/write position of t to p.

$t.Read(ch)$
> reads the character ch at $t.pos$ and increments $t.pos$ by 1. An attempt to read beyond the end of the text causes 0X to be read and $t.pos$ is not incremented.

t.Write(ch)
> inserts the character *ch* at *t.pos* and increments *t.pos* by 1.

t.Load(r)
> loads the text *t* from a file (rider *r*).

t.Store(r)
> stores the text *t* in a file (rider *r*).

Text buffer

The central data structure of texts is the *text buffer*. In its simplest form, it is an array of characters. However, the insertion and deletion of characters must be efficient; thus we make use of the following observation:

The array is not completely filled. It consists of a sequence of characters and a gap that extends from the position after the last character to the end of the array. Inserting and deleting at the front of this gap (i.e., at the end of the text) is efficient because no characters have to be moved. Within the text, inserting and deleting are expensive operations.

The trick is to move the gap from the end of the text to within the text. Then inserting and deleting can be efficient there, too (Fig. 11.9).

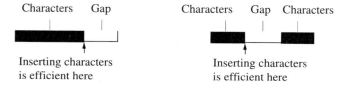

Fig. 11.9 Moving the gap from the end of the text to within the text

Whenever the insertion point in the text changes, the gap is moved to the new insertion point by a method *MoveGap*. Since multiple characters are usually inserted at the same place before the insertion point is changed, the gap seldom needs to be moved. For clients of the class *Text*, the array and the position of the gap remain hidden, of course.

Growing and shrinking

The length of arrays is fixed. But to permit a text to grow to an arbitrary length without wasting storage on small texts, we must permit the array to grow and shrink. We do this in the following way: If the array is completely filled, we create a larger array and copy the old one into the new. If the text length is less than half the array size, we create a smaller array and copy to it. These tasks are handled by the methods *Grow* and *Shrink*.

We will now examine the implementation. Note that texts in Oberon0 are implemented differently from those in the Oberon System. In Oberon they are not in main memory, but in a file; thus they can really be of arbitrary length. This implementation is more practical, but also more complicated than the Oberon0 solution. The Oberon approach is described in [WiG92].

```
MODULE AsciiTexts;                                              Implementation of
IMPORT OS, Viewers0;                                            AsciiTexts

CONST minBufLen = 32;

TYPE
   Buffer = POINTER TO ARRAY OF CHAR;
   Text* = POINTER TO TextDesc;                                 Text
   TextDesc* = RECORD (OS.ObjectDesc)
      len-: LONGINT;       (*text length*)
      pos-: LONGINT;       (*read/write position*)
      buf: Buffer;         (*text buffer*)
      gap: LONGINT         (*index of first byte in gap*)
   END;
   NotifyInsMsg* = RECORD(OS.Message) t*:Text; beg*, end*:LONGINT END;
   NotifyDelMsg* = RECORD(OS.Message) t*:Text; beg*, end*:LONGINT END;

PROCEDURE (t: Text) MoveGap (to: LONGINT);                      Text methods
   VAR n, gapLen: LONGINT;
BEGIN
   n := ABS(to - t.gap); gapLen := LEN(t.buf^) - t.len;
   IF to > t.gap THEN OS.Move(t.buf^, t.gap + gapLen, t.buf^, t.gap, n)
   ELSIF to < t.gap THEN OS.Move(t.buf^, t.gap - n, t.buf^, t.gap + gapLen - n, n)
   END;
   t.gap := to
END MoveGap;

PROCEDURE (t: Text) Grow (size: LONGINT);
   VAR bufLen: LONGINT; old: Buffer;
BEGIN
   bufLen := LEN(t.buf^);
   IF size > bufLen THEN
      t.MoveGap(t.len);
      WHILE bufLen < size DO bufLen := 2*bufLen END;
      old := t.buf; NEW(t.buf, bufLen); OS.Move(old^, 0, t.buf^, 0, t.len)
   END
END Grow;

PROCEDURE (t: Text) Shrink;
   VAR bufLen: LONGINT; old: Buffer;
BEGIN
   bufLen := LEN(t.buf^); t.MoveGap(t.len);
   WHILE (bufLen >= 2*t.len) & (bufLen > minBufLen) DO
      bufLen := bufLen DIV 2
   END;
   old := t.buf; NEW(t.buf, bufLen); OS.Move(old^, 0, t.buf^, 0, t.len)
```

```
END Shrink;

PROCEDURE (t: Text) Clear*;
BEGIN
  NEW(t.buf, minBufLen);
  t.gap := 0; t.pos := 0; t.len := 0
END Clear;
```

see ①

```
PROCEDURE (t: Text) Insert* (at: LONGINT; t1: Text; beg, end: LONGINT);
  VAR len: LONGINT; m: NotifyInsMsg; t0: Text;
BEGIN
  IF t = t1 THEN
    NEW(t0); t0.Clear; t0.Insert(0, t1, beg, end); t.Insert(at, t0, 0, t0.len)
  ELSE len := end - beg;
    IF t.len + len > LEN(t.buf^) THEN t.Grow(t.len + len) END;
    t.MoveGap(at); t1.MoveGap(end);
    OS.Move(t1.buf^, beg, t.buf^, t.gap, len);
    INC(t.gap, len); INC(t.len, len);
    m.t := t; m.beg := at; m.end := at + len; Viewers0.Broadcast(m)
  END
END Insert;
```

see ②

see ③

```
PROCEDURE (t: Text) Delete* (beg, end: LONGINT);
  VAR m: NotifyDelMsg;
BEGIN
  t.MoveGap(end); t.gap := beg; DEC(t.len, end-beg);
  IF (t.len * 2 < LEN(t.buf^)) & (LEN(t.buf^) > minBufLen) THEN t.Shrink END;
  m.t := t; m.beg := beg; m.end := end; Viewers0.Broadcast(m)
END Delete;

PROCEDURE (t: Text) SetPos* (pos: LONGINT);
BEGIN t.pos := pos
END SetPos;

PROCEDURE (t: Text) Read* (VAR ch: CHAR);
  VAR i: LONGINT;
BEGIN
  i := t.pos;
  IF t.pos >= t.gap THEN INC(i, LEN(t.buf^) - t.len) END;
  IF t.pos < t.len THEN ch := t.buf[i]; INC(t.pos) ELSE ch := 0X END
END Read;

PROCEDURE (t: Text) Write* (ch: CHAR);
  VAR m: NotifyInsMsg;
BEGIN
  IF t.len = LEN(t.buf^) THEN t.Grow(t.len + 1) END;
  IF t.pos # t.gap THEN t.MoveGap(t.pos) END;
  t.buf[t.gap] := ch; INC(t.gap); INC(t.pos); INC(t.len);
  m.t := t; m.beg := t.gap-1; m.end := t.gap; Viewers0.Broadcast(m)
END Write;

PROCEDURE (t: Text) Load* (VAR r: OS.Rider);
  VAR len: LONGINT;
BEGIN
  t.Clear;
```

```
   r.ReadLInt(len); t.Grow(len); r.ReadChars(t.buf^, len);
   t.gap := len; t.len := len
END Load;

PROCEDURE (t: Text) Store* (VAR r: OS.Rider);
BEGIN
   t.MoveGap(t.len);
   r.WriteLInt(t.len); r.WriteChars(t.buf^, t.len)
END Store;

END AsciiTexts.
```

The most important methods of *AsciiTexts* are *Insert* and *Delete*. In ❶ *Insert*, a text segment from text *t1* is inserted in text *t* by moving the gap to the insert position and copying the text segment to this position (Fig. 11.10). First *t* might have to attain the proper length via *t.Grow*. If *t* and *t1* are identical, a temporary buffer must be used.

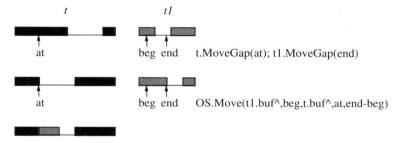

Fig. 11.10 Effects of *t.Insert(at, t1, beg, end)*

Delete works similarly. The gap is moved to the end of the text ❷ segment that is to be deleted and is then simply enlarged downward (Fig. 11.11). Finally the array in *t* is shrunk with *t.Shrink* if necessary.

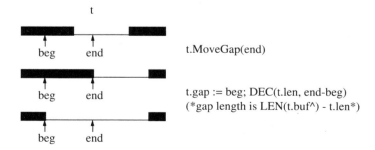

Fig. 11.11 Effects of *t.Delete(beg, end)*

❸ Whenever the text is changed, its views must be updated. Thus *Insert, Delete* and *Write* invoke the procedure *Viewers0.Broadcast* and pass it a message record that specifies how the text was modified. *Viewers0.Broadcast* distributes the message to all frames on the screen. Whichever frame displays the modified text reacts to the message by updating the modified part of the text on the screen (see Section 11.3.3).

11.3.2   Texts with Fonts and Elements (Texts0)

For simple texts, *AsciiTexts.Text* might suffice. A realistic editor, however, should support fonts and allow pictures and other elements to be inserted in the text. These features are provided by the class *Texts0.Text*, an extension of *AsciiTexts.Text*.

Interface of Texts0

```
DEFINITION Texts0;
IMPORT OS, AsciiTexts;

TYPE
   Attribute = POINTER TO AttrDesc;
   Element = POINTER TO ElemDesc;
```

Text

```
   Text = POINTER TO TextDesc;
   TextDesc = RECORD (AsciiTexts.TextDesc)
     attr-: Attribute;      (*attributes of previously read character*)
     PROCEDURE (t: Text) ChangeFont (beg, end: LONGINT; fnt: OS.Font);
     PROCEDURE (t: Text) ReadNextElem (VAR e: Element);
     PROCEDURE (t: Text) WriteElem (e: Element);
     PROCEDURE (t: Text) ElemPos (e: Element);
   END;

   AttrDesc = RECORD
     fnt-: OS.Font;      (*font of this attribute segment*)
     elem-: Element      (*if not NIL, the corrsponding character is an element*)
   END;
```

Element

```
   ElemDesc = RECORD (OS.ObjectDesc)
     w, h: INTEGER;   (*width and height of element in pixels*)
     dsc: INTEGER;    (*descender (part below the base line)*)
     PROCEDURE (e: Element) Draw (x, y: INTEGER);
     PROCEDURE (e: Element) HandleMouse
        (frame: OS.Object; x, y: INTEGER);
     PROCEDURE (e: Element) Copy (): Element;
   END;
```

Notify messages

```
   NotifyDelMsg = AsciiTexts.NotifyDelMsg;
   NotifyInsMsg = AsciiTexts.NotifyInsMsg;
   NotifyReplMsg = RECORD (OS.Message) t: Text; beg, end: LONGINT END;

END Texts0.
```

Text inherits the interface from *AsciiTexts.Text*. This means that text segments can be inserted, deleted, etc. However, the inherited methods are overridden in such a way that fonts are updated correctly and pictures and other elements can flow with the text. The following additional operations are provided:

Messages to texts

t.ChangeFont(a, b, fnt)
> changes the font of the text segment [*a..b*[to *fnt*.

t.ReadNextElem(e)
> returns the next element *e* in *t* after the position *t.pos*. Afterwards *t.pos* contains the position of the character following *e*. If no element is found, *e* = NIL and t.*pos* = *t.len*.

t.WriteElem(e)
> inserts the element *e* at *t.pos* in *t*.

pos := t.ElemPos(e)
> returns the position of the element *e* in *t* or the value *t.len* if *e* does not exist.

Which data fields are needed in *Text*? In addition to the character array, an attribute list is necessary to specify the font of each character and whether it is a plain character or an element (e.g., a picture). Each node of the attribute list represents a text segment of *len* characters in font *fnt*:

Attributes

```
TYPE
  Attribute = POINTER TO AttrDesc;
  AttrDesc = RECORD
    len: LONGINT;    (*length of attribute segment*)
    fnt: OS.Font;    (*font of attribute segment*)
    elem: Element;   (*pointer to element or NIL*)
    next: Attribute
  END;
```

Elements are represented in the text by a special character (1CX) and in the attribute list by a node of *len* = 1; the field *elem* of this node points to the actual element. For plain characters, *elem* has the value NIL. Before we turn to elements, let us consider the management of the attribute list. Fig. 11.13 shows the connection between the ASCII text and the attribute list. The attribute list is not visible to clients of *Text*.

The first node in the attribute list is a dummy that simplifies the handling of the list. Each node contains the length of the text segment that it stands for, but not its position; otherwise it would be necessary to update the positions of subsequent text segments every time a character is inserted.

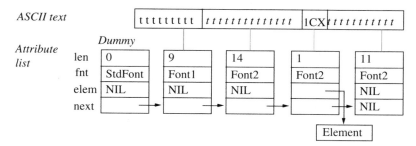

Fig. 11.13 A text with its associated attribute list

Elements

A text should also be able to contain objects that are not characters, but pictures, tables or formulas. The kinds of objects are unknown in advance; besides, we do not want to inflate texts by making them know unnecessarily many kinds of objects. Thus texts should not distinguish the objects at all, but work with an abstract class *Element*, from which picture elements, table elements and formula elements can later be derived. This keeps the editor small and makes it possible to add new kinds of elements anytime.

```
TYPE
  Element = POINTER TO ElemDesc;
  ElemDesc = RECORD (OS.ObjectDesc)
    w, h: INTEGER;  (*width and height of element in pixels*)
    dsc: INTEGER    (*descender (part below the base line)*)
  END;
```

Which operations should be possible on elements? Elements should be able to display themselves on the screen and to react to mouse clicks. They should also know how to write themselves to a file and how to read themselves in again; these are already properties of the superclass *OS.Object*. Thus elements must understand the following messages:

Messages to elements

$e.Draw(x, y)$
    draws e at position (x, y) on the screen (Fig. 11.14).
$e.HandleMouse(f, x, y)$
    causes e to react to a mouse click at position (x, y) in frame f.
$e1 := e.Copy()$
    makes a copy of e.

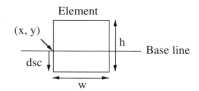

Fig. 11.14 Coordinates of an element on the screen

Most methods of *Element* are abstract and need to be overridden in subclasses.

```
MODULE Texts0;
IMPORT OS, AsciiTexts, Viewers0;

CONST ELEM = 1CX;

TYPE
  Element* = POINTER TO ElemDesc;
  Attribute* = POINTER TO AttrDesc;

  Text* = POINTER TO TextDesc;
  TextDesc* = RECORD (AsciiTexts.TextDesc)
    attr-: Attribute;          (*attributes of previously read character*)
    firstAttr: Attribute;      (*to attribute list (first node is dummy)*)
    attrRest: LONGINT          (*unread bytes in current attribute segment*)
  END;

  AttrDesc* = RECORD
    len: LONGINT;              (*length of attribute segment*)
    fnt-: OS.Font;             (*font of this attribute segment*)
    elem-: Element;            (*pointer to element descriptor or NIL*)
    next: Attribute
  END;

  ElemDesc* = RECORD (OS.ObjectDesc)
    w*, h*: INTEGER;           (*width and height in pixels*)
    dsc*: INTEGER              (*descender (part under the base line)*)
  END;

  NotifyInsMsg* = AsciiTexts.NotifyInsMsg;
  NotifyDelMsg* = AsciiTexts.NotifyDelMsg;
  NotifyReplMsg* = RECORD (OS.Message)
    t*: Text; beg*, end*: LONGINT
  END;

PROCEDURE (e: Element) Draw* (x, y: INTEGER);
END Draw;

PROCEDURE (e: Element) HandleMouse* (f: OS.Object; x, y: INTEGER);
END HandleMouse;
```

Implementation of Texts0

Element methods

```
PROCEDURE (e: Element) Copy* (): Element;
END Copy;

PROCEDURE (e: Element) Load* (VAR r: OS.Rider);
BEGIN
  r.ReadInt(e.w); r.ReadInt(e.h); r.ReadInt(e.dsc)
END Load;

PROCEDURE (e: Element) Store* (VAR r: OS.Rider);
BEGIN
  r.WriteInt(e.w); r.WriteInt(e.h); r.WriteInt(e.dsc)
END Store;
```

Text methods
see ①

```
PROCEDURE (t: Text) Split (pos: LONGINT; VAR prev: Attribute);
  VAR a, b: Attribute;
BEGIN
  a := t.firstAttr;
  WHILE (a # NIL) & (pos >= a.len) DO
    DEC(pos, a.len); prev := a; a := a.next
  END;
  IF (a # NIL) & (pos > 0) THEN
    NEW(b); b.elem := a.elem; b.fnt := a.fnt; b.len := a.len - pos; a.len := pos;
    b.next := a.next; a.next := b; prev := a
  END
END Split;
```

see ②

```
PROCEDURE (t: Text) Merge (a: Attribute);
  VAR b: Attribute;
BEGIN
  b := a.next;
  IF (b # NIL) & (a.fnt = b.fnt) & (a.len > 0) & (a.elem = NIL) & (b.elem = NIL) THEN
    INC(a.len, b.len); a.next := b.next
  END
END Merge;
```

see ③

```
PROCEDURE (t: Text) Insert*
  (at: LONGINT; t1: AsciiTexts.Text; beg, end: LONGINT);
  VAR a, b, c, d, i, j, k: Attribute; t0: Text;
BEGIN
  IF t = t1 THEN
    NEW(t0); t0.Clear; t0.Insert(0, t1, beg, end); t.Insert(at, t0, 0, t0.len)
  ELSE
    WITH t1: Text DO
      t1.Split(beg, a); t1.Split(end, b); t.Split(at, c); d := c.next;
      i := a; j := c;
      WHILE i # b DO
        i := i.next; NEW(k); k^ := i^;
        IF i.elem # NIL THEN k.elem := i.elem.Copy() END;
        j.next := k; j := k
      END;
      j.next := d; t1.Merge(b); t1.Merge(a); t.Merge(j); t.Merge(c);
      t.Insert^ (at, t1, beg, end)
    END
  END
END Insert;
```

```
PROCEDURE (t: Text) Delete* (beg, end: LONGINT);
   VAR a, b: Attribute;
BEGIN
   t.Split(beg, a); t.Split(end, b); a.next := b.next; t.Merge(a);
   t.Delete^ (beg, end)
END Delete;

PROCEDURE (t: Text) SetPos* (pos: LONGINT);
   VAR prev, a: Attribute;
BEGIN
   t.SetPos^(pos);
   a := t.firstAttr;
   WHILE (a # NIL) & (pos >= a.len) DO
      DEC(pos, a.len); prev := a; a := a.next
   END;
   IF (a = NIL) OR (pos = 0) THEN t.attr := prev; t.attrRest := 0
   ELSE t.attr := a; t.attrRest := a.len-pos
   END
END SetPos;

PROCEDURE (t: Text) Read* (VAR ch: CHAR);                    see ④
BEGIN
   t.Read^(ch);
   IF (t.attrRest = 0) & (t.attr.next # NIL) THEN
      t.attr := t.attr.next; t.attrRest := t.attr.len
   END;
   DEC(t.attrRest)
END Read;

PROCEDURE (t: Text) Write* (ch: CHAR);                       see ⑤
   VAR a, prev: Attribute; at: LONGINT;
BEGIN
   a := t.firstAttr; at := t.pos;
   WHILE (a # NIL) & (at >= a.len) DO DEC(at, a.len); prev := a; a := a.next END;
   IF (a = NIL) OR (at = 0) THEN  (*insert at end of attribute segment*)
      IF (prev = t.firstAttr) OR (prev.elem # NIL) THEN
         NEW(a); a.elem := NIL; a.fnt := prev.fnt; a.len := 1;
         a.next := prev.next; prev.next := a;
         t.Merge(a)
      ELSE INC(prev.len)
      END
   ELSE INC(a.len)
   END;
   t.Write^ (ch)
END Write;

PROCEDURE (t: Text) ReadNextElem* (VAR e: Element);
   VAR pos: LONGINT; a: Attribute;
BEGIN
   pos := t.pos + t.attrRest; a := t.attr.next;
   WHILE (a # NIL) & (a.elem = NIL) DO pos := pos + a.len; a := a.next END;
   IF a # NIL THEN e := a.elem; t.SetPos(pos+1)
   ELSE e := NIL; t.SetPos(t.len)
   END
END ReadNextElem;
```

see ⑥

```
PROCEDURE (t: Text) WriteElem* (e: Element);
  VAR x, y: Attribute; m: NotifyReplMsg;
BEGIN
  t.Write(ELEM); t.Split(t.pos - 1, x); t.Split(t.pos, y); y.elem := e;
  m.t := t; m.beg := t.pos-1; m.end := t.pos; Viewers0.Broadcast(m)
END WriteElem;

PROCEDURE (t: Text) ElemPos* (e: Element): LONGINT;
  VAR pos: LONGINT; a: Attribute;
BEGIN
  a := t.firstAttr; pos := 0;
  WHILE (a # NIL) & (a.elem # e) DO pos := pos + a.len; a := a.next END;
  RETURN pos
END ElemPos;

PROCEDURE (t: Text) ChangeFont* (beg, end: LONGINT; fnt: OS.Font);
  VAR a, b: Attribute; m: NotifyReplMsg;

  PROCEDURE Change(a: Attribute);
  BEGIN
    a.fnt := fnt;
    IF a # b THEN Change(a.next) END;
    t.Merge(a)
  END Change;

BEGIN
  IF end > beg THEN
    t.Split(beg, a); t.Split(end, b); Change(a.next); t.Merge(a);
    m.t := t; m.beg := beg; m.end := end; Viewers0.Broadcast(m)
  END
END ChangeFont;

PROCEDURE (t: Text) Clear*;
BEGIN
  t.Clear^;
  NEW(t.firstAttr); t.firstAttr.elem := NIL; t.firstAttr.next := NIL;
  t.firstAttr.fnt := OS.DefaultFont(); t.firstAttr.len := 0; t.SetPos(0)
END Clear;
```

see ⑦

```
PROCEDURE (t: Text) Store* (VAR r: OS.Rider);
  VAR a: Attribute;
BEGIN
  t.Store^(r); a := t.firstAttr.next;
  WHILE a # NIL DO
    r.WriteString(a.fnt.name);
    r.WriteObj(a.elem); r.WriteLInt(a.len);
    a := a.next
  END;
  r.Write(0X)  (*empty font name terminates attribute list*)
END Store;

PROCEDURE (t: Text) Load* (VAR r: OS.Rider);
  VAR prev, a: Attribute; name: ARRAY 32 OF CHAR; x: OS.Object;
BEGIN
```

```
    t.Load^(r);
    prev := t.firstAttr;
    LOOP
      r.ReadString(name); IF name = "" THEN EXIT END;
      NEW(a); a.fnt := OS.FontWithName(name);
      r.ReadObj(x); r.ReadLInt(a.len);
      IF x = NIL THEN a.elem := NIL ELSE a.elem := x(Element) END;
      prev.next := a; prev := a
    END;
    prev.next := NIL
END Load;

END Texts0.
```

The attribute list is managed via the operations *Split* and *Merge*. ❶
Split splits an attribute segment at position *pos* and creates two
segments (Fig. 11.15). The segment *a* to the left of the split position
is returned.

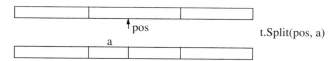

Fig. 11.15 Effects of *t.Split(pos, a)*

The inverse operation, *t.Merge(a)*, merges the segment *a* with its ❷
successor if both have the same font and do not represent elements.
   The most complicated operation of *Texts0.Text* is *Insert*. It ❸
inserts a segment of text *t1* into another text *t*. This requires temporarily splitting and remerging attribute segments, as shown in Fig.
11.16. If *t* and *t1* are the same text, a temporary buffer is used.

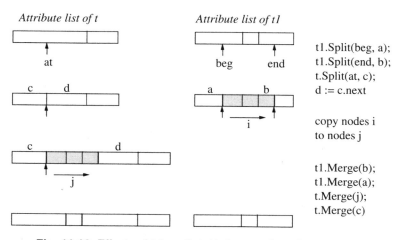

Fig. 11.16 Effects of *t.Insert(at, t1, beg, end)* on the attribute list

For the sake of simplicity, we require that both $t1$ and t be of dynamic type *Texts0.Text*. Since parameter types cannot be changed in overriding methods, $t1$ is of static type *AsciiTexts.Text*. A with statement (type guard) is necessary in order to treat $t1$ as a *Texts0.Text* object.

❹ When a character is read with *t.Read(ch)*, its attributes are stored in the field *t.attr*. As long as the characters belong to the same attribute segment, it is not necessary to reestablish *t.attr* each time a character is read. The number of unread characters in the current attribute segment is stored in a field *t.attrRest*. If *t.attrRest* is 0, *t.attr* must be set to the next attribute segment.

❺ When a character is written with *t.Write(ch)*, no attributes can be set. The font of a written piece of text can be changed with *t.ChangeFont*.

Characters that are entered at the end of an attribute segment are considered as belonging to this segment. If they are entered immediately after an element, however, a new attribute node is created (element segments must always have the length 1).

❻ Elements are inserted with a special procedure *WriteElem*. This creates a new attribute node for them.

❼ When a text is stored in a file, its attributes must be stored as well. For fonts the font name is output; elements are stored with the method *WriteObj*, which outputs the type and value of the element, as described in Section 8.3. *WriteObj* requests elements to store themselves, since only they know their internal structure. The end of the attribute list on the file is marked by an empty font name.

Structuring   What lessons can be learned from this implementation? In *AsciiTexts* and *Texts0*, classes were used as a structuring medium. They divide text management into two independent tasks: text buffer management and attribute management. In line with the principle that a component should only handle one task, these two responsibilities were assigned to different classes: text buffer management to *AsciiTexts* and attribute management to *Texts0*.

Semifinished products   *AsciiTexts.Text* is itself already a useful component. For simple texts in which fonts are not needed, this component suffices. At the same time it is a semifinished product that can be extended to a finished product as needed.

Extensibility   We have taken care to make texts extensible. The abstract class *Element* serves as a socket into which arbitrary element extensions can be plugged and used with *Text*. The Oberon System also has a text editor with extensible elements (*Write* [Szy92]); it has proven very useful and flexible. An example of an element extension is given in Section 11.5.

11.3.3 Editing Text (TextFrames0)

Now we have texts with various fonts, but we can neither display them on the screen nor edit them. We are still missing the view and controller components from the MVC concept. As in Fig. 11.7, we implement them in the class *TextFrames0.Frame*, which is derived from *Viewers0.Frame*.

A text frame is a rectangular area of the screen that handles the following tasks:

Responsibilities of text frames

(1) *Display text*. The text as a continuous stream of characters is cast in lines and displayed on the screen. Each character is represented by a rectangular pixel matrix. The characters are arranged in a line according to their widths; when an end-of-line character appears, a new line is started. If a line is wider than the frame, only as many characters are displayed as fit (Fig. 11.17).

Display text

Text (■ = end-of-line symbol)

The text ■ as a continuous ■ stream of ■ characters …

TextFrame

Fig. 11.17 Casting a text in a text frame

(2) *Process keyboard input*. Characters typed at the keyboard are inserted at the caret position, and the rest of the line is shifted right (Fig. 11.18).

Process keyboard input

Fig. 11.18 Before and after typing the character *n*

Process mouse clicks

(3) *Process mouse clicks.* If one of the three mouse buttons is pressed (ML = left, MM = middle, MR = right), the frame reacts according to Table 11.19, depending on whether the mouse pointer is in the text area or in the scroll bar of the frame.

Mouse button	In text area	In scroll bar
ML	Set caret	Scroll forward
MM	Execute command	Scroll absolutely
MR	Select	Scroll to beginning
	+ ML = delete	of text
	+ MM = copy to caret	

Table 11.19 Meaning of mouse clicks in a text frame

An MM-click causes the word clicked on to be interpreted as a command (in the form Module.Procedure) and executed. If the mouse is moved while the right button is pressed, all characters passed are selected and displayed inversely.

In forward scrolling, the text line at the height of the mouse click becomes the first line of the frame. In absolute scrolling, the vertical position of the mouse pointer in the scroll bar determines the text position from which the text is displayed in the frame. A click on the vertical center of the scroll bar causes the middle part of the text to appear at the top of the frame.

We implement text frames as a class *Frame* in a module *TextFrames0* with the following interface:

Interface of TextFrames0

```
DEFINITION TextFrames0;
IMPORT OS, Viewers0, Texts0;

TYPE
    Position = RECORD      (*position of a character ch on the screen*)
        x-, y-: INTEGER;   (*left point on base line*)
        dx-: INTEGER;      (*width of ch*)
        org-: LONGINT;     (*origin of line containing ch*)
        pos-: LONGINT      (*text position of ch*)
    END;
```

Frame

```
    Frame = POINTER TO FrameDesc;
    FrameDesc = RECORD (Viewers0.FrameDesc)
        text: Texts0.Text;     (*text displayed in this frame*)
        org-: LONGINT;         (*origin: text pos. of first char. in frame*)
```

```
    caret-: Position;            (*caret.pos < 0: no caret visible*)
    selBeg-, selEnd-: Position;    (*selBeg.pos < 0: no selection visible*)
    PROCEDURE (f: Frame) Draw;
    PROCEDURE (f: Frame) Defocus;
    PROCEDURE (f: Frame) Neutralize;
    PROCEDURE (f: Frame) Modify (dy: INTEGER);
    PROCEDURE (f: Frame) HandleKey (ch: CHAR);
    PROCEDURE (f: Frame) HandleMouse (x, y: INTEGER; buttons: SET);
    PROCEDURE (f: Frame) Handle (VAR m: OS.Message);
    PROCEDURE (f: Frame) SetCaret (pos: LONGINT);
    PROCEDURE (f: Frame) RemoveCaret;
    PROCEDURE (f: Frame) SetSelection (from, to: LONGINT);
    PROCEDURE (f: Frame) RemoveSelection;
    PROCEDURE (f: Frame) Copy (): Viewers0.Frame;
  END;

VAR
  cmdFrame-: Frame;    (*frame containing most recent command*)
  cmdPos-: LONGINT;    (*text position after most recent command*)

PROCEDURE New (t: Texts0.Text): Frame;
PROCEDURE NewMenu (name, commands: ARRAY OF CHAR): Frame;
PROCEDURE GetSelection (VAR f: Frame);

END TextFrames0.
```

The type *Position* describes the location of a character ch on the screen. It also serves to store the position of the caret and the selection. The fields x and y designate the position of ch in screen coordinates; dx is the width of ch (Figs. 11.20 and 11.22).

Position

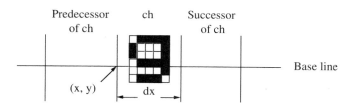

Fig. 11.20 Meaning of fields x, y and dx of type *Position*

The field *pos* gives the text position of ch; *org* specifies the origin of the line, i.e., the text position of the first character of the line containing ch.

The most important type in *TextFrames0* is the class *Frame*. Its interface is partially inherited from *Viewers0.Frame*, but some text-specific messages are added.

Messages to text frames

f.Draw
  recasts the entire text of *f*.

f.Defocus

    removes the caret by sending *f.RemoveCaret*. The focus is taken away from *f*.

f.Neutralize

    removes all marks in the frame (selection and caret) by sending *f.RemoveSelection* and *f.RemoveCaret*.

f.Modify(dy)

    shifts the lower border of *f* by *dy* and recasts any text that becomes visible.

f.HandleKey(ch)

    inserts *ch* at the caret position.

f.HandleMouse(x, y, b)

    reacts to a mouse click at the position (x, y) relative to the lower left corner of the screen. *b* is the set of pressed mouse buttons.

f.Handle(m)

    reacts to a notify message *m* sent when a text was modified (see Section 8.7).

f.SetCaret(pos)

    sets the caret to position *pos*.

f.RemoveCaret

    removes the caret.

f.SetSelection(a, b)

    sets the selection in the interval [*a..b*[.

f.RemoveSelection

    removes the selection.

f1 := f.Copy()

    returns a copy of *f*.

The procedure *New* creates a new text frame. *NewMenu* creates a new menu frame (also a text frame) that contains a viewer name and a list of commands. *GetSelection* searches all visible text frames for the latest selection and returns the frame that contains it, or NIL if no selection is visible. For this purpose each text frame must store a (nonexported) time stamp that tells when the last selection was made in this frame.

Before turning to the implementation of *TextFrames0*, which is by nature rather complex, let us examine some of the data structures more closely.

Frame metrics

The area of a text frame is divided into a text area and a scroll bar. The text area has a *margin* in which no text is displayed (Fig.11.21).

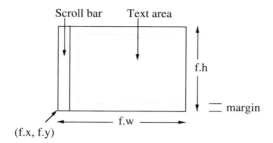

Fig. 11.21 Frame layout

Each character has a pixel pattern *pat* that is displayed on the screen in a box of width dx and height *asc+dsc* (Fig. 11.22). The character metrics $(x, y, w, h, dx, asc, dsc)$ are taken from the respective font. For an element e (e.g., a picture) this box is determined by the element's width $e.w$, its height $e.h$, and its distance $e.dsc$ from the base line (see Fig. 11.14). *Character metrics*

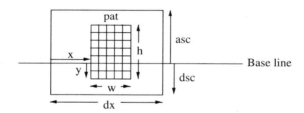

Fig. 11.22 Character metrics

The boxes of succeeding characters are strung together and form a line of text. Before a line is displayed on the screen, its metrics must be computed, i.e., its length in characters (*len*) and pixels (*wid*) as well as its height (*asc+dsc*), which is the maximum height of the individual characters or elements (Fig. 11.23). *Line metrics*

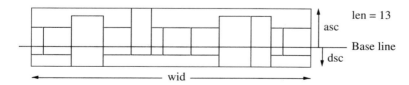

Fig. 11.23 Line metrics

The metrics of each line are stored in a line descriptor of the following form: *Line descriptors*

```
TYPE
  Line = POINTER TO LineDesc;
  LineDesc = RECORD
    len, wid: INTEGER;        (*length, width*)
    asc, dsc: INTEGER;        (*ascender, descender*)
    eol: BOOLEAN;             (*TRUE if line is terminated with EOL*)
    next: Line
  END;
```

The descriptors of the lines that are visible on the screen are linked in a circular list (Fig. 11.24). Note that a line descriptor does not contain the text of a line, but only its dimensions. The text is read anew as needed.

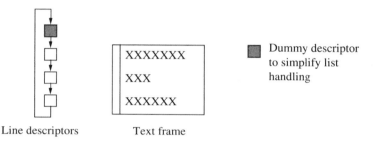

Line descriptors   Text frame

Fig. 11.24 List of line descriptors for a text frame

The reader should now be able to understand the source code of *TextFrames0*. Keep pencil and paper ready, however, for some sketches may help comprehension.

Implementation of TextFrames0

```
MODULE TextFrames0;
IMPORT OS, Viewers0, Texts0;

CONST
  EOL = 0DX; DEL = 7FX;     (*end of line character; delete character*)
  scrollW = 12;            (*width of scroll bar*)

TYPE
```

Line descriptor

```
  Line = POINTER TO LineDesc;
  LineDesc = RECORD
    len, wid, asc, dsc: INTEGER;  (*length, width, ascender, descender*)
    eol: BOOLEAN;                 (*TRUE if line is terminated with EOL*)
    next: Line
  END;
```

Screen position

```
  Position* = RECORD             (*position of a character c on the screen*)
    x-, y-, dx-: INTEGER;        (*(x,y) = left point on base line; dx = width of c*)
    org-, pos-: LONGINT;         (*origin of line containing c; text position of c*)
    L: Line                      (*line containing c*)
  END;
```

Frame

```
  Frame* = POINTER TO FrameDesc;
```

```
    FrameDesc* = RECORD (Viewers0.FrameDesc)
       text*: Texts0.Text;
       org-: LONGINT;                   (*index of first character in the frame*)
       caret-: Position;                (*caret; visible if caret.pos >= 0*)
       selBeg-, selEnd-: Position;      (*selection; visible if selBeg.pos >= 0*)
       selTime: LONGINT;                (*time stamp of selection*)
       lsp: INTEGER;                    (*space between lines*)
       margin: INTEGER;                 (*space between frame border and text*)
       lines: Line                      (*list of lines in frame (first line in dummy)*)
    END;
    SelectionMsg = RECORD (OS.Message) f: Frame END;


VAR
    cmdFrame-: Frame;                    (*frame containing the most recent command*)
    cmdPos-: LONGINT;                    (*text position after the most recent command*)
```

```
PROCEDURE GetMetric (at: Texts0.Attribute; ch: CHAR;
    VAR dx, x, y, asc, dsc: INTEGER; VAR pat: OS.Pattern);
    VAR w, h: INTEGER;
BEGIN
  IF at.elem = NIL THEN
     OS.GetCharMetric(at.fnt, ch, dx, x, y, w, h, pat);
     asc := at.fnt.maxY; dsc := - at.fnt.minY
  ELSE
     dx := at.elem.w; x := 0; y := 0; dsc := at.elem.dsc; asc := at.elem.h - dsc
  END
END GetMetric;
```

Auxiliary procedures

```
PROCEDURE MeasureLine (t: Texts0.Text; VAR L: Line);
    VAR ch: CHAR; dx, x, y, asc, dsc: INTEGER; pat: OS.Pattern;
BEGIN
  L.len := 0; L.wid := 0; L.asc := 0; L.dsc := 0; ch := " ";
  WHILE (ch # EOL) & (t.pos < t.len) DO
     t.Read(ch); INC(L.len);
     GetMetric(t.attr, ch, dx, x, y, asc, dsc, pat);
     INC(L.wid, dx);
     IF asc > L.asc THEN L.asc := asc END;
     IF dsc > L.dsc THEN L.dsc := dsc END
  END;
  L.eol := ch = EOL
END MeasureLine;
```

see ①

```
PROCEDURE DrawLine (t: Texts0.Text; len, left, right, base: INTEGER);
    VAR ch: CHAR; dx, x, y, w, h: INTEGER; pat: OS.Pattern;
BEGIN
  WHILE len > 0 DO t.Read(ch); DEC(len);
     IF t.attr.elem = NIL THEN
        OS.GetCharMetric(t.attr.fnt, ch, dx, x, y, w, h, pat);
        IF left + dx < right THEN OS.DrawPattern(pat, left + x, base + y) END
     ELSE dx := t.attr.elem.w;
        IF left + dx < right THEN t.attr.elem.Draw(left, base) END
     END;
     INC(left, dx)
  END
END DrawLine;
```

see ②

Frame methods

```
PROCEDURE (f: Frame) FlipCaret;
BEGIN
   OS.DrawPattern(OS.Caret, f.caret.x, f.caret.y - 10)
END FlipCaret;
PROCEDURE (f: Frame) FlipSelection (a, b: Position);
   VAR x, y: INTEGER; L: Line;
BEGIN
  L := a.L; x := a.x; y := a.y - L.dsc;
  WHILE L # b.L DO
     OS.InvertBlock(x, y, f.x + f.w - x, L.asc + L.dsc);
     L := L.next; x := f.x + scrollW + f.margin; y := y - f.lsp - L.asc - L.dsc
  END;
  OS.InvertBlock(x, y, b.x - x, L.asc + L.dsc)
END FlipSelection;
```

see ③

```
PROCEDURE (f: Frame) RedrawFrom (top: INTEGER);
   VAR t: Texts0.Text; L, L0: Line; y: INTEGER; org: LONGINT;
BEGIN
  (*----- find first line to be redrawn*)
  y := f.y + f.h - f.margin; org := f.org; L0 := f.lines; L := L0.next;
  WHILE (L # f.lines) & (y - L.asc - L.dsc >= top) DO
     DEC(y, L.asc + L.dsc + f.lsp); org := org + L.len; L0 := L; L := L.next
  END;
  IF y > top THEN top := y END;
  OS.FadeCursor; OS.EraseBlock(f.x, f.y, f.w, top - f.y);
  IF f.margin > 0 THEN (*draw scroll bar*)
     OS.InvertBlock(f.x + scrollW, f.y, 1, top - f.y)
  END;
  (*----- redraw lines and rebuild line descriptors; L0 is last valid line descriptor*)
  t := f.text;
  LOOP NEW(L);
     t.SetPos(org); MeasureLine(t, L);
     IF (L.len = 0) OR (y - L.asc - L.dsc < f.y + f.margin) THEN EXIT END;
     t.SetPos(org);
     DrawLine(t, L.len, f.x + scrollW + f.margin, f.x + f.w - f.margin, y - L.asc);
     org := org + L.len;
     DEC(y, L.asc + L.dsc + f.lsp); L0.next := L; L0 := L;
     IF t.pos >= t.len THEN EXIT END
  END;
  L0.next := f.lines
END RedrawFrom;
```

see ④

```
PROCEDURE (f: Frame) GetPointPos (x0, y0: INTEGER; VAR p: Position);
   VAR t: Texts0.Text; ch: CHAR; L: Line; dx, x, y, asc, dsc: INTEGER;
      pat: OS.Pattern;
BEGIN
  (*----- find line containing y0*)
  L := f.lines.next; p.y := f.y + f.h - f.margin; p.org := f.org;
  WHILE (L # f.lines) & (y0 < p.y - L.asc - L.dsc - f.lsp) & L.eol DO
     DEC(p.y, L.asc + L.dsc + f.lsp); p.org := p.org + L.len; L := L.next
  END;
  DEC(p.y, L.asc);
  (*----- find character containing x0*)
  p.x := f.x + scrollW + f.margin; p.L := L; p.pos := p.org;
  t := f.text; t.SetPos(p.pos);
```

```
      LOOP
         IF p.pos >= t.len THEN p.dx := 0; EXIT END;
         t.Read(ch); GetMetric(t.attr, ch, dx, x, y, asc, dsc, pat);
         IF (ch = EOL) OR (p.x + dx > x0) THEN p.dx := dx; EXIT
         ELSE INC(p.pos); INC(p.x, dx)
         END;
      END
   END GetPointPos;
```

PROCEDURE (f: Frame) GetCharPos (pos: LONGINT; VAR p: Position);   *see* ⑤
```
      VAR t: Texts0.Text; ch: CHAR; L: Line; dx, x, y, asc, dsc: INTEGER;
         pat: OS.Pattern; i: LONGINT;
   BEGIN
      (*----- find line containing pos*)
      L := f.lines.next; p.y := f.y + f.h - f.margin; p.org := f.org; p.pos := pos;
      WHILE (L # f.lines) & (pos >= p.org + L.len) & L.eol DO
         p.org := p.org + L.len; DEC(p.y, L.asc + L.dsc + f.lsp); L := L.next
      END;
      DEC(p.y, L.asc); p.L := L;
      (*----- find character at pos*)
      p.x := f.x + scrollW + f.margin; t := f.text; t.SetPos(p.org);
      FOR i := 1 TO p.pos - p.org DO
         t.Read(ch); GetMetric(t.attr, ch, dx, x, y, asc, dsc, pat);
         INC(p.x, dx)
      END;
      IF t.pos >= t.len THEN p.dx := 0
      ELSE t.Read(ch); GetMetric(t.attr, ch, p.dx, x, y, asc, dsc, pat)
      END
   END GetCharPos;
```

PROCEDURE (f: Frame) CallCommand;   *see* ⑥
```
      VAR x, y, i: INTEGER; buttons: SET; p: Position; t: Texts0.Text;
         ch: CHAR; cmd: ARRAY 64 OF CHAR;
   BEGIN
      REPEAT OS.GetMouse(buttons, x, y) UNTIL buttons = {};
      f.GetPointPos(x, y, p); t := f.text; t.SetPos(p.org); t.Read(ch);
      REPEAT
         WHILE (t.pos < t.len) & (ch # EOL) & ((CAP(ch) < "A") OR (CAP(ch) > "Z")) DO
            t.Read(ch)
         END;
         i := 0;
         WHILE (CAP(ch) >= "A") & (CAP(ch) <= "Z") OR (ch >= "0") & (ch <= "9")
         OR (ch = ".") DO
            cmd[i] := ch; INC(i); t.Read(ch)
         END;
         cmd[i] := 0X;
      UNTIL (t.pos >= t.len) OR (ch = EOL) OR (t.pos > p.pos);
      cmdFrame := f; cmdPos := t.pos; OS.Call(cmd)
   END CallCommand;
```

PROCEDURE (f: Frame) **RemoveCaret***;
```
   BEGIN
      IF f.caret.pos >= 0 THEN f.FlipCaret; f.caret.pos := -1 END
   END RemoveCaret;
```

```
PROCEDURE (f: Frame) SetCaret* (pos: LONGINT);
  VAR p: Position;
BEGIN
  IF pos < 0 THEN pos := 0 ELSIF pos > f.text.len THEN pos := f.text.len END;
  f.SetFocus; f.GetCharPos(pos, p);
  IF p.x < f.x + f.w - f.margin THEN f.caret := p; f.FlipCaret END
END SetCaret;

PROCEDURE (f: Frame) RemoveSelection*;
BEGIN
  IF f.selBeg.pos >= 0 THEN
    f.FlipSelection(f.selBeg, f.selEnd); f.selBeg.pos := -1
  END
END RemoveSelection;

PROCEDURE (f: Frame) SetSelection* (from, to: LONGINT);
BEGIN
  f.RemoveSelection;
  f.GetCharPos(from, f.selBeg); f.GetCharPos(to, f.selEnd);
  f.FlipSelection(f.selBeg, f.selEnd); f.selTime := OS.Time()
END SetSelection;

PROCEDURE (f: Frame) Defocus*;
BEGIN f.RemoveCaret; f.Defocus^
END Defocus;

PROCEDURE (f: Frame) Neutralize*;
BEGIN f.RemoveCaret; f.RemoveSelection
END Neutralize;

PROCEDURE (f: Frame) Draw*;
BEGIN f.RedrawFrom(f.y + f.h)
END Draw;

PROCEDURE (f: Frame) Modify* (dy: INTEGER);
  VAR y: INTEGER;
BEGIN
  y := f.y; f.Modify^ (dy);
  IF y > f.y THEN f.RedrawFrom(y) ELSE f.RedrawFrom(f.y) END
END Modify;
```

see ⑦

```
PROCEDURE (f: Frame) HandleMouse* (x, y: INTEGER; buttons: SET);
  VAR p: Position; b: SET; t: Texts0.Text; ch: CHAR; f1: Frame;
BEGIN
  f.HandleMouse^ (x, y, buttons);
  t := f.text;
  IF (x < f.x + scrollW) & (buttons # {}) THEN (*----- handle click in scroll bar*)
    REPEAT OS.GetMouse(b, x, y); buttons := buttons + b UNTIL b = {};
    f.Neutralize;
    IF OS.left IN buttons THEN f.GetPointPos(x, y, p); f.org := p.org
    ELSIF OS.right IN buttons THEN f.org := 0
    ELSIF OS.middle IN buttons THEN
      t.SetPos((f.y + f.h - y) * f.text.len DIV f.h);
      REPEAT t.Read(ch) UNTIL (ch = EOL) OR (t.pos >= t.len);
      f.org := t.pos
```

```
        END;
      f.RedrawFrom(f.y + f.h)
    ELSE (*----- handle click in text area*)
      f.GetPointPos(x, y, p);
      IF OS.left IN buttons THEN
          IF p.pos # f.caret.pos THEN f.SetCaret(p.pos) END
      ELSIF OS.middle IN buttons THEN
          t.SetPos(p.pos); t.Read(ch);
          IF t.attr.elem = NIL THEN f.CallCommand
          ELSE t.attr.elem.HandleMouse(f, x, y)
          END
      ELSIF OS.right IN buttons THEN
          f.RemoveSelection;
          f.selBeg := p; f.selEnd := p; f.selTime := OS.Time();
          LOOP
              OS.GetMouse(b, x, y); buttons := buttons + b;
              IF b = {} THEN EXIT END;
              OS.DrawCursor(x, y); f.GetPointPos(x, y, p);
              IF p.pos < f.selBeg.pos THEN p := f.selBeg END;
              IF p.pos < t.len THEN INC(p.pos); INC(p.x, p.dx) END;
              IF p.pos # f.selEnd.pos THEN
                  IF p.pos > f.selEnd.pos THEN f.FlipSelection(f.selEnd, p)
                  ELSE f.FlipSelection(p, f.selEnd)
                  END;
                  f.selEnd := p
              END
          END;
          (*----- check for right-left or right-middle click*)
          IF OS.left IN buttons THEN
              t.Delete(f.selBeg.pos, f.selEnd.pos)
          ELSIF (OS.middle IN buttons)
          & (Viewers0.focus # NIL) & (Viewers0.focus IS Frame) THEN
              f1 := Viewers0.focus(Frame);
              IF f1.caret.pos >= 0 THEN
                  f1.text.Insert(f1.caret.pos, t, f.selBeg.pos, f.selEnd.pos)
              END
          END
      END
    END
  END
END HandleMouse;

PROCEDURE (f: Frame) HandleKey* (ch: CHAR);
  VAR pos: LONGINT;
BEGIN
  pos := f.caret.pos;
  IF pos >= 0 THEN
    IF ch = DEL THEN
        IF pos > 0 THEN f.text.Delete(pos - 1, pos); f.SetCaret(pos - 1) END
    ELSE f.text.SetPos(pos); f.text.Write(ch); f.SetCaret(pos + 1)
    END
  END
END HandleKey;

PROCEDURE (f: Frame) Handle* (VAR m: OS.Message);                    see ⑧
  VAR t: Texts0.Text; ch: CHAR; VAR dx, x, y, asc, dsc: INTEGER;
```

```
            pat: OS.Pattern; p: Position;
    BEGIN
      t := f.text;
      WITH
        m: Texts0.NotifyInsMsg DO
          IF m.t = t THEN
            IF m.beg < f.org THEN f.org := f.org + (m.end - m.beg)
            ELSE
              f.Neutralize; OS.FadeCursor;
              f.GetCharPos(m.beg, p);
              t.SetPos(m.beg); t.Read(ch);
              GetMetric(t.attr, ch, dx, x, y, asc, dsc, pat);
              IF (m.end = m.beg+1) & (ch # EOL) & (p.L # f.lines)
              & (asc+dsc <= p.L.asc+p.L.dsc) THEN
                IF p.x + dx <= f.x + f.w - f.margin THEN
                  OS.CopyBlock(p.x, p.y-p.L.dsc, f.x+f.w-f.margin-dx-p.x,
                    p.L.asc+p.L.dsc, p.x+dx, p.y-p.L.dsc);
                  OS.EraseBlock(p.x, p.y-p.L.dsc, dx, p.L.asc + p.L.dsc);
                  IF t.attr.elem = NIL THEN
                    OS.DrawPattern(pat, p.x + x, p.y + y)
                  ELSE t.attr.elem.Draw(p.x, p.y)
                  END
                ELSE
                  OS.EraseBlock(p.x, p.y-p.L.dsc,
                    f.x+f.w-p.x, p.L.asc+p.L.dsc)
                END;
                INC(p.L.len); INC(p.L.wid, dx)
              ELSE f.RedrawFrom(p.y + p.L.asc)
              END
            END
          END
      | m: Texts0.NotifyDelMsg DO
          IF m.t = t THEN
            IF m.end <= f.org THEN f.org := f.org - (m.end - m.beg)
            ELSE
              f.Neutralize;
              IF m.beg < f.org THEN f.org := m.beg; f.RedrawFrom(f.y + f.h)
              ELSE f.GetCharPos(m.beg, p); f.RedrawFrom(p.y + p.L.asc)
              END
            END
          END
      | m: Texts0.NotifyReplMsg DO
          IF (m.t = t) & (m.end > f.org) THEN
            f.Neutralize;
            IF m.beg < f.org THEN m.beg := f.org END;
            f.GetCharPos(m.beg, p); f.RedrawFrom(p.y + p.L.asc)
          END
      | m: SelectionMsg DO
          IF (f.selBeg.pos >= 0) & ((m.f = NIL)
          OR (m.f.selTime < f.selTime)) THEN
            m.f := f
          END
      ELSE
      END
    END Handle;
```

```
PROCEDURE New* (t: Texts0.Text): Frame;
   VAR f: Frame; fnt: OS.Font;
BEGIN
   NEW(f); f.text := t;
   f.org := 0; f.caret.pos := -1; f.selBeg.pos := -1; f.lsp := 2; f.margin := 5;
   NEW(f.lines); f.lines.next := f.lines; fnt := OS.DefaultFont();
   f.lines.asc := fnt.maxY; f.lines.dsc := - fnt.minY; f.lines.len := 0;
   RETURN f
END New;

PROCEDURE NewMenu* (name, menu: ARRAY OF CHAR): Frame;
   VAR t: Texts0.Text; f: Frame; i: INTEGER;
BEGIN
   NEW(t); t.Clear;
   i := 0; WHILE name[i] # 0X DO t.Write(name[i]); INC(i) END;
   t.Write(" "); t.Write("|"); t.Write(" ");
   i := 0; WHILE menu[i] # 0X DO t.Write(menu[i]); INC(i) END;
   f := New(t); f.margin := 0; RETURN f
END NewMenu;

PROCEDURE (f: Frame) Copy* (): Viewers0.Frame;
   VAR f1: Frame;
BEGIN f1 := New(f.text); f1.margin := f.margin; RETURN f1
END Copy;

PROCEDURE GetSelection* (VAR f: Frame);                          see ⑨
   VAR m: SelectionMsg;
BEGIN m.f := NIL; Viewers0.Broadcast(m); f := m.f
END GetSelection;

END TextFrames0.
```

MeasureLine reads a line from the current text position to the next ❶
end of line character and returns a line descriptor as shown in Fig.
11.23. The metrics of each character are obtained via *GetMetric*.

   DrawLine reads *len* characters starting at the current text ❷
position and displays them on the screen. *left* is the left margin and
right the right margin of the frame; characters that extend beyond
the right margin, are not displayed (clipping). *base* is the height of
the base line relative to the bottom of the screen. Elements are
requested to draw themselves, since the frame does not know how
to draw them.

   RedrawFrom redraws all lines starting at the vertical position ❸
top and creates new line descriptors for them. During this process,
y always points to the top of the line to be drawn, and *org* is the
text position of the first character in this line. Before a line is
drawn, its metrics are computed with *MeasureLine*. The space
between two lines is always *f.lsp* in this implementation. If *f* is not a
menu frame (*f.margin* > 0), a scroll bar is also drawn.

❹

GetPointPos computes the position p of the character on the screen that contains the point $(x0, y0)$ or that is closest to it (see Fig. 11.20).

❺

GetCharPos computes the position p of the character at text position *pos* (see Fig. 11.20).

❻

If the user clicks in the text with the middle mouse button, the word at the current position is interpreted as an Oberon command and invoked via *OS.Call*.

❼

If the mouse is in a text frame, a *HandleMouse* message is sent to the frame. (x, y) is the mouse position and *buttons* is the set of pressed mouse buttons. If a button is pressed in the scroll bar, the text is scrolled; if a button is pressed in the text area, then, depending on the button pressed, either the caret is set, a piece of text is selected, or a command is executed. If an element is clicked on with the middle mouse button, then the frame does not respond itself, but the click is passed to the element for handling. Thus an element that is unknown to the frame can react to the click in its own way. When a selection is made, a unique time stamp is stored with the selection.

❽

Most messages to text frames are implemented as methods because their receiver is known. For some messages, however, (e.g., notify messages) the receiver is unknown to the sender. Thus they must be broadcast to *all* possible receivers, whereby each receiver must determine whether the message is intended for it. Such messages are not implemented as methods, but as message records, and *Handle* is the corresponding message handler.

Each time a text is modified, a notify message is broadcast to all frames on the screen. Those frames that show the modified text respond by making the modification visible on the screen (compare Fig. 8.18).

NotifyInsMsg means that some characters were inserted in the text. The message is handled by the frame f if the frame's own text *f.text* is the modified text $m.t$. In our implementation only the insertion of single characters was optimized. In all other cases the entire frame contents after the inserted text are redrawn.

NotifyDelMsg means that something was deleted in the text. *NotifyReplMsg* means that something was modified (e.g., the font) without changing the length of the text. To keep the implementation simple *NotifyDelMsg* and *NotifyReplMsg* cause the complete frame contents to be redrawn starting at the point of the modification. In the Oberon System these operations were optimized to redraw as little as possible of the frame contents. This is complicated, however, and was omitted in Oberon0.

Finally, *Handle* interprets *SelectionMsg* (see below): If the selection of f is newer than that of *m.f*, *m.f* is replaced by f.

GetSelection determines the latest selection in all visible text ➒ frames. For this purpose, a message record of type *SelectionMsg* is broadcast to all frames. Text frames respond by entering themselves in this record if they contain a selection that is newer than the latest selection so far. At the end of the broadcast the message record contains the frame with the latest selection.

From an object-oriented point of view, three things are particularly interesting about *TextFrames0*:

What can be learned?

(1) *Genericity*
A text frame can be installed into a viewer and is handled correctly by it although viewers do not know text frames. Viewers work with abstract frames, of which a text frame is just one possible variant.

(2) *MVC concept*
A text frame is the view and controller component of a text editor. Modifications to the text cause a notify message to be sent to all frames. The implementation of the message interpreter *Handle* shows how text frames react to it. The broadcast of a message to multiple receivers is the major application of message records.

(3) *Arbitrary elements in texts*
Text frames must display and manipulate elements. Since they do not know what kinds of elements exist, they work with variables of the abstract class *Element* that may contain any kind of elements at run time.

11.3.4 Main Module of Text Editor (Edit0)

What we still need is a main module that creates a text frame and installs it into a viewer, and that provides various other commands to the user. We call this module *Edit0*; it provides the following three commands:

Edit0.Open f

Opens a viewer with a text frame and displays the text file *f* in it.

Edit0.Store

This command is invoked from the menu of a viewer *v*. The contents of the text frame in *v* are stored in a file whose name is the name of the viewer *v*. (The name of a viewer is displayed at the beginning of the associated menu frame.)

Edit0.ChangeFont n

Changes the font of the last text selection to the font with the name *n*.

To read the command arguments, *Edit0* uses an object of type *IO.Scanner*. The module *IO* is an input/output module that is described in Appendix C.

Implementation of Edit0

```
MODULE Edit0;
IMPORT OS, IO, TextFrames0, Texts0, Viewers0;

PROCEDURE Open*;
   VAR s: IO.Scanner; t: Texts0.Text; menu, cont: TextFrames0.Frame;
      v: Viewers0.Viewer; f: OS.File; r: OS.Rider;
BEGIN
   s.SetToParameters; s.Read;
   IF s.class = IO.name THEN
      menu := TextFrames0.NewMenu(s.str,
         "Viewers0.Close  Viewers0.Copy  Edit0.Store");
      NEW(t);
      f := OS.OldFile(s.str);
      IF f = NIL THEN t.Clear
      ELSE OS.InitRider(r); r.Set(f, 0); t.Load(r)
      END;
      cont := TextFrames0.New(t);
      v := Viewers0.New(menu, cont)
   END
END Open;

PROCEDURE Store*;
   VAR v: Viewers0.Viewer; s: IO.Scanner; f: OS.File; r: OS.Rider;
BEGIN
   v := Viewers0.ViewerAt(TextFrames0.cmdFrame.y);
   s.Set(v.menu(TextFrames0.Frame).text, 0);
   s.Read; (*read viewer name*)
   IF s.class = IO.name THEN
      v.Neutralize;
      f := OS.NewFile(s.str); OS.InitRider(r); r.Set(f, 0);
      v.cont(TextFrames0.Frame).text.Store(r);
      OS.Register(f)
   END
END Store;
```

```
PROCEDURE ChangeFont*;
  VAR s: IO.Scanner; f: TextFrames0.Frame;
BEGIN
  s.SetToParameters; s.Read;
  TextFrames0.GetSelection(f);
  IF (f # NIL) & (s.class = IO.name) THEN
    f.text.ChangeFont(f.selBeg.pos, f.selEnd.pos, OS.FontWithName(s.str))
  END
END ChangeFont;

END Edit0.
```

11.4 A Graphics Editor

In addition to text viewers, we would like to have viewers in which graphics can be edited. It should be possible to draw, move, select and delete various figures such as rectangles, lines and circles.

A graphics editor is also an interactive program that is structured according to the MVC concept. The model here is a graphics of type *Shapes0.Graphic*, which handles a list of figures of type *Shapes0.Shape*. The view and the controller are combined in the class *GraphicFrames0.Frame*, which can be installed in a viewer of type *Viewers0.Viewer*. The main module is *Draw0* (Fig. 11.25).

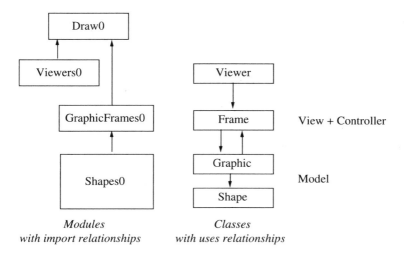

Modules
with import relationships

Classes
with uses relationships

Fig. 11.25 Modules and classes of the graphics editor

Whenever the model is changed by drawing, selecting or deleting a figure, all its views must be updated. As with the text editor, this is done via notify messages that are sent to all frames by the model.

11.4.1   Figures (Shapes0)

The module *Shapes0* handles drawings (class *Graphic*) as the data model of the editor. Just as a text consists of characters and elements, a drawing consists of figures. A drawing should be able to contain any figures, including ones that are defined later. Thus *Graphic* cannot know the kinds of figures, but must work with an abstract class *Shape*. The interface of *Shapes0* follows:

interface of
Shapes0

```
DEFINITION Shapes0;
IMPORT OS, Viewers0;

TYPE
```

Shape

```
  Shape = POINTER TO ShapeDesc;
  ShapeDesc = RECORD (OS.ObjectDesc)
    selected: BOOLEAN;      (*TRUE: shape is selected*)
    PROCEDURE (s: Shape) SetBox (x, y, w, h: INTEGER);
    PROCEDURE (s: Shape) GetBox (VAR x, y, w, h: INTEGER);
    PROCEDURE (s: Shape) Draw (f: Viewers0.Frame);
    PROCEDURE (s: Shape) Move (dx, dy: INTEGER);
    PROCEDURE (s: Shape) Neutralize;
    PROCEDURE (s: Shape) SetSelection (x, y, w, h: INTEGER);
    PROCEDURE (s: Shape) Copy (): Shape;
  END;
```

Graphic

```
  Graphic = POINTER TO GraphicDesc;
  GraphicDesc = RECORD
    shapes: Shape;
    PROCEDURE (g: Graphic) Insert (s: Shape);
    PROCEDURE (g: Graphic) DeleteSelected;
    PROCEDURE (g: Graphic) MoveSelected (dx, dy: INTEGER);
    PROCEDURE (g: Graphic) Draw (f: Viewers0.Frame);
    PROCEDURE (g: Graphic) Neutralize;
    PROCEDURE (g: Graphic) SetSelection (x, y, w, h: INTEGER);
    PROCEDURE (g: Graphic) GetBox (VAR x, y, w, h: INTEGER);
    PROCEDURE (g: Graphic) Copy (): Graphic;
    PROCEDURE (g: Graphic) Load (VAR r: OS.Rider);
    PROCEDURE (g: Graphic) Store (VAR r: OS.Rider);
  END ;

  NotifyChangeMsg = RECORD (OS.Message) g: Graphic END ;

VAR curShape: ARRAY 32 OF CHAR;  (*name of current shape type*)

PROCEDURE InitGraphic (VAR g: Graphic);
END Shapes0.
```

Messages to
figures

$s.SetBox(x, y, w, h)$

computes the position and size of figure s based on its enclosing rectangle (x, y, w, h).

s.GetBox(x, y, w, h)

   returns the smallest rectangle (x, y, w, h) that encloses s.

s.Draw(f)

   draws s at its current position in frame f.

s.Move(dx, dy)

   moves s by the vector (dx, dy).

s.Neutralize

   removes any selection from s.

s.SetSelection(x, y, w, h)

   selects s if it is totally within the rectangle (x, y, w, h).

s1 := s.Copy()

   returns a copy of s.

g.Insert (s)   *Messages to*

   inserts the figure s in the graphics g.   *graphics*

g.DeleteSelected

   deletes all selected figures in g.

g.MoveSelected (dx, dy)

   moves all selected figures in g by the vector (dx, dy).

g.Draw (f)

   requests all figures in g to draw themselves at their position in
   frame f.

g.Neutralize

   deselects all figures in g.

g.SetSelection (x, y, w, h)

   selects all figures of the graphics g that are totally within the
   rectangle (x, y, w, h).

g.GetBox (x, y, w, h)

   returns the smallest rectangle that encloses all figures in the
   graphics g.

g1 := g.Copy()

   returns a copy of g.

g.Load (r)

   loads the graphics g from the rider r.

g.Store (r)

   stores the graphics g on the rider r.


```
MODULE Shapes0;                                       Implementation of
IMPORT OS, Viewers0;                                  Shapes0

TYPE
   Shape* = POINTER TO ShapeDesc;                     Shape
   ShapeDesc* = RECORD (OS.ObjectDesc)
      selected*: BOOLEAN;  (*TRUE: shape is selected*)
```

```
                        next: Shape
                      END;
```

Graphic
```
                      Graphic* = POINTER TO GraphicDesc;
                      GraphicDesc* = RECORD
                        shapes*: Shape
                      END;

                      NotifyChangeMsg* = RECORD (OS.Message) g*: Graphic END;

                    VAR
                      curShape*: ARRAY 32 OF CHAR;  (*name of current shape type*)
```

Shape methods
```
                    PROCEDURE (s: Shape) SetBox* (x, y, w, h: INTEGER);
                    BEGIN s.selected := FALSE;
                    END SetBox;

                    PROCEDURE (s: Shape) Draw* (f: Viewers0.Frame);
                    END Draw;

                    PROCEDURE (s: Shape) Move* (dx, dy: INTEGER);
                    END Move;

                    PROCEDURE (s: Shape) SetSelection* (x, y, w, h: INTEGER);
                    END SetSelection;

                    PROCEDURE (s: Shape) Neutralize*;
                    BEGIN s.selected := FALSE
                    END Neutralize;

                    PROCEDURE (s: Shape) GetBox* (VAR x, y, w, h: INTEGER);
                    END GetBox;

                    PROCEDURE (s: Shape) Copy* (): Shape;
                    END Copy;
```

Graphic methods
```
                    PROCEDURE InitGraphic* (VAR g: Graphic);
                    BEGIN g.shapes := NIL
                    END InitGraphic;

                    PROCEDURE (g: Graphic) Insert* (s: Shape);
                      VAR msg: NotifyChangeMsg;
                    BEGIN
                      s.next := g.shapes; g.shapes := s; msg.g := g; Viewers0.Broadcast(msg)
                    END Insert;

                    PROCEDURE (g: Graphic) DeleteSelected*;
                      VAR s, s0: Shape; msg: NotifyChangeMsg;
                    BEGIN
                      s := g.shapes; s0 := NIL;
                      WHILE s # NIL DO
                        IF s.selected THEN
                          IF s0 = NIL THEN g.shapes := s.next ELSE s0.next := s.next END
                        ELSE s0 := s
                        END;
```

```
      s := s.next
    END;
    msg.g := g; Viewers0.Broadcast(msg)
END DeleteSelected;

PROCEDURE (g: Graphic) MoveSelected* (dx, dy: INTEGER);
    VAR s: Shape; msg: NotifyChangeMsg;
BEGIN
    s := g.shapes;
    WHILE s # NIL DO
      IF s.selected THEN s.Move(dx, dy) END;
      s := s.next
    END;
    msg.g := g; Viewers0.Broadcast(msg)
END MoveSelected;

PROCEDURE (g: Graphic) Draw* (f: Viewers0.Frame);
    VAR s: Shape;
BEGIN
    s := g.shapes;  WHILE s # NIL DO s.Draw(f); s := s.next END
END Draw;

PROCEDURE (g: Graphic) Neutralize*;
    VAR s: Shape; msg: NotifyChangeMsg; changed: BOOLEAN;
BEGIN
    s := g.shapes; changed := FALSE;
    WHILE s # NIL DO
      changed := changed OR s.selected; s.Neutralize; s := s.next
    END;
    IF changed THEN msg.g := g; Viewers0.Broadcast(msg) END
END Neutralize;

PROCEDURE (g: Graphic) SetSelection* (x, y, w, h: INTEGER);
    VAR s: Shape; msg: NotifyChangeMsg;
BEGIN
    s := g.shapes;
    WHILE s # NIL DO s.SetSelection(x, y, w, h); s := s.next END;
    msg.g := g; Viewers0.Broadcast(msg)
END SetSelection;

PROCEDURE (g: Graphic) GetBox* (VAR x, y, w, h: INTEGER);
    VAR x0, y0, w0, h0: INTEGER; s: Shape;
BEGIN
    x := 0; y := 0; w := 12; h := 12;
    s := g.shapes;
    IF s # NIL THEN s.GetBox(x, y, w, h); s := s.next END;
    WHILE s # NIL DO
      s.GetBox(x0, y0, w0, h0);
      IF x0 < x THEN INC(w, x - x0); x := x0 END;
      IF y0 < y THEN INC(h, y - y0); y := y0 END;
      IF x0 + w0 > x + w THEN w := x0 + w0 - x END;
      IF y0 + h0 > y + h THEN h := y0 + h0 - y END;
      s := s.next
    END;
END GetBox;
```

```
PROCEDURE (g: Graphic) Copy* (): Graphic;
  VAR s, a, b: Shape; g1: Graphic;
BEGIN
  NEW(g1); g1.shapes := NIL;
  s := g.shapes;
  WHILE s # NIL DO
    a := s.Copy(); a.next := NIL;
    IF g1.shapes = NIL THEN g1.shapes := a ELSE b.next := a END;
    b := a; s := s.next
  END;
  RETURN g1
END Copy;

PROCEDURE (g: Graphic) Load* (VAR r: OS.Rider);
  VAR s, last: Shape; x: OS.Object;
BEGIN
  last := NIL;
  REPEAT
    r.ReadObj(x);
    IF x = NIL THEN s := NIL ELSE s := x(Shape) END;
    IF last = NIL THEN g.shapes := s ELSE last.next := s END;
    last := s
  UNTIL x = NIL  (*terminated by a NIL shape*)
END Load;

PROCEDURE (g: Graphic) Store* (VAR r: OS.Rider);
  VAR s: Shape;
BEGIN
  s := g.shapes;
  WHILE s # NIL DO r.WriteObj(s); s := s.next END;
  r.WriteObj(NIL)
END Store;

BEGIN
  curShape := ""
END Shapes0.
```

11.4.2   Editing Figures (GraphicFrames0)

A graphics frame displays figures on the screen and reacts to
mouse clicks by creating, moving, selecting or deleting figures. To
keep the example small, we do not support resizing of figures.

Meaning of mouse buttons
The mouse buttons have the following meaning: If the left
button is pressed while the mouse is dragged, a new figure is
drawn in the enclosing rectangle. If the mouse is dragged with the
middle button pressed, the entire drawing in the frame is moved; if
the middle and the left button are pressed simultaneously
(interclick), only the selected figures are moved. The right button
permits selection. When the mouse is moved with the right button
pressed, all figures enclosed in the selection rectangle are selected

(i.e., filled with a color); if the left button is interclicked, the selected figures are deleted.

To allow moving the entire drawing on the screen without changing the coordinates of all figures, a graphics frame has a coordinate system with the origin ($orgX$, $orgY$) relative to the lower left corner of the frame (Fig. 11.26). The coordinates of the figures are relative to this origin, so that moving the origin moves the entire drawing.

Coordinate system

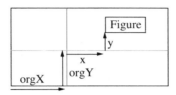

Fig. 11.26 Graphics frame with origin (*orgX*, *orgY*)

Graphics frames are implemented in module *GraphicFrame0*, which has the following interface:

```
DEFINITION GraphicFrames0;
IMPORT Viewers0, OS, Shapes0;

TYPE
   Frame = POINTER TO FrameDesc;
   FrameDesc = RECORD (Viewers0.FrameDesc)
      orgX, orgY: INTEGER;
      graphic: Shapes0.Graphic;
      PROCEDURE (f: Frame) Draw;
      PROCEDURE (f: Frame) Neutralize;
      PROCEDURE (f: Frame) Modify (y: INTEGER);
      PROCEDURE (f: Frame) Copy (): Viewers0.Frame;
      PROCEDURE (f: Frame) HandleMouse (x, y: INTEGER; buttons: SET);
      PROCEDURE (f: Frame) Handle (VAR m: OS.Message);
      PROCEDURE (f: Frame) InvertBlock (x, y, w, h: INTEGER);
   END ;

PROCEDURE New (graphic: Shapes0.Graphic): Frame;
END GraphicFrames0.
```

Interface of GraphicFrames0

Most of the interface of *Frame* is inherited from the base class *Viewers0.Frame*. Only one method is new:

f.InvertBlock(x, y, w, h)
> inverts the block (x, y, w, h) in frame *f*. x and y are relative to the origin ($orgX$, $orgY$). If the block extends beyond the border of the frame, it is clipped. *InvertBlock* can also be used to draw horizontal and vertical lines ($w=1$ or $h=1$).

Implementation of
GraphicFrames0

```
MODULE GraphicFrames0;
IMPORT OS, Viewers0, Shapes0;

TYPE
```

Frame

```
  Frame* = POINTER TO FrameDesc;
  FrameDesc* = RECORD (Viewers0.FrameDesc)
    orgX*, orgY*: INTEGER;      (*origin*)
    graphic*: Shapes0.Graphic   (*shapes in this frame*)
  END;
```

see ①

```
PROCEDURE (f: Frame) InvertBlock* (x, y, w, h: INTEGER);
BEGIN
  INC(x, f.x + f.orgX); INC(y, f.y + f.orgY);
  IF x < f.x THEN DEC(w, f.x - x); x := f.x END;
  IF x + w > f.x + f.w THEN w := f.x + f.w - x END;
  IF y < f.y THEN DEC(h, f.y - y); y := f.y END;
  IF y + h > f.y + f.h THEN h := f.y + f.h - y END;
  IF (w > 0) & (h > 0) THEN OS.InvertBlock(x, y, w, h) END
END InvertBlock;
```

see ②

```
PROCEDURE (f: Frame) Draw*;
BEGIN
  OS.FadeCursor;
  OS.EraseBlock(f.x, f.y, f.w, f.h);
  f.graphic.Draw(f)
END Draw;

PROCEDURE (f: Frame) Modify* (y: INTEGER);
BEGIN f.Modify^ (y); f.Draw
END Modify;
```

see ③

```
PROCEDURE (f: Frame) HandleMouse* (x, y: INTEGER; buttons: SET);
  VAR w, h, dx, dy: INTEGER; obj: OS.Object; s: Shapes0.Shape;
    changed: BOOLEAN;

    PROCEDURE Track(VAR x, y, w, h, dx, dy: INTEGER; VAR buttons: SET);
      VAR b: SET; x1, y1: INTEGER;
    BEGIN
      REPEAT
        OS.GetMouse(b, x1, y1); buttons := buttons + b;
        OS.DrawCursor(x1, y1)
      UNTIL b = {};
      dx := x1 - x; dy := y1 - y; w := ABS(dx); h := ABS(dy);
      IF x1 < x THEN x := x1 END;
      IF y1 < y THEN y := y1 END;
      DEC(x, f.x + f.orgX); DEC(y, f.y + f.orgY)
    END Track;
BEGIN changed := FALSE;
  IF OS.left IN buttons THEN
    Track(x, y, w, h, dx, dy, buttons);
    (*----- generate new shape with type curShape*)
    OS.NameToObj(Shapes0.curShape, obj);
    IF obj # NIL THEN
      s := obj(Shapes0.Shape); s.SetBox(x, y, w, h); f.graphic.Insert(s)
    END
```

```
    ELSIF OS.middle IN buttons THEN
        Track(x, y, w, h, dx, dy, buttons);
        IF OS.left IN buttons THEN (*----- MM+ML click: move selected figures*)
            f.graphic.MoveSelected(dx, dy)
        ELSE (*----- MM click: move origin*)
            INC(f.orgX, dx); INC(f.orgY, dy); f.Draw
        END
    ELSIF OS.right IN buttons THEN
        f.Neutralize; Track(x, y, w, h, dx, dy, buttons);
        f.graphic.SetSelection(x, y, w, h);
        IF OS.left IN buttons THEN (*----- MR+ML click: delete selected shapes*)
            f.graphic.DeleteSelected
        END
    END
END HandleMouse;

PROCEDURE (f: Frame) Handle* (VAR m: OS.Message);                    see ④
BEGIN
    WITH m: Shapes0.NotifyChangeMsg DO
        IF f.graphic = m.g THEN f.Draw END
    ELSE
    END
END Handle;

PROCEDURE (f: Frame) Neutralize*;
BEGIN
    f.graphic.Neutralize
END Neutralize;

PROCEDURE New* (graphic: Shapes0.Graphic): Frame;
    VAR f: Frame;
BEGIN
    NEW(f); f.graphic := graphic;
    f.orgX := 0; f.orgY := 0;
    RETURN f
END New;

PROCEDURE (f: Frame) Copy* (): Viewers0.Frame;
    VAR f1: Frame;
BEGIN
    f1 := New(f.graphic); f1.orgX := f.orgX; f1.orgY := f.orgY; RETURN f1
END Copy;

END GraphicFrames0.
```

Graphics frames normally offer a set of drawing primitives. These ❶
are methods that allow drawing dots, rectangles, etc. into the
frame. Their arguments are in coordinates relative to the origin
$(orgX, orgY)$ and are transformed to screen coordinates. In this
example there is only one drawing primitive, *InvertBlock*, which
also handles clipping.

   Draw redraws the entire frame contents. To keep the imple- ❷
mentation simple, this occurs with each modification in the frame.

In practice this would not be acceptable; provisions would have to be made to assure that only those parts of the frame are redrawn that actually changed.

❸ *HandleMouse* interprets mouse clicks as described above. *Track* computes the start and end points of a mouse movement while a button is pressed. The coordinates of these points are transformed to coordinates relative to the origin of the frame (orgX, orgY).

It is interesting to see how figures are entered by the user. When the user moves the mouse while pressing the left button, the frame must react by creating a new figure and displaying it. But which figure is to be drawn? A rectangle? A circle? The frame is not aware of rectangles or circles, but only of abstract figures. It must revert to a trick: It creates a figure of the type whose name is currently stored in the global variable *Shapes0.curShape*. The procedure *OS.NameToObj* is used to create from a type name an object of that type. Any new module that wants its own figures to be drawn simply installs the name of the respective figure class in *curShape* (see Section 11.4.4). This makes the editor create figures that it does not know at all.

In systems that do not offer this possibility, *curShape* can be implemented as a variable of type *Shape*, which at any time contains an object of the current figure type. When the editor has to draw a figure, it copies this object and draws the copy.

❹ *Handle* is the message handler for graphics frames. It handles *NotifyChange* messages that are sent to all frames when a figure is modified.

11.4.3   Main Module of Graphics Editor (Draw0)

Draw0 provides two commands:

Draw0.Open f
> Opens a viewer with a graphics frame and displays in it the contents of file *f*.

Draw0.Store
> This command is invoked from the menu of a viewer *v*. The contents of the graphics frame in *v* are stored in a file whose name is the name of the viewer *v*.

Implementation of Draw0

```
MODULE Draw0;
IMPORT OS, IO, Texts0, TextFrames0, Shapes0, GraphicFrames0, Viewers0;
```

```
PROCEDURE Open*;
   VAR s: IO.Scanner; v: Viewers0.Viewer;
      menu: TextFrames0.Frame; cont: GraphicFrames0.Frame;
      file: OS.File; r: OS.Rider; g: Shapes0.Graphic;
BEGIN
   s.SetToParameters; s.Read;
   IF s.class = IO.name THEN
      menu := TextFrames0.NewMenu
         (s.str, "Viewers0.Close  Viewers0.Copy  Draw0.Store");
      NEW(g); Shapes0.InitGraphic(g); file := OS.OldFile(s.str);
      IF file # NIL THEN OS.InitRider(r); r.Set(file, 0); g.Load(r) END;
      cont := GraphicFrames0.New(g);
      v := Viewers0.New(menu, cont)
   END
END Open;


PROCEDURE Store*;
   VAR v: Viewers0.Viewer; s: IO.Scanner; file: OS.File; r: OS.Rider;
BEGIN
   v := Viewers0.ViewerAt(TextFrames0.cmdFrame.y);
   s.Set(v.menu(TextFrames0.Frame).text, 0); s.Read;
   IF s.class = IO.name THEN
      file := OS.NewFile(s.str); OS.InitRider(r); r.Set(file, 0);
      v.cont(GraphicFrames0.Frame).graphic.Store(r);
      OS.Register(file)
   END
END Store;

END Draw0.
```

11.4.4 Rectangles as Special Figures (Rectangles0)

The graphics editor developed so far can only work with abstract figures. It can be extended, however, by deriving concrete figure classes for rectangles, circles and lines from the abstract figure class *Shape*. Each concrete figure class is implemented in a separate module that can be added to the existing editor (Fig. 11.27).

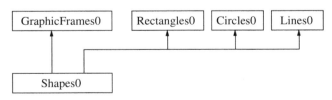

Fig. 11.27 Module hierarchy with figure extensions

The Oberon System even permits adding modules like *Rectangles0* at run time while the editor is already loaded. This allows a user to dynamically adapt the functionality of the editor as needed.

As an example of a figure extension, we look at the module *Rectangles0*, in which rectangles are implemented. Its interface is:

Interface of Rectangles0

```
DEFINITION Rectangles0;
IMPORT Shapes0;
TYPE
    Rectangle = POINTER TO RectDesc;
    RectDesc = RECORD (Shapes0.ShapeDesc) END;
PROCEDURE Set;
END Rectangles0.
```

The class *Rectangle* has the same interface as *Shapes0.Shape*. In the implementation of *Rectangle*, however, the abstract methods are overridden. The command *Rectangles0.Set* makes the editor draw a rectangle when it tries to create a new figure.

Implementation of Rectangles0

Rectangle

```
MODULE Rectangles0;
IMPORT OS, Viewers0, Shapes0, GraphicFrames0;

TYPE
    Rectangle* = POINTER TO RectDesc;
    RectDesc* = RECORD (Shapes0.ShapeDesc)
        x, y, w, h: INTEGER
    END;

PROCEDURE (r: Rectangle) SetBox* (x, y, w, h: INTEGER);
BEGIN
    r.SetBox^ (x, y, w, h);
    r.x := x; r.y := y; r.w := w; r.h := h
END SetBox;

PROCEDURE (r: Rectangle) Draw* (f: Viewers0.Frame);
BEGIN
    WITH f: GraphicFrames0.Frame DO
        IF r.selected THEN
            f.InvertBlock(r.x, r.y, r.w, r.h)
        ELSE
            f.InvertBlock(r.x, r.y, r.w, 1);
            f.InvertBlock(r.x, r.y + r.h - 1, r.w, 1);
            f.InvertBlock(r.x, r.y + 1, 1, r.h - 2);
            f.InvertBlock(r.x + r.w - 1, r.y + 1, 1, r.h - 2)
        END
    END
END Draw;

PROCEDURE (r: Rectangle) Move* (dx, dy: INTEGER);
BEGIN
    INC(r.x, dx); INC(r.y, dy)
END Move;
```

```
PROCEDURE (r: Rectangle) SetSelection* (x, y, w, h: INTEGER);
BEGIN
   r.selected := (r.x >= x) & (r.x+r.w <= x+w) & (r.y >= y) & (r.y+r.h <= y+h)
END SetSelection;

PROCEDURE (r: Rectangle) GetBox* (VAR x, y, w, h: INTEGER);
BEGIN x := r.x; y := r.y; w := r.w; h := r.h
END GetBox;

PROCEDURE (r: Rectangle) Copy* (): Shapes0.Shape;
   VAR r1: Rectangle;
BEGIN
   NEW(r1);
   r1.selected := r.selected; r1.x := r.x; r1.y := r.y; r1.w := r.w; r1.h := r.h;
   RETURN r1
END Copy;

PROCEDURE (r: Rectangle) Load* (VAR R: OS.Rider);
BEGIN R.ReadInt(r.x); R.ReadInt(r.y); R.ReadInt(r.w); R.ReadInt(r.h)
END Load;

PROCEDURE (r: Rectangle) Store* (VAR R: OS.Rider);
BEGIN R.WriteInt(r.x); R.WriteInt(r.y); R.WriteInt(r.w); R.WriteInt(r.h)
END Store;

PROCEDURE Set*;
BEGIN Shapes0.curShape := "Rectangles0.RectDesc"
END Set;

END Rectangles0.
```

The command *Rectangles0.Set* stores the name of the rectangle type in the global variable *Shapes0.curShape*. The editor uses this type name in the creation of a new figure. After the invocation of *Rectangles0.Set*, the editor thus draws rectangles.

11.5 Embedding Graphics in Texts

The next step is to integrate pictures in texts and let them flow with the text during editing. Fortunately we have provided texts with the ability to handle arbitrary elements. Pictures are thus a special kind of element—graphic elements.

How must a graphic element behave? It is installed with the command *GraphicElems0.Insert*, which creates an empty graphic element (displayed as a blank rectangle) and inserts it in the text at the caret position. When the element is clicked with the middle mouse button, a graphic viewer opens that displays the drawing contained in the element. This viewer permits editing. The drawing

Graphic elements

can be written back to the element by clicking on the command *GraphicElems0.Update* in the menu of the graphic viewer (Fig. 11.28).

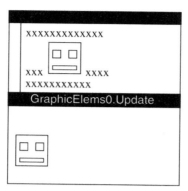

Text frame with an element

Graphic frame.
Is opened in response to a middle click at the element.

Fig. 11.28 Behavior of graphic elements

A graphic element is a subclass of *Texts0.Element*. It contains a list of figures that can be displayed in a graphics frame.

Temporary graphics frame

How is a graphic element displayed in the midst of a text frame? At the position where the element is to appear in the text, a (temporary) graphics frame is placed with the dimensions of the element. In this frame the element, i.e., its figures, can be displayed. The frame must only be there while the contents of the element are drawn; otherwise it can be removed. Thus one graphics frame suffices for all graphic elements.

We implement graphic elements in the module *GraphicElems0* with the following interface:

Interface of GraphicElems0

```
DEFINITION GraphicElems0;
IMPORT Texts0;

TYPE
    Element = POINTER TO ElemDesc;
    ElemDesc = RECORD (Texts0.ElemDesc) END;

PROCEDURE Insert;
PROCEDURE Update;

END GraphicElems0.
```

The class *GraphicElems0.Element* has the same interface as its abstract base class *Texts0.Element*. The inherited methods are overridden to provide the required behavior for graphic elements.

```
MODULE GraphicElems0;
IMPORT OS, Texts0, Shapes0, GraphicFrames0, TextFrames0, Viewers0;

TYPE
  Element* = POINTER TO ElemDesc;
  ElemDesc* = RECORD (Texts0.ElemDesc)
    orgX, orgY: INTEGER;
    graphic: Shapes0.Graphic;
  END;
  UpdateFrame = POINTER TO UpdateFrameDesc;
  UpdateFrameDesc = RECORD (GraphicFrames0.FrameDesc)
    text: Texts0.Text;
    e: Element
  END;

VAR f: GraphicFrames0.Frame;
  (*reused within a text frame whenever a graphic element has to be redrawn*)

PROCEDURE (e: Element) Copy* (): Texts0.Element;
  VAR res: Element;
BEGIN NEW(res); res^ := e^; res.graphic := e.graphic.Copy(); RETURN res
END Copy;

PROCEDURE (e: Element) Draw* (x, y: INTEGER);
BEGIN
  f.x := x; f.y := y; f.w := e.w; f.h := e.h;
  f.orgX := e.orgX; f.orgY := e.orgY; f.graphic := e.graphic;
  f.Draw
END Draw;

PROCEDURE (e: Element) HandleMouse* (f: OS.Object; x, y: INTEGER);
  VAR v: Viewers0.Viewer; menu: TextFrames0.Frame;
    cont: UpdateFrame; buttons: SET;
BEGIN
  REPEAT OS.GetMouse(buttons, x, y) UNTIL buttons = {};
  menu := TextFrames0.NewMenu
    ("", "Viewers0.Close  Viewers0.Copy  GraphicElems0.Update");
  NEW(cont);
  cont.graphic := e.graphic;
  cont.orgX := e.orgX + 10; cont.orgY := e.orgY + 10;
  cont.text := f(TextFrames0.Frame).text; cont.e := e;
  v := Viewers0.New(menu, cont)
END HandleMouse;

PROCEDURE (e: Element) Load* (VAR r: OS.Rider);
BEGIN
  e.Load^ (r);
  r.ReadInt(e.orgX); r.ReadInt(e.orgY);
  NEW(e.graphic); Shapes0.InitGraphic(e.graphic); e.graphic.Load(r)
END Load;

PROCEDURE (e: Element) Store* (VAR r: OS.Rider);
BEGIN e.Store^ (r); r.WriteInt(e.orgX); r.WriteInt(e.orgY); e.graphic.Store(r)
END Store;
```

Implementation of GraphicElems0

Element

see ①

see ②

```
PROCEDURE Insert*;
    VAR e: Element; f: TextFrames0.Frame;
BEGIN
    IF Viewers0.focus # NIL THEN
        f := Viewers0.focus(TextFrames0.Frame);
        IF (f # NIL) & (f.caret.pos >= 0) THEN
            NEW(e); e.w := 12; e.h := 12; e.dsc := 0;
            NEW(e.graphic); Shapes0.InitGraphic(e.graphic);
            e.orgX := 0; e.orgY := 0;
            f.text.SetPos(f.caret.pos); f.text.WriteElem(e)
        END
    END
END Insert;
```

see ③

```
PROCEDURE Update*;
    VAR v: Viewers0.Viewer; f: UpdateFrame; e: Element;
        m: Texts0.NotifyReplMsg; x, y: INTEGER; pos: LONGINT;
BEGIN
    v := Viewers0.ViewerAt(TextFrames0.cmdFrame.y);
    f := v.cont(UpdateFrame);
    e := f.e; pos := f.text.ElemPos(e);
    IF pos < f.text.len THEN
        f.graphic.GetBox(x, y, e.w, e.h);
        e.graphic := f.graphic; e.orgX := - x ; e.orgY := - y;
        m.t := f.text; m.beg := pos; m.end := pos + 1; Viewers0.Broadcast(m)
    END
END Update;

PROCEDURE Init;
    VAR g: Shapes0.Graphic;
BEGIN NEW(g); Shapes0.InitGraphic(g); f := GraphicFrames0.New(g)
END Init;

BEGIN Init
END GraphicElems0.
```

❶   *Draw* draws the graphic element at screen position (x, y). It creates a (temporary) graphics frame of the appropriate size at this position, installs the figures in it, and sends it a *Draw* message.

❷   *HandleMouse* is invoked when a graphic element is clicked with the middle mouse button. The method opens a viewer with a frame of type *UdateFrame* and displays the figures of the element in it. The update frame remembers which element is currently being edited (*f.e*) and to which text it belongs (*f.text*). This information is necessary to restore the edited figures in the element via the *Update* command.

❸   In an *UpdateFrame f*, the figures of the element *f.e* contained in the text *f.text* are edited. *Update* writes the edited figures back to *f.e*. The size of *f.e* is determined as the smallest rectangle that encloses all the figures.

This example shows how in Oberon two initially different pro- *What can be* grams can be integrated. The following properties are important *learned?* for this:

(1) *GraphicElems0* is a separate program. Nevertheless, it has access to the text in the text editor, which is necessary in order to be able to insert elements. It also has access to the figures in a graphics frame, which is necessary in order to display the figures of an element in such a frame. Thus Oberon programs are not closed monolithic systems, but are open in the sense that exported data structures are visible to other programs (not only to other modules of the same program).

(2) Graphic elements are compatible with abstract elements and can thus be handled by the text editor. The editor communicates with them via messages rather than via procedure calls. Messages represent a looser coupling of program parts than procedure calls, which require that the caller knows the callee.

(3) Graphic elements wrap up a set of figures to make them compatible with elements (see Section 8.4)

12 Costs and Benefits of OOP

This book has attempted to show what kind of situations classes are useful for and when they should not be used. Let us summarize now: Why should we program in an object-oriented instead of a procedural way? What are the costs and the benefits of object-oriented programming? Are the benefits greater than the costs?

If a programmer is aware of the strengths and the limits of object-oriented programming and uses classes consciously, then the benefits by far outweigh the costs. However, costs can quickly rise if classes are used thoughtlessly, particularly in situations where they do not simplify matters, but rather add complexity.

12.1 Benefits of OOP

We expect a programming technique to help us in solving problems. The greatest problem in programming is complexity. The larger and more complex a program is, the more important it becomes to decompose it into small, comprehensible parts. To master complexity, we must abstract away from details. Classes are a suitable tool for that:

Mastering complexity

- Classes permit the construction of handy components with simple interfaces that abstract away from implementation details.
- Data and operations form an entity and are not spread over a program, as with procedural techniques.
- The locality of code and data improves the readability and maintainability of software.

- Information hiding protects against unauthorized access to critical data.

Extensibility   Object-oriented programming makes it possible to build extensible systems. This is one of its great advantages and distinguishes OOP from conventional programming techniques. Extensibility means that an existing system can be made to work with new components without having to be modified. Components can be even added at run time.

Type extension and the resulting polymorphism of variables prove useful primarily in the following situations (see Chapter 7):

- Handling of heterogeneous data structures: Programs can work with variants of objects without distinguishing them. New variants can be added at any time.
- Changing behavior at run time: One object can be replaced by another at run time. This can change the behavior of an algorithm that uses this object.
- Implementation of generic components: Algorithms can be generalized so that they no longer work with just *one* kind of object.
- Completion of semifinished products: Components need not be customized for a certain application. They can be stored as semifinished products in a library and extended as needed to yield various finished products.
- Extension of frameworks: Application-independendent parts of a domain can be implemented as a framework and later extended by adding application-specific parts.

Reuse   In practice, software reuse often fails because existing components do not match new requirements. Object-oriented programming helps by making it possible to adapt components to new needs without invalidating their existing clients. This lets us enjoy all the advantages of reuse:

- We save development time that can be invested in other tasks more profitably.
- Reused components usually contain fewer errors than newly developed ones because they have already been tested repeatedly.
- When a component is used by several clients, improvements in its code take effect in multiple programs simultaneously.

- If programs rely on standard components, their structure and user interface become more uniform, which makes them more understandable and easier to use.

12.2 Costs of OOP

Object-oriented programming requires learning four things: *Learning effort*

(1) The basic concepts such as classes, inheritance and dynamic binding must be understood. For programmers that are already familiar with modules and abstract data types, this is but a small step. For others who have never used data encapsulation, this can mean a paradigm shift and require significant learning time.

(2) Reuse requires programmers to become familiar with large class libraries. This can be harder than learning a new programming language. A class library *is* actually a virtual language that can include hundreds of types and thousands of operations. In Smalltalk, for example, a significant part of its class library must be learned before practical programming can begin. This takes time.

(3) More difficult than *using* a class library is *designing* one. Class design is language design and requires experience. It is an iterative process where learning occurs through errors.

(4) It is just as difficult to learn when to use classes (see Chapter 7) and when to keep hands off. Only with the acquisition of this critical skill has one mastered object-oriented programming.

As we can see, the learning effort for the basic concepts is small, but that for the class library and for the proper use of classes can be substantial.

Since implementation details of classes are usually unknown, the programmer must rely on documentation and naming when trying to understand a class. The time gained in not having to write a class must in part be reinvested (especially in the beginning) in order to understand the class. *Comprehension problems*

The documentation of classes is more difficult than that of procedures or modules. Since every method can be overridden, the documentation must not only say what the method does, but also in which context it is invoked: overridden methods are usually not invoked by the client, but by a framework. Thus the programmer must know what conditions hold when the method is called. For abstract methods, which are empty, the documentation must even say what the overriding method is supposed to do.

In deep class hierarchies, the fields and methods of a class are usually inherited from various hierarchy levels. It is not always easy to see which fields and methods actually belong to a class. Tools such as a class browser are necessary to provide this information. If concrete classes are extended, then each method usually does little before passing the message to the base class. The implementation of an operation is thus distributed among several classes, and we have to leaf through the code to understand how it works.

Methods are usually shorter than procedures since they perform only a single operation on data. But the number of methods is accordingly higher. Short methods have the advantage of being easy to understand, but the drawback that the code to handle a message is sometimes spread out over many small methods.

Flexibility

Data abstraction limits the flexibility of clients. Clients can only carry out those operations that a class provides. They no longer have unlimited access to the data. This is usually intended. The motivation is the same as for using a high-level programming language, namely to prevent certain unclean program structures.

Data abstraction should not be overdone. The more data are hidden, the more difficult it is to extend a class. The point is not that clients should not be *allowed* to know data, but that they should not be *required* to know them in order to work with a class.

Efficiency

It is often claimed that object-oriented programming is inefficient. What is true about that? We must distinguish between run-time inefficiency, storage inefficiency, and inefficiency coming from unnecessary generality:

(1) *Run-time inefficiency.* In languages like Smalltalk, messages are interpreted at run time by searching them in one or more tables and selecting the appropriate method. Of course, this is

slow. Even with the best optimizing techniques, Smalltalk programs prove to be ten times slower than optimized C programs [Cha92].

In hybrid languages like Oberon-2, Object-Pascal and C++, sending a message only amounts to invoking a procedure variable referenced by a pointer. On certain machines, messages are only 10 percent slower than procedure calls. Since messages are rare compared to other operations in a program, their influence on run time is negligible.

However, there is another factor that influences run time: data abstraction. It denies direct access to fields of a class and requires that every operation on the data be done via methods. This costs a procedure invocation for every data access. However, when data abstraction is used only where it is necesary (i.e., not for its own sake), then the slowdown is moderate.

(2) *Storage inefficiency*. Dynamic binding and run-time type checking require information about the type of an object at run time. This information is kept in a type descriptor of which there is one per class. Each object has an invisible pointer to the type descriptor of its class. The additional storage requirement in object-oriented programs is thus one pointer per object and one type descriptor per class.

(3) *Unnecessary generality*. Inefficiency can also mean that a program has unnecessary features. A library class often has more methods than are needed. Since extraneous methods cannot be removed, they have to be carried along as dead weight. This does not affect run time, but it does inflate code size.

One alternative would be to provide a base class with only a minimum of methods, and then to implement various extensions of it that offer increasing functionality.

Another approach would be to let the linker remove superfluous methods. Such smart linkers are available for various languages and operating systems.

Oberon has another way of dealing with unnecessary generality: Program parts can be added at run time. Thus it is not necessary to load the entire program at once, but only those parts have to be loaded that are actually needed. In practice this saves more code than the removal of methods can.

Thus it cannot be said that object-oriented programming is generally inefficient. If classes are used only where they make sense, the loss of efficiency is negligible both in run time and in memory.

12.3 The Future of OOP

Will object-oriented programming survive, or is it only a fad that will die off again?

Classes have found their way into most modern programming languages. This already indicates that they are going to stay. Classes will soon belong to the standard repertoire of every programmer, just as every programmer today can handle dynamic data structures and recursion, which were also new twenty years ago. But classes are just *one* new construct among many others. We will have to learn for what situations they are suited and will use them there and only there. It is the skill of every craftsman, and more so of every engineer, to select the right tool for every task.

Object-oriented programming has given rise to a certain euphoria. Advertisements promise incredible things, and even some researchers seem to consider object-oriented programming to be the panacea that will solve all the problems of software development. This euphoria will subside. After a period of disillusionment, people will perhaps cease to speak about object-oriented programming, just as hardly anybody speaks about structured programming any more. But classes will be used quite naturally then and will be seen as what they are: components that help to build modular and extensible software.

A Oberon-2 Language Definition

A.1 Introduction

Oberon-2 is a general-purpose language in the tradition of Oberon and Modula-2. Its most important features are block structure, modularity, separate compilation, static typing with strong type checking (also across module boundaries), and type extension with type-bound procedures.

This report is not intended as a programmer's tutorial, but is deliberately kept concise. It serves as a reference for programmers, implementors, and manual writers. What remains unsaid is mostly left so intentionally, either because it can be derived from stated rules of the language, or because it would require commitment to a definition when a general commitment appears as unwise.

Section A.12.1 defines some terms that are used to express the type checking rules of Oberon-2. Where they appear in the text, they are written in italics to indicate their special meaning (e.g., the *same* type).

A.2 Syntax

An extended Backus-Naur Formalism (EBNF) is used to describe the syntax of Oberon-2: Alternatives are separated by |. Brackets [and] denote optionality of the enclosed expression, and braces { and } denote its repetition (possibly 0 times). Nonterminal symbols start with an upper-case letter (e.g., Statement). Terminal symbols either start with a lower-case letter (e.g., ident), or are written all in upper-case letters (e.g., BEGIN), or are denoted by strings (e.g., ":=").

A.3   Vocabulary and Representation

The representation of (terminal) symbols in terms of characters is defined using the ASCII set. Symbols are identifiers, numbers, strings, operators, and delimiters. The following lexical rules must be observed: Blanks and line breaks must not occur within symbols (except blanks in strings). They are ignored unless they are essential to separate two consecutive symbols. Upper-case and lower-case letters are considered distinct.

1. *Identifiers* are sequences of letters and digits. The first character must be a letter.

    ident = letter {letter | digit}.

    Examples: x   Scan   Oberon2   GetSymbol   firstLetter

2. *Numbers* are (unsigned) integer or real constants. The type of an integer constant is the minimal type to which the constant value belongs (see A.6.1). If the constant is specified with the suffix H, the representation is hexadecimal; otherwise it is decimal.

    A real number always contains a decimal point. Optionally it may also contain a decimal scale factor. The letter E (or D) means "times ten to the power of". A real number is of type REAL, unless it has a scale factor containing the letter D, in which case it is of type LONGREAL.

number	= integer	real.
integer	= digit {digit}	digit {hexDigit} "H".
real	= digit {digit} "." {digit} [ScaleFactor].
ScaleFactor	= ("E"	"D") ["+"	"-"] digit {digit}.
hexDigit	= digit	"A"	"B"	"C"	"D"	"E"	"F".
digit	= "0"	"1"	"2"	"3"	"4"	"5"	"6"	"7"	"8"	"9".

    Examples:

1991	INTEGER	1991
0DH	SHORTINT	13
12.3	REAL	12.3
4.567E8	REAL	456700000
0.57712566D-6	LONGREAL	0.00000057712566

3. *Character constants* are denoted by the ordinal number of the character in hexadecimal notation followed by the letter X.

    character = digit {hexDigit} "X".

4. *Strings* are sequences of characters enclosed in single (') or double (") quotation marks. The opening quotation mark must be the same as the closing one and must not occur within the string. The number of characters in a string is called its *length*. A string of length 1 can be used wherever a character constant is allowed and vice versa.

    string = ' " ' {char} ' " ' | " ' " {char} " ' ".

    Examples: "Oberon-2"   "Don't worry!"   "x"

5. *Operators and delimiters* are the special characters, character pairs, or reserved words listed below. The reserved words consist exclusively of capital letters and cannot be used as identifiers.

+	:=	ARRAY	IMPORT	RETURN
-	^	BEGIN	IN	THEN
*	=	BY	IS	TO
/	#	CASE	LOOP	TYPE
~	<	CONST	MOD	UNTIL
&	>	DIV	MODULE	VAR
.	<=	DO	NIL	WHILE
,	>=	ELSE	OF	WITH
;	..	ELSIF	OR	
|	:	END	POINTER	
(	)	EXIT	PROCEDURE	
[	]	FOR	RECORD	
{	}	IF	REPEAT	

6. *Comments* may be inserted between any two symbols in a program. They are arbitrary character sequences opened by the bracket (* and closed by *). Comments may be nested. They do not affect the meaning of a program.

A.4   Declarations and Scope Rules

Every identifier occurring in a program must be introduced by a declaration unless it is a predeclared identifier. Declarations also specify certain permanent properties of an object, such as whether it is a constant, a type, a variable, or a procedure. The identifier is then used to refer to the associated object.

The *scope* of an object x extends textually from the point of its declaration to the end of the *block* (module, procedure, or record) to which the declaration belongs and hence to which the object is *local*. It excludes the scopes of objects with the same name that are declared in nested blocks. The scope rules are:

1. No identifier may denote more than one object within a given scope (i.e., no identifier may be declared twice in a block).
2. An object may only be referenced within its scope.
3. A type T of the form POINTER TO $T1$ (see A.6.4) can be declared before the scope of $T1$. In this case, the declaration of $T1$ must follow in the same block to which T is local.
4. Identifiers denoting record fields (see A.6.3) or type-bound procedures (see A.10.2) are valid in record designators only.

An identifier declared in a module block may be followed by an export mark (an asterisk or a minus sign) in its declaration to indicate that it is exported. An identifier x exported by a module M may be used in other modules if they import M (see A.11). The identifier is then denoted as $M.x$ in these modules and is called a *qualified identifier*. Identifiers marked with a minus in their declaration are *read-only* in importing modules.

```
Qualident    = [ident "."] ident.
IdentDef     = ident [" * " | " - "].
```

The following identifiers are predeclared; their meaning is defined in the indicated sections:

ABS	(A.10.3)	LEN	(A.10.3)
ASH	(A.10.3)	LONG	(A.10.3)
BOOLEAN	(A.6.1)	LONGINT	(A.6.1)
CAP	(A.10.3)	LONGREAL	(A.6.1)
CHAR	(A.6.1)	MAX	(A.10.3)
CHR	(A.10.3)	MIN	(A.10.3)
COPY	(A.10.3)	NEW	(A.10.3)
DEC	(A.10.3)	ODD	(A.10.3)
ENTIER	(A.10.3)	ORD	(A.10.3)
EXCL	(A.10.3)	REAL	(A.6.1)
FALSE	(A.6.1)	SET	(A.6.1)
HALT	(A.10.3)	SHORT	(A.10.3)
INC	(A.10.3)	SHORTINT	(A.6.1)
INCL	(A.10.3)	SIZE	(A.10.3)
INTEGER	(A.6.1)	TRUE	(A.6.1)

A.5 Constant Declarations

A constant declaration associates an identifier with a constant value.

```
ConstantDeclaration  = IdentDef "=" ConstExpression.
ConstExpression      = Expression.
```

A constant expression is an expression that can be evaluated by a mere textual scan without actually executing the program. Its operands are constants (A.8) or predeclared functions (A.10.3) that can be evaluated at compile time. Examples of constant declarations are:

```
N = 100
limit = 2*N - 1
fullSet = {MIN(SET) .. MAX(SET)}
```

A.6 Type Declarations

A data type determines the set of values that variables of that type may assume, and the operators that are applicable. A type declaration associates an identifier with a type. In the case of structured types (arrays and records) it also defines the structure of variables of this type.

```
TypeDeclaration = IdentDef "=" Type.
Type = Qualident I ArrayType I RecordType I PointerType I ProcedureType.
```

Examples:

```
Table = ARRAY N OF REAL

Tree = POINTER TO Node
Node =  RECORD
    key : INTEGER;
    left, right: Tree
END

CenterTree = POINTER TO CenterNode
CenterNode = RECORD (Node)
    width: INTEGER;
    subnode: Tree
END

Function = PROCEDURE(x: INTEGER): INTEGER
```

A.6.1 Basic Types

The basic types are denoted by predeclared identifiers. The associated operators are defined in A.8.2 and the predeclared function procedures in A.10.3. The values of the given basic types are the following:

```
BOOLEAN     truth values TRUE and FALSE
CHAR        characters of the extended ASCII set (0X .. 0FFX)
SHORTINT    integers between MIN(SHORTINT) and MAX(SHORTINT)
INTEGER     integers between MIN(INTEGER) and MAX(INTEGER)
LONGINT     integers between MIN(LONGINT) and MAX(LONGINT)
REAL        real numbers between MIN(REAL) and MAX(REAL)
LONGREAL    real numbers betw. MIN(LONGREAL) and MAX(LONGREAL)
SET         sets of integers between 0 and MAX(SET)
```

Types SHORTINT, INTEGER, and LONGINT are *integer types*; types REAL and LONGREAL are *real types*; together they are called *numeric types*. They form a hierarchy: each larger type *includes* (the values of) the smaller types:

$$\text{LONGREAL} \supseteq \text{REAL} \supseteq \text{LONGINT} \supseteq \text{INTEGER} \supseteq \text{SHORTINT}$$

A.6.2 Array Types

An array is a structure consisting of a number of elements that are all of the same type, called the *element type*. The number of elements of an array is called its *length*. The elements of the array are designated by indices, which are integers between 0 and the length minus 1.

```
ArrayType  = ARRAY [Length {"," Length}] OF Type.
Length     = ConstExpression.
```

A type of the form

```
ARRAY L0, L1, ..., Ln OF T
```

is understood as an abbreviation of

```
ARRAY L0 OF
    ARRAY L1 OF
    ...
        ARRAY Ln OF T
```

Arrays declared without length are called *open arrays*. They are restricted to pointer base types (see A.6.4), element types of open array types, and formal parameter types (see A.10.1). Examples:

```
ARRAY 10, N OF INTEGER
ARRAY OF CHAR
```

A.6.3 Record Types

A record type is a structure consisting of a fixed number of elements, called *fields*, with possibly different types. The record type declaration specifies the name and type of each field. The scope of the field identifiers extends from the point of their declaration to the end of the record type, but they are also visible within designators referring to fields of record variables (see A.8.1). If a record type is exported, field identifiers that are to be visible outside the declaring module must be marked. They are called *public fields*; unmarked elements are called *private fields*.

```
RecordType  = RECORD ["("BaseType")"] FieldList {";" FieldList} END.
BaseType    = Qualident.
FieldList   = [IdentList ":" Type ].
```

Record types are extensible; i.e., a record type can be declared as an extension of another record type. In the example

```
T0 = RECORD x: INTEGER END
T1 = RECORD (T0) y: REAL END
```

T1 is a (direct) *extension* of *T0* and *T0* is the (direct) *base type* of *T1* (see A.12.1). An extended type *T1* consists of the fields of its base type and of the fields that are declared in *T1* (see A.6). Identifiers declared in the extension must be different from the identifiers declared in its base type(s). The following are examples of record type declarations:

```
RECORD
    day, month, year: INTEGER
END

RECORD
    name, firstname: ARRAY 32 OF CHAR;
    age: INTEGER;
    salary: REAL
END
```

A.6.4 Pointer Types

Variables of a pointer type P assume as values pointers to variables of some type T. T is called the *pointer base type* of P and must be a record or array type. Pointer types adopt the extension relation of their pointer base types: if a type $T1$ is an extension of T, and $P1$ is of type POINTER TO $T1$, then $P1$ is also an extension of P.

```
PointerType = POINTER TO Type.
```

If p is a variable of type P = POINTER TO T, a call of the predeclared procedure NEW(p) (see A.10.3) allocates a nameless variable of type T in free storage. If T is a record type or an array type with fixed length, the allocation has to be done with NEW(p); if T is an n-dimensional open array the allocation has to be done with NEW($p, e_0, ..., e_{n-1}$), where T is allocated with lengths given by the expressions $e_0, ..., e_{n-1}$. In either case a pointer to the allocated variable is assigned to p. p is of type P and the *referenced* variable $p\wedge$ (pronounced as *p-referenced*) is of type T.

Any pointer variable may assume the value NIL, which points to no variable at all. All pointer variables are initialized to NIL.

A.6.5 Procedure types

Variables of a procedure type T have a procedure (or NIL) as their value. If a procedure P is assigned to a variable of type T, the formal parameter lists (see A.10.1) of P and T must *match* (see A.12.1). P must not be a predeclared or type-bound procedure, nor may it be local to another procedure.

```
ProcedureType = PROCEDURE [FormalParameters].
```

A.7 Variable Declarations

Variable declarations introduce variables by defining an identifier and a data type for them.

```
VariableDeclaration = IdentList ":" Type.
```

Record and pointer variables have both a *static type* (the type with which they are declared—simply called their type) and a *dynamic type* (the type they assume at run time). For pointers and variable parameters of record type, the dynamic type may be an extension of their static type. The static type determines which fields of a record are accessible. The dynamic type is used to call type-bound procedures (see A.10.2).

The following are examples of variable declarations (refer to examples in A.6):

```
i, j, k: INTEGER
x, y: REAL
p, q: BOOLEAN
s: SET
F: Function
a: ARRAY 100 OF REAL
w: ARRAY 16 OF RECORD
      name: ARRAY 32 OF CHAR;
      count: INTEGER
   END
t, c: Tree
```

A.8 Expressions

Expressions denote rules of computation whereby constants and current values of variables are combined to compute other values by the application of operators and function procedures. Expressions consist of operands and operators. Parentheses may be used to express specific associations of operators and operands.

A.8.1 Operands

With the exception of set constructors and literal constants (numbers, character constants, or strings), operands are denoted by *designators*. A designator consists of an identifier referring to a constant, variable, or procedure. This identifier may possibly be qualified by a module identifier (see A.4 and A.11) and may be followed by selectors if the designated object is an element of a structure.

```
Designator      =  Qualident
                   {"." ident | "[" ExpressionList "]" | "^" | "(" Qualident ")"}.
ExpressionList  =  Expression {"," Expression}.
```

If a designates an array, then $a[e]$ denotes that element of a whose index is the current value of the expression e. The type of e must be an integer type. A designator of the form $a[e_0, e_1, ..., e_n]$ stands for

$a[e_0][e_1]...[e_n]$. If r designates a record, then $r.f$ denotes the field f of r or the procedure f bound to the dynamic type of r (see A.10.2). If p designates a pointer, $p^\wedge$ denotes the variable that is referenced by p. The designators $p^\wedge.f$ and $p^\wedge[e]$ may be abbreviated as $p.f$ and $p[e]$; i.e., record and array selectors imply dereferencing. If a or r are read-only, then $a[e]$ and $r.f$ are also read-only.

A *type guard* $v(T)$ asserts that the dynamic type of v is T (or an extension of T); i.e., program execution is aborted if the dynamic type of v is not T (or an extension of T). Within the designator, v is then regarded as having the static type T. The guard is applicable if

1. v is a variable parameter of record type or v is a pointer, and if
2. T is an extension of the static type of v.

If the designated object is a constant or a variable, then the designator refers to its current value. If it is a procedure, the designator refers to that procedure unless it is followed by a (possibly empty) parameter list, in which case it implies an activation of that procedure and stands for the value resulting from its execution. The actual parameters must correspond to the formal parameters as in proper procedure calls (see A.10.1).

The following are examples of designators (refer to examples in A.7):

```
i                      (INTEGER)
a[i]                   (REAL)
w[3].name[i]           (CHAR)
t.left.right           (Tree)
t(CenterTree).subnode  (Tree)
```

A.8.2 Operators

Four classes of operators with different precedences (binding strengths) are syntactically distinguished in expressions. The operator ~ has the highest precedence, followed by multiplication operators, addition operators, and relations. Operators of the same precedence associate from left to right. For example, x-y-z stands for $(x$-$y)$-z.

```
Expression         = SimpleExpression [Relation SimpleExpression].
SimpleExpression   = ["+" | "-"] Term {AddOperator Term}.
Term               = Factor {MulOperator Factor}.
Factor             = Designator [ActualParameters] | number | character
                     | string | NIL | Set | "(" Expression ")" | "~" Factor.
```

```
Set                  = "{" [Element {"," Element}] "}".
Element              = Expression [".." Expression].
ActualParameters     = "(" [ExpressionList] ")".
Relation             = "=" | "#" | "<" | "<=" | ">" | ">=" | IN | IS.
AddOperator          = "+" | "-" | OR.
MulOperator          = "*" | "/" | DIV | MOD | "&".
```

The available operators are listed in the following tables. Some operators are applicable to operands of various types, denoting different operations. In these cases, the actual operation is identified by the type of the operands. The operands must be *expression compatible* with respect to the operator (see A.12.1).

Logical operators

OR	logical disjunction	p OR q	$\equiv$ "if p then TRUE, else q end"
&	logical conjunction	p & q	$\equiv$ "if p then q, else FALSE end"
~	negation	~ p	$\equiv$ "not p"

These operators apply to BOOLEAN operands and yield a BOOLEAN result.

Arithmetic operators

+	sum
-	difference
*	product
/	real quotient
DIV	integer quotient
MOD	modulus

The operators +, -, *, and / apply to operands of numeric types. The type of the result is the type of that operand that includes the type of the other operand, except for division (/), where the result is the smallest real type that includes both operand types. When used as monadic operators, - denotes sign inversion and + denotes the identity operation. The operators DIV and MOD apply to integer operands only. They are related by the following formulas, defined for any x and positive divisor y:

```
x = (x DIV y) * y + (x MOD y)
0 ≤ (x MOD y) < y
```

Examples:

x	y	x DIV y	x MOD y
5	3	1	2
-5	3	-2	1

Set operators

+	union
-	difference $(x - y = x * (-y))$
*	intersection
/	symmetric set difference $(x / y = (x-y) + (y-x))$

Set operators apply to operands of type SET and yield a result of type SET. The monadic minus sign denotes the complement of x; i.e., $-x$ denotes the set of integers between 0 and MAX(SET) that are not elements of x.

A set constructor defines the value of a set by listing its elements between braces. The elements must be integers in the range 0..MAX(SET). A range $a..b$ denotes all integers in the interval $[a, b]$.

Relational operators

=	equal
#	unequal
<	less
<=	less or equal
>	greater
>=	greater or equal
IN	set membership
IS	type test

Relations yield a BOOLEAN result. The relations $=, \#, <, <=, >$, and $>=$ apply to numeric types, CHAR, (open) character arrays, and strings. The relations $=$ and $\#$ also apply to BOOLEAN and SET, as well as to pointer and procedure types (including the value NIL). x IN s stands for "x is an element of s". x must be of an integer type and s of type SET. v IS T stands for "the dynamic type of v is T (or an extension of T)" and is called a *type test*. It is applicable if

1. v is a variable parameter of record type or v is a pointer, and if
2. T is an extension of the static type of v.

The following are examples of expressions (refer to examples in A.7):

1991	INTEGER
i DIV 3	INTEGER
~p OR q	BOOLEAN
(i+j) * (i-j)	INTEGER
s - {8, 9, 13}	SET
i + x	REAL
a[i+j] * a[i-j]	REAL

```
(0<=i) & (i<100)          BOOLEAN
t.key = 0                 BOOLEAN
k IN {i..j-1}             BOOLEAN
w[i].name <= "John"       BOOLEAN
t IS CenterTree           BOOLEAN
```

A.9 Statements

Statements denote actions. There are elementary and structured statements. Elementary statements are not composed of any parts that are themselves statements. They are the assignment, the procedure call, the return, and the exit statement. Structured statements are composed of parts that are themselves statements. They are used to express sequencing and conditional, selective, and repetitive execution. A statement may also be empty, in which case it denotes no action. The empty statement is included in order to relax punctuation rules in statement sequences.

```
Statement =
    [ Assignment | ProcedureCall | IfStatement | CaseStatement |
    WhileStatement | RepeatStatement | ForStatement | LoopStatement |
    WithStatement | EXIT | RETURN [Expression] ].
```

A.9.1 Assignments

Assignments replace the current value of a variable with a new value specified by an expression. The expression must be *assignment compatible* with the variable (see A.12.1). The assignment operator is written as ":=" and pronounced as *becomes*.

```
Assignment = Designator ":=" Expression.
```

If an expression e of type T_e is assigned to a variable v of type T_v, the following happens:

1. If T_v and T_e are record types, only those fields of T_e are assigned which also belong to T_v (*projection*); the dynamic type of v must be the same as the static type of v and is not changed by the assignment.
2. If T_v and T_e are pointer types, the dynamic type of v becomes the dynamic type of e.
3. If T_v is ARRAY n OF CHAR and e is a string of length $m<n$, $v[i]$ becomes e_i for $i = 0..m-1$ and $v[m]$ becomes 0X.

The following are examples of assignments (refer to examples in A.7):

```
i := 0
p := i = j
x := i + 1
k := log2(i+j)
F := log2                    (* see A.10.1 *)
s := {2, 3, 5, 7, 11, 13}
a[i] := (x+y) * (x-y)
t.key := i
w[i+1].name := "John"
t := c
```

A.9.2 Procedure Calls

A procedure call activates a procedure. It may contain a list of actual parameters which replace the corresponding formal parameters defined in the procedure declaration (see A.10). The correspondence is established by the positions of the parameters in the actual and formal parameter lists. There are two kinds of parameters: *variable* and *value parameters*.

If a formal parameter is a variable parameter, the corresponding actual parameter must be a designator denoting a variable. If it denotes an element of a structured variable, the component selectors are evaluated when the formal/actual parameter substitution takes place, i.e., before the execution of the procedure. If a formal parameter is a value parameter, the corresponding actual parameter must be an expression. The value of this expression is assigned to the formal parameter (see also A.10.1).

```
ProcedureCall = Designator [ActualParameters].
```

Examples:

```
WriteInt(i*2+1)      (* see A.10.1 *)
t.Insert("John")     (* see A.11 *)
INC(w[k].count)
```

A.9.3 Statement Sequences

Statement sequences denote the sequence of actions specified by the component statements which are separated by semicolons.

```
StatementSequence = Statement {";" Statement}.
```

A.9.4 If Statements

```
IfStatement =   IF Expression THEN StatementSequence
                {ELSIF Expression THEN StatementSequence}
                [ELSE StatementSequence]
                END.
```

If statements specify the conditional execution of guarded statement sequences. The boolean expression preceding a statement sequence is called its *guard*. The guards are evaluated in sequence of occurrence until one evaluates to TRUE, whereafter its associated statement sequence is executed. If no guard is satisfied, the statement sequence following the symbol ELSE is executed, if there is one. Example:

```
IF (ch >= "A") & (ch <= "Z") THEN ReadIdentifier
ELSIF (ch >= "0") & (ch <= "9") THEN ReadNumber
ELSIF (ch = " ' ") OR (ch = ' " ') THEN ReadString
ELSE SpecialCharacter
END
```

A.9.5 Case Statements

Case statements specify the selection and execution of a statement sequence according to the value of an expression. First the case expression is evaluated; then that statement sequence is executed whose case label list contains the obtained value. The case expression must either be of an integer type that *includes* the types of all case labels, or both the case expression and the case labels must be of type CHAR. Case labels are constants, and no value may occur more than once. If the value of the expression does not match any label, the statement sequence following the symbol ELSE is selected, if there is one; otherwise the program is aborted.

```
CaseStatement   = CASE Expression OF Case {"|" Case}
                  [ELSE StatementSequence] END.
Case            = [CaseLabelList ":" StatementSequence].
CaseLabelList   = CaseLabels {"," CaseLabels}.
CaseLabels      = ConstExpression [".." ConstExpression].
```

Example:
```
CASE ch OF
    "A" .. "Z": ReadIdentifier
|   "0" .. "9": ReadNumber
|   " ' ", ' " ': ReadString
ELSE SpecialCharacter
END
```

A.9.6 While Statements

While statements specify the repeated execution of a statement sequence while the boolean expression (its *guard*) yields TRUE. The guard is checked before every execution of the statement sequence.

```
WhileStatement = WHILE Expression DO StatementSequence END.
```

Examples:

```
WHILE i > 0 DO i := i DIV 2; k := k + 1 END
WHILE (t # NIL) & (t.key # i) DO t := t.left END
```

A.9.7 Repeat Statements

A repeat statement specifies the repeated execution of a statement sequence until a condition specified by a boolean expression is satisfied. The statement sequence is executed at least once.

```
RepeatStatement = REPEAT StatementSequence UNTIL Expression.
```

A.9.8 For Statements

A for statement specifies the repeated execution of a statement sequence for a fixed number of times while a progression of values is assigned to an integer variable called the *control variable* of the for statement.

```
ForStatement =   FOR ident ":=" Expression TO Expression
                 [BY ConstExpression] DO StatementSequence END.
```

The statement

```
FOR v := low TO high BY step DO statements END
```

is equivalent to

```
v := low; temp := high;
IF step > 0 THEN
    WHILE v <= temp DO statements; v := v + step END
ELSE
    WHILE v >= temp DO statements; v := v + step END
END
```

low must be *assignment compatible* with v (see A.12.1), *high* must be *expression compatible* (i.e., comparable) with v, and *step* must be a nonzero constant expression of an integer type. If *step* is not specified, it is assumed to be 1. Examples:

```
FOR i := 0 TO 79 DO k := k + a[i] END
FOR i := 79 TO 1 BY -1 DO a[i] := a[i-1] END
```

A.9.9 Loop Statements

A loop statement specifies the repeated execution of a statement sequence. It is terminated upon execution of an exit statement within that sequence (see A.9.10).

```
LoopStatement = LOOP StatementSequence END.
```

Example:

```
LOOP
    ReadInt(i);
    IF i < 0 THEN EXIT END;
    WriteInt(i)
END
```

Loop statements are useful to express repetitions with several exit points or cases where the exit condition is in the middle of the repeated statement sequence.

A.9.10 Return and Exit Statements

A return statement indicates the termination of a procedure. It is denoted by the symbol RETURN, followed by an expression if the procedure is a function procedure. The type of the expression must be *assignment compatible* (see A.12.1) with the result type specified in the procedure heading (see A.10).

Function procedures require the presence of a return statement indicating the result value. In proper procedures, a return statement is implied by the end of the procedure body. Any explicit return statement therefore appears as an additional (probably exceptional) termination point.

An exit statement is denoted by the symbol EXIT. It specifies termination of the enclosing loop statement and continuation with the statement following that loop statement. Exit statements are contextually, although not syntactically, associated with the loop statement that contains them.

A.9.11 With Statements

With statements execute a statement sequence depending on the result of a type test and apply a type guard to every occurrence of the tested variable within this statement sequence.

```
WithStatement  = WITH Guard DO StatementSequence
    {"|" Guard DO StatementSequence}
    [ELSE StatementSequence] END.
Guard = Qualident ":" Qualident.
```

If v is a variable parameter of record type or a pointer variable, and if it is of a static type $T0$, the statement

```
WITH v: T1 DO S1 | v: T2 DO S2 ELSE S3 END
```

has the following meaning: if the dynamic type of v is $T1$, then the statement sequence $S1$ is executed, where v is regarded as if it had the static type $T1$; else if the dynamic type of v is $T2$, then $S2$ is executed, where v is regarded as if it had the static type $T2$; else $S3$ is executed. $T1$ and $T2$ must be extensions of $T0$. If no type test is satisfied and if an else clause is missing, the program is aborted. Example:

```
WITH t: CenterTree DO i := t.width; c := t.subnode END
```

A.10 Procedure Declarations

A procedure declaration consists of a *procedure heading* and a *procedure body*. The heading specifies the procedure identifier and the *formal parameters*. For type-bound procedures it also specifies the *receiver* parameter. The body contains declarations and statements. The procedure identifier is repeated at the end of the procedure declaration.

There are two kinds of procedures: *proper procedures* and *function procedures*. The latter are activated by a function designator as a constituent of an expression and yield a result that is an operand of the expression. Proper procedures are activated by a procedure call. A procedure is a function procedure if its formal parameters specify a result type. The body of a function procedure must contain a return statement that defines its result.

All constants, variables, types, and procedures declared within a procedure body are *local* to the procedure. Since procedures may be declared as local objects, too, procedure declarations may be nested. The call of a procedure within its declaration implies recursive activation.

Objects declared in the environment of the procedure are also visible in those parts of the procedure in which they are not concealed by locally declared objects with the same name.

```
ProcedureDeclaration  =  ProcedureHeading ";" ProcedureBody ident.
ProcedureHeading      =  PROCEDURE [Receiver] IdentDef
                         [FormalParameters].
ProcedureBody         =  DeclarationSequence
                         [BEGIN StatementSequence] END.
DeclarationSequence   =  {CONST {ConstantDeclaration ";"}
                         | TYPE {TypeDeclaration ";"}
                         | VAR {VariableDeclaration ";"} }
                         {ProcedureDeclaration ";"
                         | ForwardDeclaration ";"}.
ForwardDeclaration    =  PROCEDURE " ^ " [Receiver] IdentDef
                         [FormalParameters].
```

If a procedure declaration specifies a receiver parameter, the procedure is considered to be bound to a type (see A.10.2). A *forward declaration* serves to allow forward references to a procedure whose actual declaration appears later in the text. The formal parameter lists of the forward declaration and the actual declaration must *match* (see A.12.1).

A.10.1 Formal Parameters

Formal parameters are identifiers declared in the formal parameter list of a procedure. They correspond to actual parameters specified in the procedure call. The correspondence between formal and actual parameters is established when the procedure is called. There are two kinds of parameters, *value* and *variable* parameters, indicated in the formal parameter list by the absence or presence of the keyword VAR. Value parameters are local variables to which the value of the corresponding actual parameter is assigned as an initial value. Variable parameters correspond to actual parameters that are variables, and they stand for these variables. The scope of a formal parameter extends from its declaration to the end of the procedure block in which it is declared. A function procedure without parameters must have an empty parameter list. It must be called by a function designator whose actual parameter list is empty, too. The result type of a function procedure can be neither a record nor an array.

```
FormalParameters    = "(" [FPSection {";" FPSection}] ")" [":" Qualident].
FPSection           = [VAR] ident {"," ident} ":" Type.
```

Let T_f be the type of a formal parameter f (not an open array) and T_a the type of the corresponding actual parameter a. For variable parameters, T_a must be the *same* as T_f, or T_f must be a record type and T_a an extension of T_f. For value parameters, a must be *assignment compatible* with f (see A.12.1).

If T_f is an open array, then a must be *array compatible* with f (see A.12.1). The lengths of f are taken from a. The following are examples of procedure declarations:

```
PROCEDURE ReadInt(VAR x: INTEGER);
    VAR i: INTEGER; ch: CHAR;
BEGIN i := 0; Read(ch);
    WHILE ("0" <= ch) & (ch <= "9") DO
        i := 10*i + (ORD(ch)-ORD("0")); Read(ch)
    END;
    x := i
END ReadInt

PROCEDURE WriteInt(x: INTEGER); (*0 <= x <100000*)
    VAR i: INTEGER; buf: ARRAY 5 OF INTEGER;
BEGIN i := 0;
    REPEAT buf[i] := x MOD 10; x := x DIV 10; INC(i) UNTIL x = 0;
    REPEAT DEC(i); Write(CHR(buf[i] + ORD("0"))) UNTIL i = 0
END WriteInt

PROCEDURE WriteString(s: ARRAY OF CHAR);
    VAR i: INTEGER;
BEGIN i := 0;
    WHILE (i < LEN(s)) & (s[i] # 0X) DO Write(s[i]); INC(i) END
END WriteString;

PROCEDURE log2(x: INTEGER): INTEGER;
    VAR y: INTEGER; (*assume x>0*)
BEGIN
    y := 0; WHILE x > 1 DO x := x DIV 2; INC(y) END;
    RETURN y
END log2
```

A.10.2 Type-Bound Procedures

Globally declared procedures may be associated with a record type declared in the same module. The procedures are said to be *bound* to the record type. The binding is expressed by the type of the *receiver* in the heading of a procedure declaration. The receiver may be either a variable parameter of record type T or a value parameter of type POINTER TO T (where T is a record type). The procedure is bound to the type T and is considered local to it.

```
ProcedureHeading  = PROCEDURE [Receiver] IdentDef [FormalParameters].
Receiver          = "(" [VAR] ident ":" ident ")".
```

If a procedure P is bound to a type $T0$, it is implicitly also bound to any type $T1$ that is an extension of $T0$. However, a procedure P ' (with the same name as P) may be explicitly bound to $T1$, in which case it overrides the binding of P. P ' is considered a *redefinition* of P for $T1$. The formal parameters of P and P ' must *match* (see A.12.1). If P and $T1$ are exported (see A. 4), P ' must be exported, too.

If v is a designator and P is a type-bound procedure, then $v.P$ denotes that procedure P that is bound to the dynamic type of v (*dynamic binding*). Note that this may be a different procedure than the one bound to the static type of v. v is passed to P's receiver according to the parameter passing rules specified in A.10.1.

If r is a receiver parameter declared with type T, $r.P \wedge$ denotes the (redefined) procedure P bound to the base type of T.

In a forward declaration of a type-bound procedure, the receiver parameter must be of the *same* type as in the actual procedure declaration. The formal parameter lists of both declarations must *match* (A.12.1).

Examples:

```
PROCEDURE (t: Tree) Insert (node: Tree);
    VAR p, father: Tree;
BEGIN
    p := t;
    REPEAT father := p;
        IF node.key = p.key THEN RETURN END;
        IF node.key < p.key THEN p := p.left ELSE p := p.right END
    UNTIL p = NIL;
    IF node.key < father.key THEN father.left := node
    ELSE father.right := node
    END;
    node.left := NIL; node.right := NIL
END Insert;

PROCEDURE (t: CenterTree) Insert (node: Tree);  (*redefinition*)
BEGIN
    WriteInt(node(CenterTree).width);
    t.Insert^ (node)  (* calls the Insert procedure bound to Tree *)
END Insert;
```

A.10.3 Predeclared Procedures

The following table lists the predeclared procedures. Some are generic procedures, i.e., they apply to several types of operands. v stands for a variable, x and n for expressions, and T for a type.

Function procedures

Name	Argument type	result type	Function
ABS(x)	numeric type	type of x	absolute value
ASH(x, n)	x, n: integer type	LONGINT	arithmetic shift ($x * 2^n$)
CAP(x)	CHAR	CHAR	x is letter: corresp.onding capital letter
CHR(x)	integer type	CHAR	character with ordinal number x
ENTIER(x)	real type	LONGINT	largest integer not greater than x
LEN(v, n)	v: array; n: integer constant	LONGINT	length of v in dimension n (first dim. = 0)
LEN(v)	v: array	LONGINT	equivalent to LEN(v, 0)
LONG(x)	SHORTINT	INTEGER	identity
	INTEGER	LONGINT	identity
	REAL	LONGREAL	identity
MAX(T)	T = basic type	T	maximum value of type T
	T = SET	INTEGER	maximum element of a set
MIN(T)	T = basic type	T	minimum value of type T
	T = SET	INTEGER	0
ODD(x)	integer type	BOOLEAN	x MOD 2 = 1
ORD(x)	CHAR	INTEGER	ordinal number of x
SHORT(x)	LONGINT	INTEGER	identity
	INTEGER	SHORTINT	identity
	LONGREAL	REAL	identity (truncation possible)
SIZE(T)	any type	integer type	number of bytes required by T

Proper procedures

Name	Argument types	Function
COPY(x, v)	x: char. array, string; v: char. array	$v := x$
DEC(v)	integer type	$v := v - 1$
DEC(v, n)	v, n: integer type	$v := v - n$
EXCL(v, x)	v: SET; x: integer type	$v := v - \{x\}$
HALT(x)	integer constant	terminate program
INC(v)	integer type	$v := v + 1$
INC(v, n)	v, n: integer type	$v := v + n$
INCL(v, x)	v: SET; x: integer type	$v := v + \{x\}$
NEW(v)	pointer to record or fixed array	allocate $v \wedge$
NEW($v, x_0, \ldots, x_n$)	v: pointer to open array; x_i: int. type	allocate $v \wedge$ with lengths $x_0 .. x_n$

COPY allows the assignment between (open) character arrays with different types. If necessary, the source is shortened to the target length minus one. The target is always terminated by the character 0X. In HALT(x), the interpretation of x is left to the underlying system implementation.

A.11 Modules

A module is a collection of declarations of constants, types, variables, and procedures, together with a sequence of statements for the purpose of assigning initial values to the variables. A module constitutes a text that is compilable as a unit.

```
Module     = MODULE ident ";" [ImportList] DeclarationSequence
             [BEGIN StatementSequence] END ident ".".
ImportList = IMPORT Import {"," Import} ";".
Import     = [ident ":="] ident.
```

The import list specifies the names of the imported modules. If a module A is imported by a module M and A exports an identifier x, then x is referred to as $A.x$ within M. If A is imported as $B := A$, the object x must be referenced as $B.x$. This allows short alias names in qualified identifiers. Identifiers that are to be exported (i.e., that are to be visible in client modules) must be marked by an export mark in their declaration (see A. 4).

The statement sequence following the symbol BEGIN is executed when the module is added to a system (loaded), which is done after the imported modules have been loaded. It follows that cyclic import of modules is illegal. Individual (parameterless and exported) procedures can be activated from the system, and these procedures serve as *commands* (see A.12.4).

```
MODULE Trees;

    IMPORT Texts, Oberon;
    (* exports: Tree, Node, Insert, Search, Write, Init *)
    (* exports read-only: Node.name *)

    TYPE
        Tree* = POINTER TO Node;
        Node* = RECORD
            name-: POINTER TO ARRAY OF CHAR;
            left, right: Tree
        END;

    VAR w: Texts.Writer;
```

```
PROCEDURE (t: Tree) Insert* (name: ARRAY OF CHAR);
   VAR p, father: Tree;
BEGIN p := t;
   REPEAT father := p;
      IF name = p.name^ THEN RETURN END;
      IF name < p.name^ THEN p := p.left ELSE p := p.right END
   UNTIL p = NIL;
   NEW(p); p.left := NIL; p.right := NIL;
   NEW(p.name, LEN(name)+1); COPY(name, p.name^);
   IF name < father.name^ THEN father.left := p
   ELSE father.right := p
   END
END Insert;

PROCEDURE (t: Tree) Search* (name: ARRAY OF CHAR): Tree;
   VAR p: Tree;
BEGIN p := t;
   WHILE (p # NIL) & (name # p.name^) DO
      IF name < p.name^ THEN p := p.left ELSE p := p.right END
   END;
   RETURN p
END Search;

PROCEDURE (t: Tree) Write*;
BEGIN
   IF t.left # NIL THEN t.left.Write END;
   Texts.WriteString(w, t.name^); Texts.WriteLn(w);
   Texts.Append(Oberon.Log, w.buf);
   IF t.right # NIL THEN t.right.Write END
END Write;

PROCEDURE Init* (VAR t: Tree);
   VAR t: Tree;
BEGIN
   NEW(t.name, 1); t.name[0] := 0X; t.left := NIL; t.right := NIL
END Init;

BEGIN Texts.OpenWriter(w)
END Trees.
```

A.12 Appendices to the Language Definition

A.12.1 Definition of Terms

Integer types	SHORTINT, INTEGER, LONGINT
Real types	REAL, LONGREAL
Numeric types	*integer types*, *real types*

Same types
Two variables a and b with types T_a and T_b are of the *same type* if
1. T_a and T_b are both denoted by the same type identifier, or
2. T_a is declared to equal T_b in a type declaration of the form $T_a = T_b$, or
3. a and b appear in the same identifier list in a variable, record field, or formal parameter declaration and are not open arrays.

Equal types
Two types T_a and T_b are *equal* if
1. T_a and T_b are the *same* type, or
2. T_a and T_b are open array types with *equal* element types, or
3. T_a and T_b are procedure types whose formal parameter lists *match*.

Type inclusion
Numeric types *include* (the values of) smaller numeric types according to the following hierarchy:

$$\text{LONGREAL} \supseteq \text{REAL} \supseteq \text{LONGINT} \supseteq \text{INTEGER} \supseteq \text{SHORTINT}$$

Type extension (base type)
Given a type declaration $T_b = \text{RECORD} (T_a) \ldots \text{END}$, T_b is a *direct extension* of T_a, and T_a is a *direct base type* of T_b. A type T_b is an *extension* of a type T_a (T_a is a *base type* of T_b) if
1. T_a and T_b are the *same* types, or
2. T_b is a direct extension of an extension of T_a
If $P_a = \text{POINTER TO } T_a$ and $P_b = \text{POINTER TO } T_b$, P_b is an extension of P_a (P_a is a base type of P_b) if T_b is an extension of T_a.

Assignment compatibility

An expression e of type T_e is *assignment compatible* with a variable v of type T_v if one of the following conditions holds:

1. T_e and T_v are the *same* type.
2. T_e and T_v are numeric types and T_v includes T_e.
3. T_e and T_v are record types and T_e is an extension of T_v and the dynamic type of v is T_v .
4. T_e and T_v are pointer types and T_e is an extension of T_v.
5. T_v is a pointer or a procedure type and e is NIL.
6. T_v is ARRAY n OF CHAR, e is a string constant with m characters, and $m < n$.
7. T_v is a procedure type and e is the name of a procedure whose formal parameters *match* those of T_v.

Expression compatibility

For a given operator, the types of its operands are expression compatible if they conform to the following table (which also shows the result type of the expression). Type $T1$ must be an extension of type $T0$:

Operator	1st Operand	2nd Operand	Result Type
+ - *	numeric	numeric	smallest numeric type including both opd. types
/	numeric	numeric	smallest real type including both opd. types
DIV MOD	integer	integer	smallest integer type including both opd. types
+ - * /	SET	SET	SET
OR & ~	BOOLEAN	BOOLEAN	BOOLEAN
= # < <= > >=	numeric	numeric	BOOLEAN
	CHAR	CHAR	BOOLEAN
	character array, string	character array, string	BOOLEAN
= #	BOOLEAN	BOOLEAN	BOOLEAN
	SET	SET	BOOLEAN
	NIL, pointer type $T0$ or $T1$	NIL, pointer type $T0$ or $T1$	BOOLEAN
	NIL, procedure type T	NIL, procedure type T	BOOLEAN
IN	integer	SET	BOOLEAN
IS	type $T0$	type $T1$	BOOLEAN

Array compatibility

An actual parameter a of type T_a is *array compatible* with a formal parameter f of type T_f if

1. T_f and T_a are the *same* type, or

2. T_f is an open array, T_a is any array, and their element types are *array compatible*, or
3. T_f is ARRAY OF CHAR and a is a string.

Matching formal parameter lists

Two formal parameter lists *match* if

1. they have the same number of parameters, and
2. they have either the *same* function result type or none, and
3. parameters at corresponding positions have *equal* types, and
4. parameters at corresponding positions are both either value or variable parameters.

A.12.2 Syntax of Oberon-2

```
Module        = MODULE ident ";" [ImportList] DeclSeq
                [BEGIN StatSeq] END ident ".".
ImportList    = IMPORT [ident ":="] ident {"," [ident ":="] ident} ";".
DeclSeq       = { CONST {IdentDef "=" ConstExpr ";" }
                | TYPE {IdentDef "=" Type ";"}
                | VAR {IdentList ":" Type";"}}
                {ProcDecl ";" | ForwardDecl ";"}.
ProcDecl      = PROCEDURE [Receiver] IdentDef [FormalPars] ";" DeclSeq
                [BEGIN StatSeq] END ident.
ForwardDecl   = PROCEDURE "^" [Receiver] IdentDef [FormalPars].
FormalPars    = "(" [FPSection {";" FPSection}] ")" [":" Qualident].
FPSection     = [VAR] ident {"," ident} ":" Type.
Receiver      = "(" [VAR] ident ":" ident ")".
Type          = Qualident
                | ARRAY [ConstExpr {"," ConstExpr}] OF Type
                | RECORD ["("Qualident")"] FieldList {";" FieldList} END
                | POINTER TO Type
                | PROCEDURE [FormalPars].
FieldList     = [IdentList ":" Type].
StatSeq       = Statement {";" Statement}.
Statement     = [  Designator ":=" Expr
                |  Designator ["(" [ExprList] ")"]
                |  IF Expr THEN StatSeq {ELSIF Expr THEN StatSeq}
                   [ELSE StatSeq] END
                |  CASE Expr OF Case {"|" Case} [ELSE StatSeq] END
                |  WHILE Expr DO StatSeq END
                |  REPEAT StatSeq UNTIL Expr
                |  FOR ident ":=" Expr TO Expr [BY ConstExpr] DO StatSeq END
                |  LOOP StatSeq END
                |  WITH Guard DO StatSeq {"|" Guard DO StatSeq}
                   [ELSE StatSeq] END
                |  EXIT
                |  RETURN [Expr]  ].
Case          = [CaseLabels {"," CaseLabels} ":" StatSeq].
CaseLabels    = ConstExpr [".." ConstExpr].
Guard         = Qualident ":" Qualident.
ConstExpr     = Expr.
Expr          = SimpleExpr [Relation SimpleExpr].
SimpleExpr    = ["+" | "-"] Term {AddOp Term}.
Term          = Factor {MulOp Factor}.
Factor        = Designator ["(" [ExprList] ")"] | number | character
                | string | NIL | Set | "(" Expr ")" | " ~ " Factor.
Set           = {" [Element {"," Element}] "}".
Element       = Expr [".." Expr].
Relation      = "=" | "#" | "<" | "<=" | ">" | ">=" | IN | IS.
AddOp         = "+" | "-" | OR.
MulOp         = " * " | "/" | DIV | MOD | "&".
Designator    = Qualident {"." ident | "[" ExprList "]" | " ^ "  | "(" Qualident ")"}.
ExprList      = Expr {"," Expr}.
IdentList     = IdentDef {"," IdentDef}.
Qualident     = [ident "."] ident.
IdentDef      = ident [" * " | "-"].
```

A.12.3 The Module SYSTEM

The module SYSTEM contains certain types and procedures that are necessary to implement *low-level* operations particular to a given computer and/or operating system. These include, for example, facilities for accessing devices that are controlled by the computer, and facilities to break the type compatibility rules otherwise imposed by the language definition.

It is strongly recommended that the use of the module SYSTEM be restricted to specific modules (called *low-level* modules). Such modules are inherently nonportable and unsafe, but easily recognized due to the identifier SYSTEM appearing in their import list. The following specifications hold for the implementation of Oberon-2 on the Ceres computer.

Module SYSTEM exports a type BYTE with the following characteristics: Variables of type CHAR or SHORTINT can be assigned to variables of type BYTE. If a formal variable parameter is of type ARRAY OF BYTE, then the corresponding actual parameter may be of any type.

Another type exported by module SYSTEM is the type PTR. Variables of any pointer type may be assigned to variables of type PTR. If a formal variable parameter is of type PTR, the corresponding actual parameter may be any pointer type. If the actual parameter is a pointer to a record type T the address of the type descriptor of T is passed as the actual parameter.

The procedures contained in module SYSTEM are listed in the following tables. Most of them correspond to single instructions compiled as in-line code. For details, the reader is referred to the processor manual. v stands for a variable, x, y, a, and n for expressions, and T for a type.

Function procedures

Name	Argument types	Result type	Function
ADR(v)	any	LONGINT	address of variable v
BIT(a, n)	a: LONGINT; n: *integer*	BOOLEAN	bit n of Mem[a]
CC(n)	*integer* constant	BOOLEAN	condition n ($0 \leq n \leq 15$)
LSH(x, n)	x: *integer*, CHAR, BYTE; n: *integer*	type of x	logical shift
ROT(x, n)	x: *integer*, CHAR, BYTE; n: *integer*	type of x	rotation
VAL(T, x)	T, x: any type	T	x interpreted as of type T

Proper procedures

Name	Argument types	Function
GET(a, v)	a: LONGINT;	$v := M[a]$
	v: any basic type, pointer, procedure type	
PUT(a, x)	a: LONGINT;	$M[a] := x$
	x: any basic type, pointer, procedure type	
GETREG(n, v)	n: *integer* constant;	$v := \text{Register}_n$
	v: any basic type, pointer, procedure type	
PUTREG(n, x)	n: *integer* constant;	$\text{Register}_n := v$
	x: any basic type, pointer, procedure type	
MOVE($a0$, $a1$, n)	$a0$, $a1$: LONGINT; n: *integer*	$M[a1..a1 +n\text{-}1] := M[a0..a0 +n\text{-}1]$
NEW(v, n)	v: any pointer; n: *integer*	allocate n bytes of memory; assign its address to v

A.12.4 The Oberon Environment

Oberon-2 programs usually run in an environment that provides *command activation, garbage collection, dynamic loading* of modules, and certain *run-time data structures.* Although not part of the language, this environment contributes to the power of Oberon-2 and is to some degree implied by the language definition. This section describes the essential features of a typical Oberon environment and provides implementation hints. More details can be found in [WiG92], [Rei91], and [PHT91].

Commands

A command is any parameterless procedure P that is exported from a module M. It is denoted by $M.P$ and can be activated under this name from the shell of the operating system. In Oberon, a user invokes commands instead of programs or modules. This gives the user a finer grain of control and allows modules with multiple entry points. When a command $M.P$ is invoked, the module M is dynamically loaded unless it is already in memory and the procedure P is executed. When P terminates, M remains loaded. All global variables and data structures that can be reached from global pointer variables in M retain their values. When P (or another command of M) is invoked again, it may continue to use these values.

The following module demonstrates the use of commands. It implements an abstract data structure *Counter* that encapsulates a counter variable and provides commands to increment and print its value.

```
MODULE Counter;
IMPORT Texts, Oberon;

VAR
    counter: LONGINT;
    w: Texts.Writer;

PROCEDURE Add*; (*takes a numeric argument from the command line*)
    VAR s: Texts.Scanner;
BEGIN
    Texts.OpenScanner(s, Oberon.Par.text, Oberon.Par.pos);
    Texts.Scan(s);
    IF s.class = Texts.Int THEN INC(counter, s.i) END
END Add;

PROCEDURE Write*;
BEGIN
    Texts.WriteInt(w, counter, 5); Texts.WriteLn(w);
    Texts.Append(Oberon.Log, w.buf)
END Write;

BEGIN counter := 0; Texts.OpenWriter(w)
END Counter.
```

The user may execute the following two commands:

Counter.Add   n   adds value *n* to variable *counter*
Counter.Write   writes current value of *counter* to screen

Since commands are parameterless, they have to get their arguments from the operating system. In general, commands are free to take arguments from anywhere (e.g., from the text following the command, from the most recent selection, or from a marked viewer). The command *Add* uses a scanner (a data type provided by the Oberon system) to read the value that follows it on the command line.

When *Counter.Add* is invoked for the first time, the module *Counter* is loaded and its body is executed. Every call of *Counter.Add n* increments the variable *counter* by *n*. Every call of *Counter.Write* writes the current value of *counter* to the screen.

Since a module remains loaded after the execution of its commands, there must be an explicit way to unload it (e.g., when the user wants to substitute a recompiled version for the loaded version.) The Oberon system provides a command to do that.

Dynamic Loading of Modules

A loaded module may invoke a command of a still unloaded module by calling the loader and passing the name of the desired command as a parameter. The specified module is then dynamically loaded and the designated command is executed. Dynamic loading allows the user to start a program as a small set of basic modules and to extend it by adding further modules at run time as the need becomes evident.

A module $M0$ may cause the dynamic loading of a module $M1$ without importing it. $M1$ may of course import and use $M0$, but $M0$ need not know about the existence of $M1$. $M1$ can be a module that is designed and implemented long after $M0$.

Garbage Collection

In Oberon-2, the predeclared procedure NEW is used to allocate data blocks in free memory. There is, however, no way to explicitly dispose of an allocated block. Rather, the Oberon environment uses a *garbage collector* to find the blocks that are not referenced by a pointer any more and to make them available for allocation again.

A garbage collector frees a programmer from the nontrivial task of deallocating data structures correctly and thus helps to avoid errors. However, it requires information about dynamic data at run time.

Browser

The interface of a module (the declaration of the exported objects) is extracted from the module by a *browser*, which is a separate tool of the Oberon environment. For example, the browser produces the following interface of the module *Trees* from A.11.

```
DEFINITION Trees;
    TYPE
       Tree = POINTER TO Node;
       Node = RECORD
          name: POINTER TO ARRAY OF CHAR;
          PROCEDURE (t: Tree) Insert (name: ARRAY OF CHAR);
          PROCEDURE (t: Tree) Search (name: ARRAY OF CHAR): Tree;
          PROCEDURE (t: Tree) Write;
       END;
```

PROCEDURE Init (VAR t: Tree);
END Trees.

For a record type, the browser also collects all procedures bound to this type and shows their declaration in the record type declaration.

Run-Time Data Structures

Certain information about records has to be available at run time: The dynamic type of records is needed for type tests and type guards. A table with the addresses of the procedures bound to a record is needed for calling them using dynamic binding. Finally, the garbage collector needs information about the locations of pointers in dynamically allocated records. All that information is stored in *type descriptors*, of which there is one for every record type at run time. The following paragraphs show a possible implementation of type descriptors.

The dynamic type of a record corresponds to the address of its type descriptor. For dynamically allocated records, this address is stored in a *type tag*, which precedes the actual record data and is invisible to the programmer. If *t* is a variable of type *CenterTree* (see the example in A.6), Figure A.12.1 shows one possible implementation of the run-time data structures.

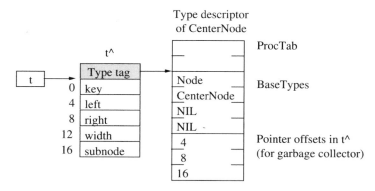

Fig. A.12.1 A variable *t* of type *CenterTree*, the record *t*^ of type *CenterNode*, and its type descriptor

Since both the table of procedure addresses and the table of pointer offsets must have a fixed offset from the type descriptor address, and since both may grow when the type is extended and further procedures and pointers are added, the tables are located at the opposite ends of the type descriptor and grow in different directions.

A type-bound procedure $t.P$ is called as $t.tag.ProcTab[Index_P]$. The procedure table index of every type-bound procedure is known at compile time. A type test v IS T is translated into $v.tag.BaseTypes[ExtensionLevel_T] = TypeDescrAdr_T$. Both the extension level of a record type and the address of its type descriptor are known at compile time. For example, the extension level of *Node* is 0 (it has no base type), and the extension level of *CenterNode* is 1.

B The Module *OS*

OS is a cover module for various constants, types, variables and procedures of the Oberon System that are used in examples throughout this book. It serves to keep the interface between the examples and the Oberon System small and permits us to avoid a description of the complete Oberon module library. (Interested readers are referred to [Rei91].)

```
DEFINITION OS;                                                              Interface of OS
    IMPORT Display, Files, Fonts; (*Oberon modules that are not explained here*)

    CONST
        right = 0; middle = 1; left = 2; (*mouse button codes*)
        ticks = 300; (*OS.Time returns the time in units of 1/ticks seconds*)

    TYPE
        File = Files.File;
        Font = Fonts.Font;
        Message = RECORD END; (*base type for all message records*)
        Object = POINTER TO ObjectDesc;
        Pattern = Display.Pattern;

        Rider = RECORD (Files.Rider) (*read/write position in a file*)         Rider
            PROCEDURE (VAR r: Rider) Set (f: Files.File; pos: LONGINT);
            PROCEDURE (VAR r: Rider) Read (VAR x: CHAR);
            PROCEDURE (VAR r: Rider) ReadString (VAR s: ARRAY OF CHAR);
            PROCEDURE (VAR r: Rider) ReadInt (VAR x: INTEGER);
            PROCEDURE (VAR r: Rider) ReadLInt (VAR x: LONGINT);
            PROCEDURE (VAR r: Rider) ReadObj (VAR x: Object);
            PROCEDURE (VAR r: Rider) ReadChars
                (VAR x: ARRAY OF CHAR; n: LONGINT);
            PROCEDURE (VAR r: Rider) Write (x: CHAR);
            PROCEDURE (VAR r: Rider) WriteString (s: ARRAY OF CHAR);
            PROCEDURE (VAR r: Rider) WriteInt (x: INTEGER);
            PROCEDURE (VAR r: Rider) WriteLInt (x: LONGINT);
            PROCEDURE (VAR r: Rider) WriteObj (x: Object);
            PROCEDURE (VAR r: Rider) WriteChars
                (VAR x: ARRAY OF CHAR; n: LONGINT);
        END;
        ObjectDesc = RECORD                                                    Object
```

```
                    PROCEDURE (x: Object) Load (VAR r: Rider);
                    PROCEDURE (x: Object) Store (VAR r: Rider);
                  END;

                  VAR
                    Caret-: Pattern;
                    screenH-, screenW-: INTEGER; (*screen height and width in pixels*)
```

Screen operations
```
                  PROCEDURE CopyBlock (sx, sy, w, h, dx, dy: INTEGER);
                  PROCEDURE FillBlock (x, y, w, h: INTEGER);
                  PROCEDURE EraseBlock (x, y, w, h: INTEGER);
                  PROCEDURE InvertBlock (x, y, w, h: INTEGER);
                  PROCEDURE DrawPattern (pat: Pattern; x, y: INTEGER);
                  PROCEDURE DrawCursor (x, y: INTEGER);
                  PROCEDURE FadeCursor;
```

Font operations
```
                  PROCEDURE DefaultFont (): Font;
                  PROCEDURE FontWithName (name: ARRAY OF CHAR): Font;
                  PROCEDURE GetCharMetric (f: Font; ch: CHAR;
                    VAR dx, x, y, w, h: INTEGER; VAR pat: Pattern);
```

Mouse and
keyboard
operations
```
                  PROCEDURE AvailChars (): INTEGER;
                  PROCEDURE ReadKey (VAR ch: CHAR);
                  PROCEDURE GetMouse (VAR buttons: SET; VAR x, y: INTEGER);
```

File operations
```
                  PROCEDURE NewFile (name: ARRAY OF CHAR): File;
                  PROCEDURE OldFile (name: ARRAY OF CHAR): File;
                  PROCEDURE Register (f: File);
                  PROCEDURE InitRider (VAR r: Rider);
```

Miscellaneous
```
                  PROCEDURE NameToObj (name: ARRAY OF CHAR; VAR obj: Object);
                  PROCEDURE Move (VAR fromBuf: ARRAY OF CHAR; from: LONGINT;
                    VAR toBuf: ARRAY OF CHAR; to, n: LONGINT);
                  PROCEDURE Time (): LONGINT;
                  PROCEDURE Call (command: ARRAY OF CHAR);

                  END OS.
```

Screen operations $CopyBlock\ (sx, sy, w, h, dx, dh)$

copies the rectangular screen area (sx, sy, w, h) to (dx, dy, w, h).

$FillBlock\ (x, y, w, h)$

fills the rectangular screen area (x, y, w, h).

$EraseBlock\ (x, y, w, h)$

deletes the rectangular screen area (x, y, w, h).

$InvertBlock\ (x, y, w, h)$

inverts the rectangular screen area (x, y, w, h).

$DrawPattern\ (pat, x, y)$

copies the rectangular bit pattern pat to the screen position with left bottom corner (x, y).

$DrawCursor\ (x, y)$
> moves the mouse pointer to position (x, y).

$FadeCursor$
> hides the mouse pointer.

$f := DefaultFont\ ()$ *Font operations*
> returns the standard font.

$f := FontWithName\ (n)$
> returns the font with the name n.

$GetCharMetric\ (fnt, ch, dx, x, y, w, h, pat)$
> returns the character metrics (x, y, w, h, dx) and the bit pattern
> pat of the character ch in font fnt. The meaning of the metrics is
> shown in Fig. 11.22.

$n := AvailChars\ ()$ *Mouse and*
> returns the number of characters in the keyboard buffer.   *keyboard*

$ReadKey\ (ch)$ *operations*
> reads and removes the next character ch from the keyboard
> buffer. If the buffer is empty, the method stalls until a cha-
> racter is typed in.

$GetMouse\ (b, x, y)$
> returns the mouse coordinates (x, y) relative to the lower left
> corner of the screen as well as the set b of pressed mouse
> buttons ($0 = right$, $1 = middle$, $2 = left$).

$f := NewFile\ (n)$ *File operations*
> creates a new (temporary) file f with name n and opens it.

$f := OldFile\ (n)$
> opens an existing file f with name n. If no such file exists, $f =$
> NIL.

$Register\ (f)$
> transforms the temporary file f created with $NewFile$ into a
> permanent file.

$InitRider\ (r)$
> initializes the rider r (see Section 8.3).

$r.Set\ (f, pos)$ *Methods of class*
> sets rider r to position pos in file f.   *Rider*

$r.Read\ (ch)$
> reads character ch from rider r.

$r.ReadInt\ (x)$
> reads integer x from rider r.

r.ReadLInt (x)
> reads long integer x from rider r.

r.ReadString (s)
> reads string s (stored in compressed form) from rider r.

r.ReadChars (buf, len)
> reads *len* characters from rider r into buffer *buf*.

r.ReadObj (obj)
> creates and reads an arbitrary object written with *WriteObj* and returns it in *obj* (see Section 8.3).

r.Write (ch)
> writes character *ch* to rider r.

r.WriteInt (x)
> writes integer x to rider r.

r.WriteLInt (x)
> writes long integer x to rider r.

r.WriteString (s)
> writes string s in compressed form to rider r.

r.WriteChars (buf, len)
> writes *len* characters from buffer *buf* to rider r.

r.WriteObj (obj)
> writes an arbitrary object *obj* to rider r (see Section 8.3).

Other operations *NameToObj (name, obj)*
> The parameter *name* is a string of the form "M.T". *NameToObj* creates a record of type *T* exported by module *M* and returns a pointer to it in *obj*. If the module or type name is incorrect or the created object is not assignment compatible with *obj*, NIL is returned.

Move (buf0, pos0, buf1, pos1, len)
> copies *len* bytes from *buf0[pos0]* to *buf1[pos1]*.

t := Time ()
> returns the elapsed time since system start in $1/ticks$ seconds (*ticks* being a constant declared in *OS*).

Call (cmd)
> activates the command *cmd* and loads the module containing the command if it is not already loaded.

C The Module *IO*

Module *IO* handles simple input/output of numbers, characters and strings. Input is handled via a scanner that is able to read various symbols in a text. Output is via procedures.

To read a text, a scanner *s* is set to the desired text position via *s.Set*. Successive symbols can be read via *s.Read*.

For output, a text *t* must be assigned to the variable *out* and its write position must be set via *t.SetPos*. Output routines write to the text *out* starting at position *out.pos*.

```
DEFINITION IO;
    IMPORT Texts0;

    CONST none = 0; integer = 1; name = 2; string = 3; char = 4;

    TYPE
        Scanner = RECORD
            text-: Texts0.Text;             (*text to which scanner is set*)
            class-: INTEGER;                (*class of recognized symbol*)
            int-: LONGINT;                  (*filled if class=integer*)
            str-: ARRAY 32 OF CHAR;         (*filled if class=string or name*)
            ch-: CHAR;                      (*filled if class=char*)
            PROCEDURE (VAR s: Scanner) Set (t: Texts0.Text; pos: LONGINT);
            PROCEDURE (VAR s: Scanner) SetToParameters;
            PROCEDURE (VAR s: Scanner) Read;
            PROCEDURE (VAR s: Scanner) Eot (): BOOLEAN;
            PROCEDURE (VAR s: Scanner) Pos (): LONGINT;
        END ;

    VAR out: Texts0.Text;  (*output procedures write to this text*)

    PROCEDURE Ch (ch: CHAR);
    PROCEDURE Str (s: ARRAY OF CHAR);
    PROCEDURE Int (x: LONGINT; w: INTEGER);
    PROCEDURE Real (x: REAL; w: INTEGER);
    PROCEDURE NL;

END IO.
```

Interface of IO

Scanner

Output routines

Scanner $s.Set(t, pos)$
messages   sets the scanner s to position pos in text t.
                   $s.SetToParameters$
                           sets the scanner s to the text after the last command clicked.
                           This permits reading of command parameters.
                   $s.Read$
                           reads the next symbol from the current scanner position and
                           returns its value in $s.int$, $s.str$ or $s.ch$. $s.class$ specifies the kind
                           of symbol read. Blanks are skipped. Examples:

Input	*Kind of Symbol*	*Value in*
\<eot\>	s.class = none	–
123	s.class = integer	s.int
-123	s.class = integer	s.int
xxx	s.class = name	s.str
xxx.yyy	s.class = name	s.str
"xxx"	s.class = string	s.str (no quotes)
other	s.class = char	s.ch

           $bool := s.Eof ()$
                   returns TRUE if no more symbols can be read from the
                   scanner s, otherwise FALSE.
           $pos := s.Pos ()$
                   returns the current text position of the scanner s.

Output routines $Str(s)$
                   outputs the string s.
                   $Ch(ch)$
                   outputs the character ch.
                   $Int(i, w)$
                           outputs the signed integer i right-justified in a character field
                           of width w.
                   $Real(r, w)$
                           outputs the real number r in a character field of width w (e.g.,
                           $Real(123.45, 7) = 0.12E02$).
                   NL
                           causes a line feed.

D How to Get Oberon

The Oberon System, including the Oberon-2 compiler and various *Oberon*
tools such as a text editor, a graphics editor and a browser, is
available at no cost. It can either be obtained via *ftp* from ETH
Zurich or ordered from Springer-Verlag on diskette.

The Oberon System is currently available for Sun SPARC- *Platforms*
Station, DECstation, IBM RS/6000, Apple Macintosh II and IBM-
PC (MS-DOS). Oberon-2 compilers are currently available for Sun
SPARCStation, DECstation and IBM RS/6000.

The parameters for the ftp program are: *ftp*

Ftp host name:	neptune.inf.ethz.ch
Internet address:	129.132.101.33
Login name:	ftp
Password:	<your e-mail address>
Ftp directory:	Oberon

Oberon can also be purchased from Springer-Verlag on diskette. *Diskette*
Please specify the computer version.

In addition to this book on Oberon-2 and its application in *Documentation*
object-oriented programming, the following books serve as a documentation of Oberon:

- *N. Wirth and M. Reiser Programming in Oberon. Steps beyond
  Pascal and Modula-2. Addison-Wesley 1992*
  Tutorial for the Oberon programming language and concise
  language reference.

- *M. Reiser: The Oberon System. User Guide and Programmer's
  Manual. Addison-Wesley, 1991*
  User manual for the programming environment and reference
  for the standard module library.

- *N. Wirth and J. Gutknecht: Project Oberon. Addison-Wesley, 1992*
  Program listings with explanations for the whole Oberon
  System, including the compiler for the NS32000.

Oberon0

The source code for Oberon0 described in Chapter 11 can also be
obtained at no cost so that the reader can play with it and extend
it. The source code is available via the same ftp address as
specified above. It is in the subdirectory Oberon0. If the Oberon
System is purchased on diskette, the source code of Oberon0 is
included.

Bibliography

[Abb83]   Abbott R.: Program Design by Informal English Descriptions. Communications of the ACM, 26 (11), 1983

[BDMN79]   Birtwistle G.M., Dahl O.-J., Myhrhaug B., Nygaard K.: Simula Begin, Studentlitteratur, Lund, Sweden, 1979

[BeC89]   Beck K., Cunningham W.: A Laboratory for Teaching Object-Oriented Thinking. Proceedings OOPSLA'89. SIGPLAN Notices, 24 (10), 1989

[Boo91]   Booch G.: Object-Oriented Design with Applications. Benjamin Cummings, 1991

[Bud91]   Budd T.: Object-Oriented Programming. Addison-Wesley, 1991

[Cha92]   Chambers C.: The Design and Implementation of the SELF Compiler, an Optimizing Compiler for Object-Oriented Programming Languages. Ph.D. thesis, Stanford, 1992

[CoY90]   Coad P., Yourdon E.: Object-Oriented Analysis. Prentice Hall, 1990

[Deu89]   Deutsch P.: Design Reuse and Frameworks in the Smalltalk-80 System. In Biggerstaff T.J., Perlis A.J. (ed.): Software Reusability, Volume 2, ACM Press, 1989

[DoD83]   Reference Manual for the Ada Programming Language (ANSI/MIL-STD-1815A), United States Departement of Defense, Washington D.C., 1983

[GWM88]　　Gamma E., Weinand A., Marty R.: ET++ – An Object-Oriented Application Framework in C++. Proceedings OOPSLA'88, SIGPLAN Notices, 23 (11), 1988

[GoR83]　　Goldberg A., Robson D.: Smalltalk-80, The Language and its Implementation. Addison-Wesley, 1983

[Hof90]　　Hoffman D.: On Criteria for Module Interfaces. IEEE Trans. on Software Engineering, 16 (5), 1990

[JoF88]　　Johnson R.E., Foote B.: Designing Reusable Classes. Journal of Object-Oriented Programming, June/July 1988

[KrP88]　　Krasner G., Pope S.: A Cookbook for Using the MVC User Interface Paradigm in Smalltalk. Journal of Object-Oriented Programming Aug./Sep. 1988

[Mey86]　　Meyer B.: Genericity versus Inheritance. Proceedings OOPSLA'86, SIGPLAN Notices, 21 (11), 1986

[Mey87]　　Meyer B.: Object-Oriented Software Construction. Prentice Hall, 1987

[Par72]　　Parnas D.L.: On the Criteria to be Used in Decomposing Systems into Modules, Communications of the ACM, 15 (12), 1972

[PHT91]　　Pfister C., Heeb B., Templ J.: Oberon Technical Notes. Computer Science Report 156, ETH Zürich, March 1991

[RBP91]　　Rumbaugh J., Blaha M., Premerlani W., Eddy F., Lorensen W.: Object-Oriented Modeling and Design. Prentice Hall, 1991

[Rei91]　　Reiser M.: The Oberon System; Users Guide and Programmers Manual. Addison-Wesley, 1991

[ReW92]　　Reiser M., Wirth N.: Programming in Oberon. Steps Beyond Pascal and Modula-2. Addison-Wesley, 1992

[Sch86]　　Schmucker K.J.: Object-Oriented Programming for the Macintosh. Hayden, 1986

[Sed88]　　Sedgewick R.: Algorithms. Addison-Wesley, 1988

[ShM88]　　Shlaer S., Mellor S.: Object-Oriented Systems Analysis: Modeling the World in Data. Yourdon Press, 1988

[Str86]   Stroustrup B.: The C++ Programming Language, Addison-Wesley, 1986 (second edition 1991)

[Str89]   Stroustrup B.: Multiple Inheritance for C++. Proceedings EUUG Spring Conference, Helsinki, May 1989

[Swe85]   Sweet R.E.: The Mesa Programming Environment. SIGPLAN Notices, 20 (7), 1985

[Szy92]   Szyperski C.A.: Write–ing Applications. Proceedings of Tools Europe 92, Dortmund, 1992

[Web89]   Webster B.F.: The NeXT Book. Addison-Wesley, 1989

[WiG92]   Wirth N., Gutknecht J.: Project Oberon. The Design of an Operating System and Compiler. Addison-Wesley, 1992

[Wir71]   Wirth N.: Program Development by Stepwise Refinement. Communications of the ACM, 14, (4), 1971

[WiW89]   Wirfs-Brock A., Wilkerson B.: Variables Limit Reusability. Journal of Object-Oriented Programming, May/June 1989

[WWW90]   Wirfs-Brock R., Wilkerson R., Wiener L.: Designing Object-Oriented Software. Addison-Wesley, 1990

Index

3360

DATE DUE